Things We Said Today

CONVERSATIONS

with the Beatles

Things We Said Today

CONVERSATIONS

with the Beatles

Geoffrey and Vrnda Giuliano

ADAMS MEDIA CORPORATION
Holbrook, Massachusetts

Published by
Adams Media Corporation
260 Center Street, Holbrook, MA 02343

ISBN: 1-55850-800-7

Printed in the United States of America.

J I H G F E D C B

Things we said today : conversations with the Beatles /
Geoffrey and Vrnda Giuliano.
p.   cm.
Includes index.
ISBN 1-55850-800-7 (pbk.)
1. Beatles. 2. Rock musicians—England—Interviews.
I. Giuliano, Geoffrey. II. Giuliano, Vrnda. III. Beatles.
ML421.B4A5   1997
782.42166'092'2—dc21
[B]   97-2579
CIP
MN

This book is available at quantity discounts for bulk purchases.
For information, call 1-800-872-5627 (in Massachusetts, 781-767-8100).

Visit our home page at http://www.adamsmedia.com

Visit the author's web sites at http://www.neonblue.com/indigo
and http://www.neonblue.com/sri

Dedication

· · · · · · · · · · · · ·

To Max Muller, and Vivian Stanshall.

Max Mueller
1823–1900

Max Mueller was perhaps the world's best known Indologist.
His extensive work drew attention to the ancient *Vedic*
literatures and awakened general interest in Indology.

Vivian Stanshall
1943–1995

Vivian Stanshall was one of this century's most
original comedic minds who, as the headmaster of
the fabled Bonzo Dog Doo Dah Band elevated affable lunacy
and intellectual whimsy to high art. He will be sadly missed
by his many friends.

Contents
· · · · · · · · · · ·

Note: All pieces conducted by Geoffrey Giuliano are noted by the use of the author's first name in the interviews. The remainder of the content of this book consists of either press conference, press releases, or other "fair use" and public domain materials. A complete list of all sources has been kept on file by the authors.

Acknowledgments

Associate Researchers: Sesa Nichole Giuliano and Deborah Lynn Black

Intern: Devin Giuliano

The authors would like to thank the following people for their kindness in helping to realize this book.

Stefano Castino

Delta Music

Gaura Daya Dasa Bramchari

Srivas Dasa Bramachari

Tamal Krishna Das Bramachari

Theodore Bush

Avalon and India Giuliano

Her Grace Nandini Devi Dasi

His Divine Grace A.C. Bhativedanta Swami Prabhupada

His Holiness Jagannatha Dasa Puripada

His Holiness Radha Govinda Maharaja

Kashi Nath Narayan Jones

New Navadvipa Vaishnava Community

SRI/The Spiritual Realization Institute of America

Vrndarani Devi Dasi

Dr. Ronald Zucker

The George Martin (London, October 31, 1995) and Derek Taylor interviews were conducted and kindly provided by Dr. Bob Hieronimus of 21st Century Radio's Hieronimus & Co. We thank them for the use of this material and highly recommend their intelligent and insightful radio series. Thanks also to Good Day Sunshine for the use of some additional quotations.

Preface
STEP INSIDE LOVE

. . . .

I met the Beatles once upon a Beatle time. STEP INSIDE LOVE they said, and so we did. They had a "Beat," you see, with new melodies and new words and faces and clothes that looked you straight in the eye, staring right back at you. No messing about—you were "transported" to where you wanted to be. STEP INSIDE LOVE YEAH—YEAH—YEAH it was all fab gear. STEP INSIDE LOVE. . . . That's if you can! "We could've sold-out the stadium five times over already—There's never been anything like it!!" (Check newspapers for details) STEP INSIDE LOVE. Oh, we loved your success. We dipped into our pockets like never before. STEP INSIDE LOVE ". . . and sign here, Boys." STEP INSIDE LOVE, LONDON—NEW YORK—PARIS—ROME (Oh, how you Roamed). STEP INSIDE LOVE Nineteen something—something and the Tax Man appeared. STEP INSIDE LOVE YEAH—YEAH—YEAH STEP INSIDE LOVE. All hail, to The Magical History Four! You had nothing to fear except each other's lust (need) for a green independence, or so it seemed—STEP ALONGSIDE LOVE Waiting to find a direction, "As time goes by." STEP OUTSIDE LOVE For a *new* experience—Both Beatle and Bonzo stopped barking—cooling down relationships as well as the amps. STEP INSIDE LOVE We loved you, Beatles. YEAH—YEAH—YEAH!

"LEGS" LARRY SMITH*
TORONTO 1985

---

* "Legs" Larry Smith, the charismatic drummer for the brilliant Bonzo Dog Doo Dah Band, is a close friend of George Harrison.

Introduction

ONE SWEET DREAM
• • • • • • • • • • • • • • • • • •
"There is nothing new except what is forgotten. —Anon.

Unlike almost anyone else who made their mark as popular entertainers, the Beatles were unique in their ability to so accurately funnel their life experience into both their music and engaging public statements. As armchair philosophers, the Fab Four weren't bad, honestly shoveling their hard-won perceptions into everything they did. In comparison to today's self-involved crop of empty-headed crooners, John, Paul, George, and even Ringo have generally had something interesting to say.

When George Harrison was asked why the so-called current potentate pop stars didn't really impart too much of importance in their music anymore, he reeled off, "Because they don't know anything, do they?" Let's face it, even as bargain-basement gurus, such perennial lightweights as Whitney Houston, Michael Jackson, and even the great, hollow, sex-obsessed diva Madonna are pretty darn sad.

Ardently adhering to the "tell us something we don't know" school, we tip our hats to the revelations of past prophets like Dylan, the Incredible String Band, the Moody Blues, Pete Townshend, and Jimi Hendrix—but we take it off to the Beatles. As two very impressionable heads of wet cement back in the late sixties and early seventies, we first experienced a staggering array of new ideas emanating from these four engaging philosopher/kings, stumbling over such imperatives as women's liberation (listen to "Getting Better" and "Woman Is the Nigger of the World"), belief in God (check out "Within You Without You," "I Will," "Across the Universe," "Let It Be," and George's "Let It Roll"), psychedelics as a key to entry-level self-realization ("Tomorrow Never Knows," "Fixing a Hole," and "A Day in the Life"), hip politics (boot up "Taxman," "Revolution," "Give Ireland Back to the Irish," and "Awaiting on You All") and, of course, good old-fashioned boy/girl romance ("Dear Prudence," "For You Blue," "Norwegian Wood," and literally dozens more).

Apart from the marvelous music, the boys had quite a lot of interest to *say* as well. Remember John's headline-grabbing Bed-Ins, Paul's 1967 statement on the relative merits of all-natural LSD, or George's stint as the materially exhausted, wannabe Hare Krishna? All things considered, the Beatles were really quite wonderful geezers. Rank amateurs as aspiring Gods, but bloody insightful musicians with open hearts and minds to match. Here, then, are a few primary examples of the really good things the Fabmen have had to say over the years on such varied subjects as God, drugs, music, their acrimonious breakup, and even themselves. We hope you enjoy it. Have Bol.

GEOFFREY AND VRNDA GIULIANO
SRI/THE SPIRITUAL REALIZATION INSTITUTE
EASTER 1997

XIII

CHAPTER ONE

You're Such a Lovely Audience/The Beatles

The Beatles and Harold Wilson
PRESS CONFERENCE
London, March 1964

HAROLD WILSON: To keep out of politics, I'll just repeat what the *Times'* musical correspondent recently said about the Beatles, referring to their music as "distinctively indigenous in character" and "most imaginative and inventive." I'm sure the *Times'* correspondent spoke for all of us when he said of our friends, the Beatles, "Harmonically they are most intriguing with their chains of pentatonic clusters."

GEORGE HARRISON: It's very nice indeed, especially to get one [award] each because we usually have great trouble cutting them in four. I'd just like to say thank you very much, it's a great honor.

HAROLD WILSON: And now Paul . . .

PAUL MCCARTNEY: Same goes for me. Thank you very much for giving me this silver heart, but I still think you should have given one to good old Mr. Wilson!

RINGO STARR: Anyone who knows us knows I'm the one who never speaks. So I'd just like to say thanks a lot.

JOHN LENNON: I'd just like to say the same as the others. Thank you for the purple heart.

RINGO: Silver! *Silver!*

JOHN: Oh, sorry about that, Harold! We'd like to sincerely thank you all and we've got to go now because the fellow on our new film wants us and he says it's costing him a fortune. Thank you!

The Beatles

PRESS CONFERENCE
•••••••••••••••••••
London, 1965

QUESTION: We're with the Beatles at their latest press conference. They're here to tell us all about their new film. Where did the title come from?

JOHN: Out of Dick Lester's mouth it came.

RINGO: I thought it came out of his shoe?

PAUL: Well, Dick, kind of went up to us one at a time punching us, saying it's gonna be called *Help!*. And we said yeah, that's a great idea. We'll call it that and that's how it all came about.

QUESTION: Why did you have so much trouble with the title? I know you originally had a different name, what finally made *Help!* the one?

PAUL: Because it sounds about the best I say. Just sounds right. There you are. It fits the story because people are trying to get us all through it. We need a bit of help, you see.

QUESTION: How does this second film differ from the first?

JOHN: Well, it's in color for a start and there's a lot more happening in this. The last one was sort of a documentary, but this one is a real film, *almost*.

QUESTION: Do you have any different problems in this one, George, as opposed to *A Hard Day's Night*?

GEORGE: A couple of more yes. For a start we had a big idol and a lot of trick things, you see. We didn't have any tricks in the last film, did we, John?

JOHN: We didn't have any tricks in the last film, no!

PAUL: The business about the idol was that it was supposed to rise from the water and it wouldn't. It wouldn't because the water was always too rough. We had a bit of trouble with that.

QUESTION: Does this idol have anything to do with you, Ringo?

RINGO: I can't tell you what the plot is, but here's some of the questions that will be answered. Why was the high priest of the terrible goddess Kali interested in the Beatles? What did they want of them? They certainly weren't fans!

QUESTION: What happens to you in the picture?

RINGO: I'm chased by a gang of thugs all the way through it, actually.

JOHN: Yeah, they seem to be chasing Ringo and then there's two leading scientists who hope to rule the world. And an Eastern beauty saves our lives from time to time.

PAUL: All I can say is, "Will John live to sleep in his pit again? For instance, will Paul ever get back to his united organ?

QUESTION: I guess you're veteran movie stars at this point, but do you like making movies? Is it difficult for you?

PAUL: I think all of us really enjoy it. It's something different. And we've all forgotten how difficult it was standing round the set all day. You forget things like that. We're not used to doing a film which is all new for us. We've only done one before this. It's just good seeing us get together watching it sort of make it's self, it's very exciting, lovely.

QUESTION: I understand the movie brings us several new songs.

JOHN: There's about seven, Paul and I wrote eleven and we chose seven.

QUESTION: Is there a title song?

JOHN: Yeah, it's called "Help!" We think it's one of the best we've written.

PAUL: It's sung at the beginning and end of the picture.

QUESTION: George, how do you like this business of getting up early in the morning and being made up?

GEORGE: That's a bit of a drag. Apart from that and the waiting around we have a great laugh, don't we, fellas?

JOHN: Yes, we do.

RINGO: Yeah, it's great, as George said, except getting up in the morning, it's always difficult to do something you hate.

PAUL: Especially when you go to bed about three in the morning! It's pretty difficult to get up at six, however, since we never go to bed at three in the morning. It's difficult when you go to bed late. Some nights you do, some you don't.

QUESTION: Ringo, you're a newlywed, what do you expect from marriage?

RINGO: What do I expect? I don't expect anything. I just love being married. I love my wife and just want her to be there all the time. There's no one to say we can't do this and can't do that. I'm the boss, we just do it. There's no one to tell us. It's marvelous because we both belong to each other and you can share everything. It's a great thing being married. I enjoy it, but I'm not an authority, I've only been married a month. I love it. It's something you can't explain. It's only people who are married that know it.

The Beatles

PRESS CONFERENCE
. . . .
North America, 1964–1966

QUESTION: Do you believe in lunacy?

RINGO STARR: Yeah; it's healthy.

QUESTION: But aren't you embarrassed by it all?

RINGO: No, it's crazy.

QUESTION: Do you think it's wrong to set such a bad example to teenagers, smoking the way you do?

RINGO: It's better than being alcoholics.

QUESTION: What do you think of the criticism that you are not very good?

GEORGE HARRISON: We're not!

QUESTION: You've admitted to being agnostics. Are you also irreverent?

PAUL McCARTNEY: We are agnostics, so there is no point in being irreverent.

QUESTION: What impresses you most about America?

JOHN LENNON: Bread.

PAUL: Going on buses.

QUESTION: How do you like this welcome?

RINGO: So this is America. They all seem out of their minds!

QUESTION: Why are your speaking voices different from your singing voices?

GEORGE: We don't have a musical background.

QUESTION: Do you like fish and chips?

RINGO: Yes, but I like steak and chips better.

QUESTION: How tall are you?

RINGO: Two feet, nine inches.

QUESTION: Would you like to walk down the street without being recognized?

JOHN: We used to do that with no money in our pockets. There's no point in it.

QUESTION: Are you scared when crowds scream at you?

JOHN: More so in Dallas than in other places, perhaps.

QUESTION: Is it true you can't sing?

JOHN: (*Points to George*) Not me. Him!

QUESTION: Why don't you smile, George?

GEORGE: I'll hurt me lips.

QUESTION: What's your reaction to a Seattle psychiatrist's opinion that you are a menace?

GEORGE: Psychiatrists are a menace.

QUESTION: What's this about an annual illness, George?

GEORGE: I get cancer every year.

QUESTION: Where would you like to go if all the security wasn't necessary?

JOHN: Harlem.

QUESTION: Do you plan to record any anti-war songs?

JOHN: All of our songs are anti-war.

QUESTION: When you do a new song, how do you decide who sings lead?

JOHN: We just get together and whoever knows most of the words sings lead.

QUESTION: What do you think you've contributed to the musical field?

RINGO: Records.

GEORGE: A laugh and a smile.

QUESTION: How does it feel, putting on the whole world?

RINGO: We enjoy it.

PAUL: We aren't really putting you on.

GEORGE: Just a bit of it.

JOHN: How does it feel to be put on?

QUESTION: How do you feel about the nightclub, Arthur, named after your hair-style?

GEORGE: I was proud, until I saw the club.

QUESTION: What do you consider the most important thing in life?

GEORGE: Love.

QUESTION: Do you resent fans ripping up your sheets for souvenirs?

RINGO: I don't mind. So long as I'm not in them while the ripping is going on.

PAUL: I once knew a fellow on the Dingle who had two dads. He used to call them number one dad and number two dad. Now apparently, number one dad wasn't nice. He used to throw the boy on the fire, which can develop a lot of complexes in a young lad.

RINGO: I remember my uncle putting a red-hot poker on me, and that's no lie. He was trying to frighten me.

PAUL: Tell me, Ringo, do all your relatives go around applying red-hot pokers to you?

JOHN: It's the only way they can identify them.

PAUL: Ringo comes from a depressed area.

JOHN: Some people call it the slums.

RINGO: No, the slums are a bit farther.

QUESTION: John, are you an intellectual?

JOHN: I get spasms of being intellectual. I read a bit about politics but I don't think I'd vote for anyone. No message from any of those phoney politicians is coming through to me.

QUESTION: What's the most unusual request you've had?

JOHN: I wouldn't like to say.

QUESTION: Do you like topless bathing suits?

RINGO: We've been wearing them for years.

QUESTION: Girls rushed toward my car because it had press identification and they thought I met you. How do you explain this phenomenon?

JOHN: You're lovely to look at.

QUESTION: Were you worried about the oversized roughnecks who tried to infiltrate the airport crowd on your arrival?

RINGO: That was us!

QUESTION: How do you add up success?

JOHN, PAUL, GEORGE, RINGO: Money!

QUESTION: Are you ever in any danger during your concerts?

PAUL: I was got once by a cigarette lighter. Clouted me right in the eye and closed my eye for the stay. In Chicago a purple and yellow stuffed animal, a red rubber ball, and a skipping rope were plopped on stage. I had to kick a carton of

Winston's out of the way when I played. And I saw a cigarette lighter go flying past me in Detroit's Olympia Stadium.

QUESTION: Don't you worry about all that?

PAUL: It's okay, as long as they throw light stuff, like paper.

QUESTION: Do you care what the public thinks about your private lives?

RINGO: There's a woman in the United States who predicted the plane we were traveling on would crash. Now a lot of people would like to think we were scared into saying a prayer. What we did, actually, was drank.

QUESTION: What do you think of the space shots?

JOHN: Seen one, you've seen them all.

QUESTION: What do you think about the pamphlet calling you communists?

PAUL: Us, communists? Why we can't be communists. We're the world's number one capitalists. Imagine us, communists!

QUESTION: Would you ever accept a girl in your group if she could sing, play an instrument, and wear the Beatle haircut?

RINGO: How tall is she?

QUESTION: Beatle-licensed products have grossed millions of dollars in America alone, Beatle wigs, Beatle hats, Beatle T-shirts, Beatle egg cups, Beatlenut ice cream . . .

RINGO: Anytime you spell beetle with an "a" in it, we get money.

QUESTION: What are your favorite programs on American television?

PAUL: "News In Espanol" from Miami. Popeye, Bullwinkle. All the cultural stuff.

JOHN: I like American TV because you can get eighteen stations, but you can't get a good picture on any of them.

QUESTION: You were at the Playboy Club last night. What did you think of it?

PAUL: The Playboy and I are just good friends.

QUESTION: George, is the place you were brought up a bit like Greenwich Village?

GEORGE: No, more like the Bowery.

QUESTION: Aren't you tired of all the hocus-pocus? Wouldn't you rather sit on your fat wallets?

PAUL: When we get tired, we take fat vacations on our fat wallets.

QUESTION: Do you get much fan mail?

RINGO: About two thousand letters a day.

JOHN: And we're going to answer every one of them!

QUESTION: Do any of you have ulcers?

GEORGE: None we've noticed.

QUESTION: How come you were turned back by immigration?

JOHN: We had to be deloused.

QUESTION: What is your favorite food?

RINGO: I'm hung up on burgers.

GEORGE: All four of us are mad about hero sandwiches.

PAUL: I have a yen for grilled cheese.

JOHN: George and I usually wait until someone else to order, then say, "I'll have that, too."

QUESTION: How do you feel about the invasion of your privacy all the time?

RINGO: The only time it bothers us is when they get us to the floor and really mangle us.

QUESTION: Do you worry about smoking in public? Do you think it might set a bad example for your younger fans?

GEORGE: We don't set examples. We smoke because we've always smoked. Kids don't smoke because we do. They smoke because they want to. If we changed, we'd be putting on an act.

RINGO: (*Whispering*) We even drink.

QUESTION: What careers would you individually have chosen had you not become entertainers?

RINGO: A hairdresser.

GEORGE: I had a short go at being an electrician's apprentice, but I kept blowing things up, so I got dumped.

JOHN: No comment.

QUESTION: Who would the Beatles like to meet more than anyone else?

RINGO: Santa Claus.

QUESTION: Paul, you look like my son.

PAUL: You don't look a bit like my mother.

QUESTION: Why aren't you wearing a hat?

GEORGE: Why aren't you wearing a tie?

QUESTION: Is it true that on one flight the stewardess broke up a pillow fight among you guys and got clobbered?

GEORGE: I'm not really sure where she got hit, but she did make us break it up, though.

GEORGE: Remember that house we stayed in at Harlech? There was a woman who had a dog with no legs. She used to take it out in the morning for a slide.

QUESTION: Do teenagers scream at you because they are, in effect, revolting against their parents?

PAUL: They've been revolting for years.

JOHN: I've never noticed them revolting.

QUESTION: Do you have any special messages for the Prime Minister and your parents?

JOHN: Hello, Alec.

GEORGE: Hello, Muddah.

RINGO: Hello, fellas.

QUESTION: Do you have any special advice for teenagers?

JOHN: Don't get pimples.

QUESTION: Did you really use four-letter words on the tourists in the Bahamas?

JOHN: What we actually said was "Gosh."

PAUL: We may have also said, "Heavens!"

JOHN: Couldn't have said that, Paul. More than four letters.

QUESTION: What would you do if the fans got past the police lines?

GEORGE: Die laughing.

QUESTION: Why don't all four of the Beatles ever sing together?

GEORGE: Well, we try to start out together anyway.

QUESTION: What does each Beatle consider his two most valued possessions?

JOHN: Our lives.

QUESTION: What do you do with your money?

RINGO: We bury it.

GEORGE: We hide it.

PAUL: We don't see it. It goes to our office.

JOHN: We pay a lot of taxes.

QUESTION: What are your feelings on the "hints of queerness" American males found in the Beatles during the early days of your climb to popularity?

PAUL: There's more terror of that hint of queerness, of homosexuality, here than in England, where long hair is more accepted. Our whole promotion made us look silly. But we've had a chance to talk to people since then and they can see were not thick little kids.

QUESTION: Has success spoiled the Beatles?

JOHN: Well, you don't see us running out and buying bowler hats, do you? I think we've pretty well succeeded in remaining ourselves.

PAUL: The great thing about it is, you don't have big worries any more when you've got where we have—only little ones, like whether the plane is going to crash.

QUESTION: What do you plan to do after this?

RINGO: What else is there to do?

QUESTION: What excuse do you have for your collar-length hair?

JOHN: Well, it just grows out yer head.

QUESTION: Which of you is really bald?

GEORGE: We're all bald. And I'm deaf and dumb.

QUESTION: Do you ever think of getting a haircut?

GEORGE: No, luv, do you?

QUESTION: How do you feel about teenagers imitating you with Beatle wigs?

JOHN: They're not imitating us, because we don't wear Beatle wigs.

QUESTION: Where did you get your hairstyle?

PAUL: From Napoleon. And Julius Caesar, too. We cut it any time we feel like it.

RINGO: We may do it now.

QUESTION: Are you wearing wigs or real hair?

RINGO: Hey, where's the police?

PAUL: Take her out!

GEORGE: Our hair's real. What about yours, lady?

QUESTION: What would happen if you all switched to crewcuts?

JOHN: It would probably be the end of the act.

QUESTION: Are you going to get haircuts over in America?

RINGO: What d'you mean? We got them yesterday.

QUESTION: Does your hair require any special attention?

JOHN: Inattention is the main thing.

QUESTION: What do you look like with your hair back on your foreheads?

JOHN: You just don't do that, mate. You feel naked if you do that, like you don't have any trousers on.

QUESTION: Don't you feel icky and dirty with your hair so long, flopping in your eyes and down your neck?

JOHN: We've got combs.

QUESTION: What is the biggest threat to your careers, the atom bomb or dandruff?

RINGO: The atom bomb. We've already got dandruff.

QUESTION: Why are you disinterested in politics?

JOHN: We're not. We just think politicians are disinteresting.

QUESTION: What do you think of the Vietnam war?

JOHN: We think of it every day. We don't like it. We don't agree with it. We think it's wrong. But there is not much we can do about it. All we can do is say we don't like it.

QUESTION: What is your opinion of Americans who go to Canada to avoid the draft?

JOHN: We're not allowed opinions.

PAUL: Anyone who feels that fighting is wrong has the right not to go in the army.

JOHN: We all just don't agree with war. There's no need for anyone to kill for any reason.

GEORGE: "Thou shalt not kill" means *that*! Not, "Amend section A." There's no reason whatsoever. No one can force you to kill anyone if you don't want to.

CHAPTER TWO

A Ring on Every Finger/ FABS, Etc.

The Beatles
VITAL STATISTICS

BIRTHDAYS:

John Winston Lennon (October 9, 1940, deceased)

James Paul McCartney (June 18, 1942)

George Harrison (February 25, 1943)

Richard Starkey (July 7, 1940)

Yoko Ono (February 18, 1933)

Linda McCartney (September 24, 1942)

Pattie Harrison (March 17, 1944)

Olvia Arias (1948)

Maureen Starkey (August 4, 1944, deceased)

Barbara Bach (August 27, 1949)

WEDDING BELLS:

John Lennon and Cynthia Powell (August 23, 1962) (divorced November 8, 1968)

John Lennon and Yoko Ono (March 20, 1969)

Paul McCartney and Linda Louise Eastman (March 12, 1969)

George Harrison and Patricia Ann Boyd (January 21, 1966) (divorced 1970)

George Harrison and Olvia Trinidad Arias (September 7, 1978)

Ringo Starr and Maureen Cox (February 11, 1965) (divorced July 1975)

Ringo Starr and Barbara Bach (April 27, 1981)

BEATLE BABIES:

John Charles Julian Lennon (April 8, 1963)

Kyoko Cox (August 8, 1963)

Sean Ono Taro Lennon (October 9, 1975)

Heather McCartney (December 30, 1962)

Mary McCartney (August 28, 1969)

Stella McCartney (September 13, 1971)

James Louis McCartney (September 12, 1977)

Dhani Harrison (August 1, 1978)

Zak Starkey (December 12, 1965)

Jason Starkey (August 19, 1967)

Lee Starkey (November 11, 1970)

Also Known As:

John: Dr. Dream; Dr. Winston O'Ghurkin; Dr. Winston O'Reggae; Dwarf McDougal; Hon. John St. John Johnson; Kaptain Kundalini; Mel Torment; Rev. Fred Ghurkin; Rev. Thumbs Ghurkin; Dr. Winston O'Boogie; John O'Cean; and Joel Nohnn.

Paul: Paul Ramon; Bernard Webb and Apollo C. Vermouth.

George: Carl Harrison; George H.; Hari Georgeson; Jai Raj Harisein; George Harryson; L'Angelo Misterioso; George O'Hara; George O'Hara-Smith; Ohnothinmagen; P. Roducer; and Son of Harry.

Ringo: R.S.; Richie; Richie Snare; and Billy Shears.

The Beatles
EQUIPMENT
1963–1970

GUITARS:

SIX STRING:
Fender: Esquire; Stratocaster
Gibson: ES-345TD; Lap Guitar; Les Paul; SG Standard
Gretsch: Country Gentleman; Duo-Jet; 6120; Tennessean
Hofner Club 40
Rickenbacker: 325; 420
Epiphone Casino
Solid 7
Futurama

TWELVE STRING:
Rickenbacker: 320–12; 360–12; 360–12WB
Vox Mando

ACOUSTIC:

SIX STRING:
Gibson: J–160E; J–160E N; J–200
Martin: D–18; D–28
Epiphone Ft79
Spanish hollowbody

TWELVE STRING:
Framus 5/024 Hootenanny/12

BASS:
Hofner: President 500/5; Violin 500/1
Burns Solidbody
Fender Jazz
Rickenbacker 4001S

SIX STRING BASS:
Fender: Jazz; VI

MPLIFIERS:
ox: white AC–10; AC–15; AC–30; AC–50; AC–100; Bristol Bass T–60; Super
Beatle V11142
El Pico
Fender: Large Bassman; White Bassman; Princeton; Showman; Twin Reverb
Gibson: Les Paul GA–40
Gretsch Chet Atkins
Truvoice

KEYBOARDS:
Electric
Vox: Continental V–301; double keyboard Continental V–303
Hammond B–3
Hohner Pianet N
Mellotron
Moog Synthesizer

ACOUSTIC:
Harmonium
Grand Bluthner
Steinway: Grand; Baby Grand
Upright Chappell

DRUMS:
Premier: HiFi; Royal–Ace
Ludwig Super Classic

HARMONICAS:
Hohner H–H: 265; 267; 270; 1896

RINGO AND PAUL ON THE *BEATLES' ANTHOLOGY* London, 1996

The songs are what's important and, of course, how we played on them, but ultimately it's down to the writers.

RINGO

• • •

It was better when there were three of us than when Ringo said, "Oh, I've done my bit," and left me and George to do it. Me and George, as artists, had a bit more tension.

PAUL

• • •

We were four guys who really loved each other. We were stuck with each other and that wasn't a bad thing. It was a lifesaver. There were four of us and there were four brothers. We were the Four Musketeers. And everybody saved everybody else at some point.

RINGO

• • •

Ringo said, it might be very joyous [getting together], that's Ringo's words, this ancient Ringo language, "It might be very joyous." And in fact it was quite a pleasant experience.

PAUL

• • •

We all went through a lot of rubbish with each other, suing each other, not being friends, not liking each other. To look back, we did have a lot of fun. We were very close. So it was very therapeutic in a way. What's

even better was that George, Paul, and I got back together over the past couple of years to become friends and buddies again. It would have been nicer if John had been there, but of course, he's gone.

RINGO

• • •

It was great. It was a lot of fun. The emotional part, of course, was because we had John coming out of the speakers when we were doing "Free As a Bird." We had to get over that, and then we had a lot of fun.

It's sort of taken us three or four years to put our peace together so we'd been meeting up here and there and gradually it got more and more and we spent more and more time with each other, so it was a lot of fun. We had a lot of reminiscences and a lot of laughs.

RINGO

• • •

There was a real nice moment when we were doing "Real Love" and I was trying to learn the piano bit, and Ringo sat down on the drums, jamming along. It was like none of us had ever been away.

PAUL

• • •

It's always been a little messy, always the hint of continuing tension. We sort of brought it around and tied it up again in a very good way. Once we get together, hanging out and being friends again, there's not much trouble at all. We laugh a lot.

The one thing that struck me was that the only people who don't look at me as if I'm a Beatle are Paul and George. And I don't look at them like that either. It's very refreshing.

RINGO

• • •

We are the only ones who really know each other. We know what it was like. They are the only two that don't look at me like I'm a Beatle. They look at me like I'm a Ringo and I look at him like he's a Paul, or he's a George.

RINGO

• • •

In the beginning it was pretty emotional because the three of us were there and John's voice was there, but he wasn't there himself. So we had to get over that. You've heard the story. We felt John had gone out for a cup of tea, and we carried on without him, which used to happen. One of us wouldn't be there. We worked very hard, so did Jeff [Lynn], to pull it together.

RINGO

• • •

It's still a great sadness for all of us because, you know, the three of us got pretty close again and still there's that empty hole, you know, that's John.

RINGO

• • •

"Free As a Bird" is great and I'm not just saying that because I'm on it. It's an amazing Beatle track. I listened and thought, "It sounds just like *them!*" I'd taken myself away from it for so long it was like listening to it as an outsider. It's brilliant. I think you could say they made it in 1967.

RINGO

• • •

At the playback I said, it sounds like we hadn't stopped. It sounds like we didn't stop at all. No years in between.

RINGO

• • •

I don't think we'll tour. That's a whole new deal *if* we put it together. It's very difficult to go out as the Beatles, as John isn't around. We could go out as Ringo, George, and Paul. That would be the only way we could go out. But we didn't even really get into talking about that. I know everyone gets excited because we've been offered billions of dollars, but it's not really a question of doing it for the money.

RINGO

• • •

[People say we're doing this reunion for the cash] but that's not strictly true. I'm sitting here in Monte Carlo. You know, [the media] writes anything they like. They don't have a lot of facts. Our records have always sold. Every year we're selling a couple of million anyway.

RINGO

• • •

The music is the legacy the Beatles left. Not all the madness. *It's the music.* It was always that. The music is the Beatles!

RINGO

THE BEATLES
Remembering the Music

This was one of the first songs I ever finished. I was only about eighteen and we gave it to the Fourmost. I think it was the first song of my own I ever attempted with the group.

JOHN, "HELLO LITTLE GIRL"

• • •

"Love You To" was one of the first tunes I wrote for sitar. "Norwegian Wood" was an accident as far as the sitar part was concerned, but this was the first song where I consciously tried to use the sitar and tabla on the basic track: I over-dubbed the guitars and vocal later."

GEORGE, "LOVE YOU TO"

• • •

I used to wish I could write songs like the others—and I've tried, but I just can't. I can get the words all right, but whenever I think of a tune and sing it to them they always say, "Yeah, it sounds like such-a-thing," and when they point it out I see what they mean. But I did get a part credit as a composer on "What Goes On."

RINGO, "WHAT GOES ON"

• • •

That's me again, with the first backwards tape on any record anywhere. Before Hendrix, before the Who, before *any* fucker. Maybe there was that record about "They're coming to take me away, haha"; maybe *that* came out before "Rain," but it's not the same thing.

JOHN, "RAIN"

• • •

"All Too Much" was written in a childlike manner from realizations that appeared during and after some LSD experiences and which were later confirmed in meditation.

GEORGE, "ALL TOO MUCH"

• • •

That's me, 'cuz of the *Yellow Submarine* people, who were gross animals apart from the guy who drew the paintings for the movie. They lifted all the ideas for the movie out of our heads and didn't give us any credit. We had nothing to do with that movie and we sort of resented them. It was the third movie that we owed United Artists. Brian set it up and we had nothing to do with it. But I liked the movie, the artwork. They wanted another song, so I knocked off "Hey Bulldog." It's a good-sounding record that means nothing.

JOHN, "HEY BULLDOG"

• • •

Oh, that was written about a guy in Maharishi's meditation camp who took a short break to go shoot a few poor tigers, and then came back to commune with God. There used to be a character called Jungle Jim, and I combined him with Buffalo Bill. It's a sort of teenage social-comment song and a bit of a joke. Yoko's on that one, I believe, singing along.

JOHN, "THE CONTINUING STORY OF BUNGALOW BILL"

• • •

George Martin's contribution was quite a big one, actually. The first time he really ever showed he could see beyond what we were offering him was "Please Please Me." It was originally conceived as a Roy Orbison–type thing, you know. George Martin said, "Well, we'll put the tempo up." He lifted the tempo and we all thought that was much better and it became a big hit.

PAUL, *"PLEASE PLEASE ME"*

• • •

I was trying to write about an affair without letting me wife know, so it was very gobbledegook. I was sort of composing from my experiences, girls' flats, things like that.

I wrote it at Kenwood. George had just got the sitar and I said, "Could you play this piece?" We went through many different versions of the song, but it was never right and I was getting very angry about it, it wasn't coming out like I wanted. Finally I said, "Well, I just want to do it like this." So they let me go and I played the guitar very loudly into the mike and sang it at the same time. Then George had the sitar and I asked him if could he play the piece I'd written but he wasn't sure because he hadn't done much on the sitar but was willing to have a go. I think we did it in sections.

JOHN, *"NORWEGIAN WOOD"*

• • •

"The Inner Light" came, really, from "Within You, Without You." There was a David Frost show on television about meditation, the Maharishi Mahesh Yogi was interviewed on tape with John Lennon and myself live, and amongst many others in the audience was Juan

Mascaro, who is the Sanskrit teacher at Cambridge University. He wrote me a letter later saying ". . . a few days ago two friends from abroad gave me the recording of your song 'Within You, Without You.' I am very happy, it is a moving song and may it move the souls of millions; and there is more to come, as you are only beginning on the great journey."

GEORGE, *"THE INNER LIGHT"*

• • •

That was a piece of unfinished music that I turned into a comedy record with Paul. I was waiting for him in his house and I saw the phone book was on the piano with the words, "You know the name, look up the number." That was like a logo and I just changed it. It was going to be a Four Tops kind of song—the chord changes are like that—but it never developed and we made a joke of it. Brian Jones is playing saxophone on it."

JOHN, *"YOU KNOW MY NAME (LOOK UP MY NUMBER)"*

• • •

I knew it would get connotations, but it really was a children's song. I just loved the idea of kids singing it. With "Yellow Submarine" the whole idea was, "If someday I came across some kids singing it, that will be it," so it had to be very easy, there isn't a single big word. Kids will understand it much easier than adults. "In the town where I was born/lived a man who sailed to sea/And he told us of his life in the land of submarines." That's really the beginning of a kids' story. There's some stuff in Greece like icing sugar, you eat it. It's a sweet you drop into water. It's called submarine; we had it on holiday.

PAUL, "YELLOW SUBMARINE"

• • •

I often sit at the piano, working at songs, with the telly on low in the background. If I'm a bit down and not getting much done, then the words on the telly come through. That's when I heard "Good morning, good morning"—it was a corn flakes advertisement.

JOHN, "GOOD MORNING, GOOD MORNING"

• • •

"Cold Turkey" is self-explanatory. It was banned again all over the American radio, so it never got off the ground. They were thinking I was promoting heroin. They're so *stupid* about drugs! They're always arresting smugglers or kids with a few joints in their pocket. They never face the reality. They're not looking at the *cause* of the drug problem. Why is everybody taking drugs? To escape from *what*? Is life so terrible? Do we live in such a terrible situation that we can't do anything about it without reinforcement from alcohol or tobacco or sleeping pills? A drug is a drug, you know. Why we take them is important, not who's selling it to whom on the corner.

JOHN, "COLD TURKEY"

• • •

Everybody thinks Paul wrote it, but actually John wrote it for me. He's got a lot of soul, has John.

RINGO, "STRAWBERRY FIELDS"

• • •

I think this my favorite on *The Beatles* album.

PAUL, "HAPPINESS IS A WARM GUN"

• • •

This was about my dream girl. When Paul and I wrote lyrics in the old days we used to laugh about it like the Tin Pan Alley people would. And it was only later on we tried to match the lyrics to the tune. I especially like this one. It was one of my best.

JOHN, "GIRL"

• • •

Often the backing I think of early on never quite comes off. With "Tomorrow Never Knows," I'd imagined in my head that in the background you would hear thousands of monks chanting. That was impractical, of course, so we did something different. I should have tried to get nearer my original idea, the monks singing—I realize now that was what it wanted.

JOHN, "TOMORROW NEVER KNOWS"

• • •

George Martin always has something to do with our tunes, but sometimes more than others. For instance, he wrote the end of "All You Need Is Love" and got into trouble because the "In the Mood" bit was copyrighted. It was a rather hurried session and we didn't mind giving him that to do, saying, "There's the end, we want it to go on and on." Actually what he wrote was much more disjointed, so when we put all the bits together we said, "Could we have

'Greensleeves' right on top of that little Bach thing?" And on top of that we had the "In the Mood" bit.

George is quite a sage. Sometimes he works with us, sometimes against us, but he's always looked after us. I don't think he does as much as some people think, though. He sometimes does all the arrangements and we just change them.

PAUL, *"ALL YOU NEED IS LOVE"*

● ● ●

This song is about a hole in the road where the rain gets in; a good old analogy, the hole in your make-up which lets the rain in and stops your mind from going where it will. It's you interfering with things; as when someone walks up to you and says, "I am the Son of God." And you say, "No, you're not; I'll crucify you," and you crucify him. Well, that's life, but it is not fixing a hole.

It's about fans, too: "See the people standing there/who disagree and never win/wonder why they don't get in my door." If they only knew that the best way to get in is not to do that. Because obviously anyone who is going to be straight and a real friend, a *real* person, is going to get in; but they simply stand there and give off, "We are fans, don't let us in."

Sometimes I invite them in, but it's not really cool, because I let one in and the next day she was in the *Daily Mirror* with her mother saying we were going to get married. So now we tell the fans, "Forget it."

If you're a junkie sitting in a room fixing a hole, then that's what it will

mean to you, but when I wrote it I meant if there's a crack or the room is uncolorful, then I'll paint it.

PAUL, *"FIXING A HOLE"*

● ● ●

It just came to me. Everybody was going on about karma, especially in the sixties. But it occurred to me that karma is instant as well as it influences your past and future life. There really is a reaction to what you do now. That's what people ought to be concerned about. Also, I'm fascinated by commercials and promotion as an art form. I enjoy them. So the idea of instant karma was like instant coffee: presenting something in a new form. I just liked it.

JOHN, *"INSTANT KARMA"*

● ● ●

Klaus Voorman had a harmonium in his house, which I hadn't played before. I was doodling on it, just playing to amuse myself, when "Within You" started to come. The tune came first, then I got the first sentence. It came out of what we'd been discussing that evening.

GEORGE, *"WITHIN YOU, WITHOUT YOU"*

● ● ●

Well, Dr. Roberts is a joke. There's some fellow in New York, and we'd hear people say, "You can get everything off him; any pills you want." It was a big racket, but a joke, too, about this fellow who cured everyone of everything with all these pills, tranquilizers and injections for this and that. He just kept New York high. That's what "Dr. Roberts" is all about, just a pill doctor who sees you all right. It was a joke between ourselves, but they go in *in*-jokes and come out *out*-jokes because everyone listens and puts their own thing on it, which is great. I mean, when I was young I never knew what "gilly gilly elsa feffer cats . . ." was all about, but I still enjoyed singing it. You put your own meaning at your own level to our songs, and that's what's terrific about them.

PAUL, "DR. ROBERTS"

• • •

It sounds like Elvis, doesn't it? No—no, it doesn't sound like Elvis. It *is* Elvis—even those bits where he goes very high.

RINGO, "LADY MADONNA"

• • •

Derek Taylor got held up one evening in L.A. and rang to say he'd be late. I told him on the phone that the house was in Blue Jay Way. He said he could find it okay, he could always ask a cop. Hence the song.

GEORGE, "BLUE JAY WAY"

• • •

George wrote this. Forget the Indian music and listen to the melody. Don't you think it's beautiful? It's really lovely.

PAUL, "THE INNER LIGHT"

• • •

"I was having a laugh because there'd been so much gobbledegook about *Pepper*, play it backwards while standing on your head and all that. Even now, I saw Mel Torme on TV the other day saying that "Lucy" was

written to promote drugs and so was "A Little Help from My Friends," and none of them were at all. "A Little Help from My Friends" only says "get high" in it, it's really about a little help from my friends, it's a sincere message. Paul had the line about "little help from my friends," I'm not sure, but I think he had some kind of structure for it. We wrote it pretty well 50–50, but it was certainly based on his original idea.

JOHN, "GLASS ONION"

• • •

This was just a fragment of an instrumental which we weren't too sure about, but Pattie liked it very much, so we decided to leave it on the album.

PAUL, "WILD HONEY PIE"

• • •

This was one of my favorite songs, but it's been issued in so many forms that it missed it as a record. I first gave it to the World Wildlife Fund, but they didn't do much with it, and then later we put it on the *Let It Be* album.

JOHN, "ACROSS THE UNIVERSE"

• • •

"Not Guilty" was written in 1968, although it appeared for the first time on the 1979 *George Harrison* album. I wrote it before *The Beatles* White album and it seems to be about that period: Paul—John—Apple—Rishikesh—Indian friends, etc.

GEORGE, "NOT GUILTY"

• • •

This forms part of a medley of songs which is about fifteen minutes long on *Abbey Road*. We did it this way because both John and I had a number of tunes which were potentially great but which we'd never finished.

PAUL, "SHE CAME IN THROUGH THE BATHROOM WINDOW"

• • •

That's about the Maharishi, yes. I copped out and I wouldn't write, "Maharishi what have you done, you made a fool of everyone," but now it can be told, fab listeners.

JOHN, "SEXY SADIE"

THE BEATLES
Growing Apart

We loved it like mad when we were first starting out because all we ever wanted was to go around Liverpool and be cute and popular, play our guitars and not have to work. But once it really became over the top we were forced to take a closer look. Was this what we really wanted? Shooting round the world locked in the backs of armored cars and leaping about like performing fleas in baseball arenas. After a while the Beatles simply became an excuse for people to go around behaving like animals.

GEORGE, 1983

• • •

Yoko's taken a lot of shit, her and Linda; but the Beatles' breakup wasn't their fault. It was just that suddenly we were all thirty, married and changed. We couldn't carry on living that life any more.

RINGO, 1981

• • •

By the time we got to *Let It Be*, we couldn't play the game anymore. We could see through each other and therefore we felt uncomfortable. Because up until then we really believed intensely in what we were doing. Suddenly, we didn't believe: It'd come to a point where it was no longer creating magic.

JOHN, 1970

• • •

Someday they're gonna look back at the Beatles and the Stones and all those guys as relics. The days when bands were all just men will be on the newsreels. They will be showing pictures of the guy with lipstick wriggling his ass and the four guys with the evil black make-up on their eyes trying to look raunchy. That's gonna be the in-joke of the future. It's tribal, it's gang, and it's fine. But when it continues and you're still doing it when you're forty, that means you're still only sixteen in the head.

JOHN, 1980

• • •

I could be singing "Yesterday" and wondering what we were going to have for dinner. It's like driving, that thing when you almost fall asleep at the wheel for a second. That can happen when you're performing.

PAUL, 1990

• • •

After the Beatles' last tour, which was the one where the Ku Klux Klan was burning Beatle records and I was held up as a Satanist or something . . . we decided no more touring. . . . So I said yes to Dick Lester that I would make this movie [*How I Won the War*] with him.

JOHN, 1970

BEATLES ON BEATLES

Even if I'm friends with Paul again, I'd never write with him. There's no point. I was living with Paul then, so I wrote with him. It's whoever you're living with. He writes with Linda, he's living with her, you know. So it's just natural.

JOHN

• • •

If I hadn't taken the chance and gone to Butlin's and then joined the Beatles, I'd still be on the shop floor as a fitter. I'm not really a strong-willed person. I go along with whatever is happening.

RINGO

• • •

I really don't mind people writing Beatles books as long as they get it right. As long as it's accurate. I don't want to read it unless they get it right. Our roadie, Mal, kept diaries for years, he always wrote everything that happened. The problem is the legal ownership of those diaries. They'll probably never be published.

GEORGE

• • •

It's very important to me for people to know that I actually had a mother. She just happened to have a husband who ran away to sea when the war was on and so she had it very rough for awhile.

I wasn't an orphan by any means. My mum was very much alive and well and living only a fifteen-minute walk from my aunties. I always saw her off and on. I just didn't live with her full time, that's all.

JOHN

• • •

In one way I feel pessimistic. When you see the rate that the world is being demolished—people polluting the oceans and chopping down all the forests—unless somebody puts the brakes on soon, there isn't going to be anything left. There's just going to be more and more people with less and less resources. In that respect, I feel very sad. But at the same time, I have to be optimistic.

At the bottom line, I think that even if the whole planet blew up, you'd have to think about what happens when you die. In the end, "Life goes on within you and without you." I just have a belief that this is only one little bit, the physical world is one little bit of the universe. So in the end it doesn't really matter.

GEORGE

• • •

You can't tell George anything. He's very trendy and has the right clothes and all that. But he's very narrow-minded and doesn't really have a broad view. One time I said something to George and he said, "I'm as intelligent as you, you know."

JOHN

• • •

Don't ever call me ex-Beatle McCartney again. That was a band I was with. Now I'm not with them.

PAUL

• • •

I refuse to be a leader and I'll always show my genitals or do something which prevents me from being Martin Luther King or Gandhi and getting killed.

JOHN

• • •

When the Beatles split, things got very bitter between us. We were putting out some publicity for the last album and it had a wedding photo of me and Linda, only John had crossed out the word "wedding" and written "funeral." That was too bitter. He went through a messed-up period—he was into heroin—and he thought people were ignoring him and favoring me. I think there were people turning him against me. But towards the end, we got over all that and were able to talk to each other about "How's your kids?" and "How's your cats?" He liked cats an awful lot, John. His Aunt Mimi had a lot of cats.

I still can't cope with his death. I got slagged off at the time because I just went to work like a robot and someone stuck a microphone in the car and said, "What do you think about John's death?" I can't cope with emotional stuff that easily and all I could say was, "It's a drag." It must have sounded so flippant to people when they read it in the newspapers, but I went home and we wept buckets that night and on many nights after that.

John's death caused me great grief. I loved him very much and still do.

PAUL

• • •

Yes, I was in the Beatles. Yes, we made some great records together. Yes, I love those boys. But that's the end of the story!

RINGO

• • •

You're constantly trying to remember if you're okay or not. I hate justifying myself. I remember asking George Martin once, "George, are we really going to have to keep justifying ourselves?" He said, "Yeah. Forever. . . ."

PAUL

• • •

I have a great fear of this so-called "normal" thing. You know, the ones that passed their exams, the ones who went to their jobs, the ones that didn't become rock and rollers, the ones that settled for it. Settled for "the deal." That's what I'm trying to avoid. But I'm sick of avoiding it through my own self-destruction.

I've decided now that I want to live. I'd actually decided it long before but I didn't really know what it meant until now. It's taken me however many years to get this far and I'm not about to give it up. I want to have a real go at it this time.

JOHN

• • •

The Beatles didn't really come up with anything new. They just heralded the change in consciousness that was happening in the sixties.

GEORGE

• • •

I've never claimed divinity. I've never claimed purity of soul. I've never claimed to have the answer to life. I only put out songs and answer questions as honestly as I can, no more, no less. I cannot live up to other people's expectations of me because they're illusionary. And the people who want more than I am, or than Bob Dylan is, or Mick Jagger is. . . . Whatever wind was blowing at the time [the sixties] moved the Beatles, too. I'm not saying we weren't flags on the top of a ship; but the whole boat was moving. Maybe the Beatles were in the crow's nest, shouting, "Land ho," or something like that, but we were all in the same damn boat.

JOHN

• • •

They are my brothers, you see. I'm an only child, and they're my brothers. I've always said that if I ever spend all my bread, I can just go and live with one of them, and vice versa, because we all love to spend it.

RINGO

• • •

The whole Beatles thing is like a horror story, nightmare. I don't even like to think about it.

GEORGE

• • •

I've withdrawn many times—part of me is a monk and part a performing flea! The fear in the music business is that you don't exist if you're not at Xenon with Andy Warhol. As I found out, life doesn't end when you stop subscribing to *Billboard*.

JOHN

• • •

Looking back on John, you know, he was a really great guy. I always idolized him. We always did, the group. I don't know if the others will tell you that, but he was very much our idol.

PAUL

• • •

There was a definite strained relationship right from the *White* album. There was a lot of alienation between us and him. Well, there was alienation amongst all of us. It was particularly strained because having been in a band from being kids, then suddenly we're all grown up and we've all got these other wives. That didn't exactly help. All the wives at that time really drove wedges between us. And then, after the years, when I saw John in New York, it was almost like he was crying out to me to tell me certain things or renew things, relationships, but he wasn't able to, because of the situation he was in.

I didn't often go to New York, but when I was there, I'd go see him and he was nice. He was always enthusiastic. That period where he was cooking bread and stuff, I always got an overpowering feeling from him. Almost a feeling that he wanted to say much more than he could, or than he did. You could see it in his eyes. But it was difficult. Well, you'd read all these stories—and they kept coming out all the time—about how the Beatles weren't actually anything. That they didn't mean a thing. That he [John] was the only one who had a clue about anything and the wife.

John is more like me. He got tired of fame and now he takes care of his baby.

GEORGE

• • •

We were going through Regents Park on our way to North London to do a session. We were in John's big Rolls Royce and we'd just come from his house in Weybridge. Suddenly we pulled up behind Brian [Jones], he had a hat on and all his outfit. John had a microphone set up in his car with a speaker underneath, like a police setup. John was a very funny guy and he shouted through the microphone, "Brian Jones, do not move! You are under surveillance, you are under arrest," and poor Brian leapt up about eight feet and went as white as a sheet, going, "Oh, my God. Oh, my God." Then he saw it was us. "You bastards!" It nearly killed him that day, John was so official-sounding.

After sessions we'd be careening through these villages on the way to Weybridge, shouting, "Wey hey," and driving much too fast at two or three in the morning. George would be in his Ferrari or something—he was quite a fast driver—and John and I would be following in the Rolls or the Princess. John would have his mike on and he'd be shouting to George in front, "It is foolish to resist, it is foolish to resist, pull over." It was insane. All the lights would go on in the houses as we went past, it must have freaked everybody out.

When John went to make *How I Won The War* in Spain, he took the same car, which he virtually lived in. It had blacked-out windows and you could never see who was in it, so it was just perfect. John didn't come out of it, he just used to talk to the people outside through the microphone, "Get away from the car, get away."

PAUL

• • •

Whatever made the Beatles the Beatles also made the sixties, and anybody who thinks that if John and Paul got together with George and Ringo, "the Beatles" would exist, is out of their skulls.

JOHN

• • •

The very first time we took LSD, John and I were together. And that experience and a lot of other things that happened after that, both on LSD and on the meditation trip to Rishikesh, we saw beyond each other's physical bodies, you know. That's there permanently, whether he's in a physical body or not. I mean this is the goal anyway: to realize the spiritual side. If you can't feel the spirit of some friend who's been close, then what chance have you got of feeling the spirit of Christ or Buddha or whoever else you may be interested in? "If your memory serves you well, we're going to meet again." I believe that.

GEORGE

• • •

Talking is the slowest form of communicating anyway. Music is much better. We're communicating to the outside world through our music. The office in America says the folks there listen to *Sgt. Pepper* over and over so they know what we're thinking in London.

JOHN

● ● ●

I sometimes hear myself in interviews going, "Well, I'm just a sort of ordinary guy." And I think, what will they go away thinking. "Did he really say he was an ordinary guy?" Because there's quite a lot of evidence to the contrary.

PAUL

● ● ●

I was getting into that established, fat, professional-pop-star-can-do-no-wrong, worker genius, a record every few months and that's all right. A few Hare Krishnas here and there and I've done my social bit.

JOHN

● ● ●

I didn't like her [Yoko] because she was taking my friend away.

RINGO

● ● ●

Look, [John] was a great guy, a great sense of humor and I'd do it all again. I'd go through it all again and have him slagging me off again just because he was so great; those are all the down moments, there was much more pleasure than has really come out. I had a wonderful time with one of the world's most talented people.

PAUL

● ● ●

We [the Beatles] have been having dinner together. We are friends now; it's the first time we have been this close for a long time. But it doesn't mean to say we are going to make another group or anything. You know, I could go out and try to become a superstar, and I tell you, if I went to an agent and a manager and practiced a bit, I could do it. But I don't really want to do that. That's being a kamikaze pop star, the tours and everything. I don't have to prove anything. I don't want to be in the business full-time because I'm a gardener: I plant flowers and watch them grow.

GEORGE

● ● ●

The Beatles saved the world from boredom.

GEORGE

● ● ●

He and Yoko came over to our hotel (November 1980) and we had a great time saying hello again. His head was together. His album [*Double Fantasy*] was done and we worked it out that come January, we were going into the studio together. Even though he was always treated in the press as a cynical put-down artist, John had the biggest heart of all of us. He was so up, so happy then, he blew me away.

RINGO

● ● ●

That was a songwriting partnership. We were very special. I could feel it was a special kind of thing because it was dead easy to write.

Talk about sitting around for days trying to write songs, in a matter of hours we'd feel we'd been at it too long! John and I were perfect for each other. I could do stuff he might not be in the mood for, egg him in a certain direction he might not want to go in. And he could do the same with me. If I'd go in a certain direction he didn't like, he'd just stop it like that.

PAUL

• • •

I have a problem, I must admit, when people try to get the Beatles together. They're still suggesting it, even though John is dead. They still say, "Why don't the Beatles get together?" I suppose the three of us could, but it was such a struggle to find our individual identities after the Beatles.

GEORGE

• • •

I'm not afraid of dying. . . . I'm prepared for death because I don't believe in it. I think it's just getting out of one car and getting into another.

JOHN

• • •

If John had been killed by Elvis, it would at least have had meaning.

GEORGE

• • •

Starvation in India doesn't worry me one bit. Not one iota, it doesn't, man. And it doesn't worry you if you're honest. You just pose. You don't even know it exists. You've just seen the charity ads. You can't pretend to me that an ad reaches down into the

depths of your soul and actually makes you feel more for these people than, for instance, you feel about buying a new car.

PAUL

• • •

Yeah, well, how about just a cup of tea (instead of a reunion) together? Even that, you see, to get them together; get these four people together and just put them in a room to have tea. Satellite it all around the world at twenty dollars each just to watch it and we could make a fortune. We could just sit there and say, "Well, John, what have you been doing?" But it would be difficult even to do that because everybody's left home and they're living their own lives.

GEORGE

• • •

Touring's like the army, whatever the army's like. One big sameness which you have to go through. One big mess. I can't remember any tours. We've had enough of performing forever. I can't imagine any reason which would make us do any sort of tour again.

JOHN

• • •

Names are far out. Ray Cooper, for instance. A "cooper" is a barrel maker. Larry Smith. Well, a "smith's" a blacksmith. George Harrison. You know what that means, don't you? Son of Hari!

GEORGE

• • •

John's watching over us all, you know.

RINGO

• • •

So the thing is, if you really want to get it [spiritual enlightenment] permanently, you have got to do it, you know . . . be healthy, don't eat meat, keep away from nightclubs, and meditate.

GEORGE

• • •

Having reached the end of space, you look across the wall and there's yet more space.

PAUL

• • •

Satya Sai Baba is not my guru, we're just good friends.

GEORGE

• • •

Mal Evans, our roadie, got shot by the L.A. police. It was so crazy. Mal was a big lovable bear of a roadie; he would go over the top occasionally, but we all knew him and never had any problems. The LAPD weren't so fortunate. They were just told he was upstairs with a shotgun and so they ran up, kicked the door in and shot him. His girlfriend told them, "He's upstairs, he's a bit moody and he's got a shotgun up there and he's got some downers." Had I been there I would have been able to say, "Mal, don't be silly." In fact, any of his friends could have talked him out of it without any sweat, because he was not a nutter. But his girlfriend—she was an L.A. girl—didn't know him that well. She should not have rung the cops but that's the way it

goes . . . a thump on the door, "Where is he? Where's the assailant?" Bang, bang, bang, bang! They don't ask questions, they shoot first.

PAUL

• • •

We would rather be rich than famous. That is, more rich and slightly less famous.

JOHN

• • •

We're just a bunch of crummy musicians really.

GEORGE

• • •

We always make our mistakes in public.

PAUL

• • •

PAUL: He must be kicking himself now.

JOHN: I hope he kicks himself to death.

PAUL: I don't blame him for turning us down.

ON THE BEATLES BEING TURNED DOWN BY DICK ROWE OF DECCA

We were a band who made it very big, that's all. Our best work was never recorded.

JOHN

• • •

We were being influenced by avant-garde composers. For "A Day in the Life," I suggested we should write all but fifteen bars properly so that the orchestra could read it, but where the fifteen bars began we would give the musicians a simple direction: "Start on your lowest note and eventually, at the end of the fifteen bars, be at your highest." How they got there was up to them, but it all resulted in a crazy crescendo. It was interesting because the trumpet players, always famous for their fondness for lubricating substances, didn't care, so they'd be there at the note ahead of everyone. The strings all watched each other like little sheep: "Are you going up?" Yes. "So I am." And they'd go up. "A little more?" Yes. And they'd go up a little more, all very delicate and cozy, all going up together. You listen to those trumpets. They're just freaking out.

PAUL

• • •

I'm a tidy man. I keep my socks in the socks drawer and stash in the stash box. Anything else they must have brought with them.

GEORGE

CHAPTER THREE

A Fine Natural Imbalance/ John Lennon and Yoko Ono

John Lennon
SELECTED QUOTATIONS
• •
Spain, 1966

I was just a bundle of nerves the first day on this film [*How I Won The War*]. I couldn't hardly speak, I was so nervous. My first speech was in a forest, on patrol. I was supposed to say, "My heart's not in it any more," and it wasn't. I went home and said to myself, "Either you're not going to be like that, or you're going to give up." I don't mind talking to the camera; it's the people that throw me. I feel I want to be them all, painter, writer, actor, singer, player, musician. I want to try them all and I'm lucky enough to be able to. I want to see which one turns me on. This film, apart from wanting to do it because of what it stands for, I want to see what I'll be like when I've done it.

• • •

I don't want people taking things from me that aren't really me. They make you something they want to make you, that isn't really you. They come and talk and find answers, but they're their answers, not mine. We're not the Beatles to each other, you know. It's a joke to us. If we're going out the door of a hotel, we say, "Right! Beatle John! Beatle George now! Come on, let's go!" We don't put on a false front or anything. But we know that leaving the door we turn into Beatles because everybody looking at us sees Beatles. We're not the Beatles at all. We're just us.

But we made it and we asked for it to an extent and that's how it's going to be. That's why George is in India studying the sitar, and I'm here. Because we're a bit tired of going out the door and the only way to soften the blow is just to spread out a bit.

• • •

America used to be the big youth place in everybody's imagination. America had teenagers and everywhere else just had people.

• • •

If they said, "Fight the war now," my age group would fight the war. Not that they'd want to. There might be a bit more trouble gettin' them in line, because I'd be up there shouting, "Don't do it!" It just so happens some groups playing in England are making people talk about England, but nothing else is going on. Pop music gets through to people all over the world, that's the main thing. In that respect, youth might be together a bit. The commie youth might be the same as us, and we all know that, basically, they probably are. This kind of music is helping. But there's more talk about it than is actually helping. You know, swinging London, and all that. Everybody can go around England with long hair a bit, and boys can wear flowered trousers and things. But there's still the same old nonsense going on. It's just that we're all dressed up a bit different.

John Lennon

INTERVIEW

· · · · · · · · · ·

London, 1969

QUESTION: What you're saying is that as your private lives are going to be under scrutiny anyway, you might just as well play the game and turn it to your own devices, which in this case, is to push peace.

JOHN LENNON: That's it. Everybody's talking about it, but why aren't they really *saying* it? The queens and prime ministers and all the people in the public eye. Why don't they talk about it all the time? Instead of saying we *might* have a meeting, about a meeting, about a meeting to talk about it. It's like a dirty word. Especially in America. The radicals are saying, "Kill the pigs!" The establishment knows how to play the game violence, they've been playing it for millions of years. The radicals are never going to win.

QUESTION: Your relationship with Yoko in the early period, the nude photos on your *Two Virgins* LP and your honeymoon sleep-in, almost seems rather aggressive. As if to say, "I'm going to live the way I like and I want everybody to know it!"

JOHN: No, but see, if I had tried to have a honeymoon in secret, it would have been like Jackie Kennedy, you know. She tried the secret honeymoon, but it didn't work. They didn't get one, the press got it and it became a public honeymoon. So instead of fighting it, we joined up. All we did was use that event, which would have been in the press anyway, to get the word *peace* in whatever articles they wrote. And also to be on the front pages instead of other freaks. We're friendly freaks, that's all.

QUESTION: You've said you suddenly freaked out when you first got together with Yoko.

JOHN: It appeared I'd freaked out. It appeared I'd gone mad for a while. I left home and moved in with this girl nobody knew, I hadn't been on the scene so it all happened overnight for them.

QUESTION: Are you still making records as a Beatle?

JOHN: Yeah. We're in the process of finishing off the next album and halfway through the next. So production has gone up a million percent in all fields. John and Yoko have both got books coming out, individually and together, in the States and here shortly. And there's some lithography coming out as well.

QUESTION: So this has opened up a whole new creative world for you then.

41

JOHN: I had outlets like my books *In His Own Write* and *A Spaniard in the Works*, there are people doing a play from them now. All very cute, but the point is that was two books in four years. We sort of start each other off, so it's like we've got too much to do. We really have to be selective about what we're doing these days.

QUESTION: In your recent interview in *Rolling Stone* you said, "What we're trying to do is rock'n'roll with less philosorock, because rockers is what we really are." Will you please differentiate between rock'n'roll and philosorock?

JOHN: Well, philosorock is like the psychedelia all the pop groups went through, and we went through it, too. It's valid, because it was the experience we all went through. But now, we sing, "Get back," you know. So most of the lyrics on the new album are straight: "I love you and you love me and we are all together," without the other thing. It's mainly like my new single, "Get back, don't let down, I love you, don't let me down. . . ."

John Lennon
SELECTED QUOTATIONS
London, 1969

When it all started, we said, "Listen, man, here's another field that has no quali-fications except that you've got to get down to it and want to do it and you can make it in terms of the world. You can make it without the pressure." Everybody was finding that out. I had my guitar, Mick Jagger had his in London, and Eric Burdon had his up in Newcastle. We were all going through the same changes at once. We all discovered that values didn't mean a thing and you could make it without college, education, and all of those things. It's nice to know how to read and write, but apart from that I never learned anything worth a damn.

• • •

You start with rock'n'roll in the late fifties and early sixties when all the kids, including me, were James Dean and Elvis, early paranoiac and violent. That's what happens on acid, folks. From there you start maturing, or thinking about the trip. The first effects of the drugs wear off and you start coasting along a bit and you have time to look at the trees. That developed into the actual acid scene, the psychedelic bit. When everyone was groovin' around with flowers and all that. And then of course, like any drug, it wears off and you're back to so-called reality.

• • •

Some people discovered a new reality and are still confident about the future, like the two of us. Everyone's talking about the way it's going, the decadence and the rest of it, but hardly anyone's talking about all the good that came out of the last ten years. Like the vast gathering of people at Woodstock, which was the biggest mass of people ever gathered together for anything other than war. Before, nobody had an army that big that wasn't there to kill somebody or have a violent scene like the Romans. Even a Beatle concert was more violent than that! The good things to come out of the last ten years were these peaceful movements. The bully, that's the establishment. They know how to beat people up, they know how to gas them. They have the arms and the equipment. The mistake was made when the kids started playing their game. Nobody can tell me that violence is the way. There *must* be another way. But a lot of people fell for it, and it's actually understandable, because when the bully is actually right there it's hard to say, "Turn the other cheek, baby!" When we were in touch with the kids in Berkeley, we were doing our peace demonstration in Montreal in bed and we were suddenly directly connected to them by phone. They were saying, "Help us! It's out of our control." What can we say? I haven't got any solution!

●　●　●

Ask anyone who's been in the drug scene, it's not something you can go on and on doing. It's like drink, you've got to come to terms with it. You've got to get out of it. You're left with yourself all the time whatever you do, meditation, drugs or anything. You've got to get down to your own garden and your own temple in your head, like Donovan says. It all comes down to yourself.

●　●　●

To work on this relationship with Yoko is very hard, but we've got the gift of love. But love is like a precious plant, you just can't accept it and leave it in the cupboard. You've got to keep watering it and look after it. You got to see that it's all right and nurture it.

●　●　●

I'm full of optimism because of all the contacts I've made around the world. Just knowing there are other people around who I agree with and that I'm not insane and not alone. And of course Woodstock and the Isle of Wight, all the mass meetings of youth are completely positive for me. We're all showing our flags. I'm completely positive and when I'm negative I've got Yoko. This is only the beginning. This sixties bit was just waking up in the morning and we haven't even gotten to dinner time. I can't wait, I'm so glad to be around. There's going to be more and more of us. And whatever you're thinking there Mrs. Grundy of Birmingham-on-Toast, you haven't a chance. (a) You're not going to be there when we're running it and (b) you're gonna like it when you get less frightened of it. It's going to be wonderful, and I believe it. They, *whoever they are*, don't stand a chance because you can't stop love. All those old bits from religion that say, "Love is all-powerful" are true, and that's the bit they can't do, they can't handle it.

John Lennon and Yoko Ono
PRESS CONFERENCE
. . . .
London, 1969

QUESTION: It seems strange they were going to stop you from putting on something that was going to help Biafra.

JOHN LENNON: Yeah, I don't know what their reasons are.

QUESTION: They're afraid of trouble?

JOHN: Well, the British establishment doesn't like Biafra mentioned the same as they don't like Kila mentioned because we are mainly responsible for keeping the Biafra situation going. Britain is supplying the arms and the oil companies are supplying the motive, so it's not good. Britain doesn't really want publicity about Biafra. Whatever you read about Biafra in Britain is all slanted towards the Nigerians and you never really read about the Biafran side of it. They're making out like there is a suicidal kamikaze guy in the jungle holding on to a small kingdom, and that's not the case at all. The publicity is one-sided. And of course, unless we can become aware of it and think of some gimmicks to make people actually aware of what's going on in Biafra, then we won't know about it until it's all over. But in ten years' time they'll have to release the papers—then everybody in Britain will be aware of what we did to the Biafrans, the same as we're only aware now of what we really did to the Indians. We're doing the same now as we always did, you know? It's our responsibility, all of Britain's responsibility. . . .

QUESTION: Are you conscious of a fight against the establishment?

JOHN: It's the establishment *within yourself.* The fact that I think, "Oh, if hadn't opened my mouth about peace I wouldn't have to be responsible when you ask me, 'What are you going to do next?'" So, it's the establishment in myself I'm going to fight against.

YOKO ONO: It suddenly occurred to me the establishment is really starting to be afraid of us in a way. I mean, I wouldn't really mention the details, because they do fear us, I suppose . . . so they are getting nervous.

QUESTION: I wonder if you've changed your minds about actually going into parliament to rouse it up a bit and change the thinking.

JOHN: Bernadette Devlin tried and realized that nothing could be done in that field. I don't think going into Parliament is the answer. I'm as much in politics as anybody in Parliament and I don't think you have to compromise to be a politician.

That's not the answer, that'd be just putting on another cloak. Instead of being John Lennon, the pop star, or whatever I am, I'd just be Lennon the politician. I could do no more, no less. Probably less, because there's so many rules to the game out there. I'm not playing by the rules.

QUESTION: So the up-to-date report on your peace motives and the movement you've started, is that you're very happy with the way things are going. . . .

JOHN: Well, we'd be happier if there was peace. We'd be happier if we could say, "We, the British, aren't doing anything; we're a peaceful nation." The drag about being British is that we're still imperialist even though we haven't got the power. It's still money that's causing all those people to die.

QUESTION: What about the new album, can we talk about that?

JOHN: The *Wedding Album*? It's like a home wedding album. You know, people always bring out the pictures of the wedding. These are personal photographs. There's the press's photographs of the wedding, the cartoons of the wedding, it's a package. I can hardly remember, there's so much in it. I mean, there's posters and photographs, there's a section on the press which has all the cuttings and their photographs.

QUESTION: What are your views on the press?

JOHN: I'm not against them. I can't judge the press, it's like saying, "What do you think about Americans?" They're all individuals; that's what I think about them.

QUESTION: A lot of people in show business seem anti-press.

JOHN: The thing about show business is it's a love-hate relationship. You want the publicity but you don't want the intrusion on your privacy, but you can't have both. So you can't complain, really.

QUESTION: You've accepted that?

JOHN: Yes, the acceptance was to do the bed event and make ourselves available.

YOKO: I just want to say that it's also a message of love and peace. The whole thing is a love and peace message.

QUESTION: I've seen you've got some drawings in the *Wedding Album* as well, Yoko.

YOKO: Oh, yeah, one side are my drawings of how I saw the wedding and the other side is John's view. It's like a cartoon strip. Actually this whole album is about love and peace. The record is about love and peace connecting with our wedding and honeymoon.

JOHN: The press cuttings we used are both for and against. We haven't slanted it . . .

QUESTION: John, what about the music on the album?

JOHN: One side is a recording of both Yoko and my heartbeats. Our heartbeats are bumping along there, it's kind of like African drums. And we sort of howl on top. I sing "Yoko" and she sings "John" continuously on one side. It's like an extended, very extreme John and Marsha that was out years ago. On the other side is bits and pieces, it's like a montage of songs, sounds, talk, bits of interviews from Amsterdam while we were doing our first bed event.

QUESTION: A lot of people I'm sure will be intrigued as to why you put your heartbeats on an LP.

JOHN: It's just an idea, you know. I mean, why do you put your voice on an LP?

QUESTION: So you don't actually perform any songs in the usual way?

JOHN: There's one or two snatches of song on the other side.

YOKO: But "John and Yoko," the shouting, is a very long song, actually.

JOHN: It's a very big song. It's the next progression after "Life with the Lions."

YOKO: And the heartbeat itself, the drumbeat is taken from the heartbeat, it's a very basic thing.

JOHN: Music is big propaganda. Rock'n'roll is like a mother's womb in that everybody feels good like the African drums. Instead of imitating the mother's womb, or heartbeat, we just used the actual heartbeat, that's all.

QUESTION: I read in one magazine that you looked upon Yoko as a mother. In what sense did you mean that?

JOHN: No, I said Yoko is mother, lover, daughter and everything to me and vice versa. I can lean on her like I would lean on a mother when I'm in that kind of situation and I can appreciate her. She is all women to me and I am all men to her. That's what I meant.

QUESTION: What's John to you Yoko?

YOKO: Oh father, son, lover, everything. Everything a man could possess. I'm not just saying that because he has so many strange complex sides, his limit is always shifting; it's amazing. In the morning when I wake up and I see John beside me I see him as sort of a baby or maybe a father. It's all very mixed up.

JOHN: All the things people in love go through.

YOKO: Yes, it's very beautiful.

John Lennon

London, December 1969

QUESTION: With your busy life, how do you get around to actually writing so many songs?

JOHN LENNON: If I could only get time to myself right now, instead of all this Monopoly with Northern Songs, I could probably write about thirty songs a day. As it is, I probably average about twelve a night. Paul, too, is mad on it. It's something that gets in your blood. I've got things going around in my head right now. As soon as I leave here I'm going over to Paul's place and we'll sit down and start work.

QUESTION: How do you actually write?

JOHN: The way we're writing at the moment, it's straightforward and nothing weird. Songs like "Get Back," things like that. We recorded that one on the Apple roof, but I'm not sure if that's the version that went out. We always record about ten versions, so some get lost in the end. I'm not really interested in the production of our records. In fact, I wish I didn't have to go through that whole thing. For me, the satisfaction of writing a song is in the performance of it. The production is a bore. If some guy would invent a robot to do it, it would be great. But all that "get the bass right, get the drums right" is a drag. All I want to do is get my guitar out and sing songs.

QUESTION: Would you like to do any concerts again?

JOHN: Sure, I quite fancy doing some live shows, but Ringo doesn't because he says it'll be just the same when we get on, nothing different. I can't give you any definite plans for a live show when we're not even agreed on it. We've got to come to an agreement. For a start, there's too much going on now for us to talk realistically about going on tour. In a way, that's why it's unfortunate all the publicity came out about doing live shows when it did. We were only thinking about it vaguely, but it kind of got out of hand.

QUESTION: What's on tap for the band these days, then?

JOHN: I suppose the next Great Beatle Event will be the new LP, in about eight weeks. A lot of the tracks will be like "Get Back," and a lot of that was done in a one-take kind of thing. We've done about twelve tracks, some of them are still to be re-mixed. Paul and I are now working on a kind of song montage we might do as one piece on one side. We've got two weeks to finish the whole thing, so we're really working at it.

QUESTION: What does the new music sound like?

JOHN: All the songs we're doing sound normal to me, but they might be unusual to you. There's no "Revolution No. 9," but there's a few heavy sounds. I couldn't pin us down to being on a heavy scene, or a commercial pop scene, or a straight tuneful scene. We're just into whatever's going. Just rockin' along.

QUESTION: Any idea what the next single might be?

JOHN: The follow-up to "Get Back" is "Ballad of John and Yoko." It's something I wrote and it's like an old-time ballad. The song is just the story of us getting married, going to Paris, then to Amsterdam, all that. It's "Johnny B. Paperback Writer." We don't want to release it straight away, because it might kill the sales and I suppose we're cowards that way. I don't regard it as a separate record scene . . . it's the Beatles' next single, simple as that.

QUESTION: What's the personnel?

JOHN: The story came out that only Paul and I were on the record, but I wouldn't have bothered publicizing that. It doesn't mean anything, it just so happened there were only us two there. George was abroad and Ringo was on his film and couldn't come that night. Because of that, it was a choice of either re-mixing or doing a new one, and you always go for doing a new one instead of fiddling about with an old one. So we did, and it turned out very well.

QUESTION: How do you really feel about business?

JOHN: As for all this financial business, it does get in the way of writing, but I don't find it that much of a drag. It is like Monopoly . . . what with all these bankers and played round a big table with all these heavies. You know the bit, "Then I'll give you the Strand or Old Kent Road," and you say give me two houses. Really, the outcome of this whole financial business doesn't matter. We'll still be making records and somebody will be copping some money, and we'll be copping some money, and that'll be that.

QUESTION: How do you feel about Mary Hopkins' great success?

JOHN: I don't have any involvement with Mary Hopkins' records, it's pure Paul. But there is one discovery I'd like to promote. I think I'm going to do a pop record with Yoko. I've got this other song we were singing last night, I think it'll be quite a laugh for her to do a pop record. It's one I've written myself, and it's about Yoko, but I'll just change the word Yoko to John and she can sing it about me. This TV film *Rape* we did for Austrian TV didn't get fantastic reviews, but then neither does every record the Beatles make. Hell, do you remember the reviews for "Hey Jude"? I remember Stuart Henry saying, "Oh well, you'll either like it or you won't." The critics are the same with *Rape*. It's a good film and we stand by it. There's a few people who understand it and the rest have no idea. They don't know the difference between Jean Luc Godard and Walt Disney. It's funny. The critics can accept it from Luc Godard but they can't accept it from us, because they're so hung up on who Yoko and I are and what we do, they can't see the product. But that'll die. Yoko and I will just have to overcome our image, and people'll have to judge us on our art and not the way we look. Back to songwriting, though, you can't say Paul and I are writing separately these days. We do both. When it comes to needing five hundred by Friday, you gotta get it together. I definitely find I work better when I've got a deadline. It really frightens you and you've got to churn them out. All the time arranging things in my mind. This film the Beatles made recently, of us recording and working, somebody's editing at the moment. It's sixty-eight hours, but they're trying to get it down to five for several TV specials. Or, then, it might be a movie. I don't know.

QUESTION: How do you perceive your image these days?

JOHN: This "image" thing people are always on about with the Beatles is something in Joe Public's eye. That's why it's a drag when people talk about fresh-faced Beatles like it was five years ago. We're always changing. Like the TV clip of "Get Back." Now I've got the beard, Paul is clean-shaven, and George is the one with the moustache. Even we can't keep up with our image. I come into Apple one day and there's George with a new head on. So if that's the way it is with us, I tell you, the public doesn't stand a chance of keeping up with how we look. Anyway, how we are is up to ourselves. The music is what's important, and as far as that's concerned, Yoko and I stimulate each other like crazy. For instance, did you know she'd trained as a classical musician? I didn't know that until this morning. In college she majored in classical composition. I've just written a song called "Because." Yoko was playing some classical bit and I said, "Play that backwards," and we had a tune. We'll probably write a lot more in the future. I've written with other people as well. For instance, there was a mad thing I wrote with our electronics genius, Alex. It was called "What a Shame Mary Jane Had a Pain at the Party," and was meant for the last Beatles album. It was real madness, but we never released it. I'd like to do it again. There was another song I wrote around the *Pepper* time that's still in the can, called "You Know My Name Look Up the Number." That's the only words to it. It just goes on all the way like that, and we did these mad backings. But I never did finish it. And I must.

QUESTION: What's happening with "Get Back"?

JOHN: Well, we'd been talking about it since we recorded it, and we kept saying, "That's a single." Eventually we got so fed up talking about it, we suddenly said, "Okay, that's it. Get it out tomorrow."

John Lennon
INTERVIEW
• • • • • • • • • •
Mississauga, Ontario, December 1969

MARSHALL McLUHAN*: Can you recall the occasion or the immediate reasons for getting involved in music?

JOHN LENNON: I heard Elvis Presley and that was it. There were lots of other things going on, but that was the conversion. I kind of dropped everything.

MARSHALL: You felt you could do it at least as well as he could?

JOHN: Yeah. But I thought we better get a few people together because maybe we wouldn't make it alone. So we did a team job.

MARSHALL: The British are still more team-oriented than the Americans. In terms of performance, the star system doesn't play quite as well in England. The private star.

JOHN: They have a reaction to that in England, treating their stars and entertainers like animals. We're not quite like the Americans, to be hyped by Hollywood. The attitude is be quiet, do a dance at the London Palladium and stop talking about peace. That's what we get in London.

MARSHALL: Language is a form of organized stutter. Literally, you chop your sounds up in order to talk. Now, when you sing you don't stutter, so singing is a way of stretching language into long, harmonious patterns and cycles. What do you think about the language in your songs?

JOHN: Language and song to me, apart from being pure vibrations, are like trying to describe a dream. And because we don't have telepathy, we try and describe the dream to each other, to verify to each other what we know, what we believe is inside each other. And the stuttering is right, because we can't say it. No matter how you say it, it's never how you want to say it.

MARSHALL: The moment you sing, do you feel you are communicating more?

JOHN: Yes, because the words are irrelevant.

MARSHALL: Rowan and Martin say, "We don't tell jokes; we project a mood." You're also concerned with projecting a mood and defining it. Putting down some pattern so that other people can find the pattern and participate.

---

* Marshall McLuhan was America's first well-known media guru.

JOHN: As soon as you find the pattern, you break it. Otherwise it gets boring. The Beatles' pattern is one that has to be scrapped. If it remains the same, it's a monument, or a museum, and one thing this age is about is no museums. The Beatles turned into a museum, so they have to be scrapped, deformed or challenged.

MARSHALL: They're in danger of becoming in good taste?

JOHN: They've passed that. They have to be thoroughly horsewhipped.

MARSHALL: Do you think we're moving into new rhythms and patterns?

JOHN: Just complete freedom and nonexpectation from audience, musician, or performer. And when we've had that for a hundred years, then we can talk about playing around with patterns and bars and music again. We must get away from the patterns we've had for thousands of years.

MARSHALL: Well, this means very much in the way of decentralizing our world, doesn't it?

JOHN: Yes. We must be one country and stick together. You don't have to have badges to say we're together. We're together if we're together and no stamps or flags are going to make anybody together folks.

John Lennon

EXCERPTS FROM A LETTER TO PAUL AND LINDA MCCARTNEY

Ascot, Berkshire, 1969

Bag Productions Inc.
Tittenhurst Park,
Ascot, Berkshire.
Ascot 23022

Dear Linda and Paul,

. . . You really think the press are beneath me/you? . . . *Linda* who do you think we/you are? The self "indulgent" who "doesn't realize who he is hurting" bit. I hope you realized what shit you and the rest of my "kind and unselfish" friends laid on Yoko and me, since we've been together . . . Linda, if you don't care what I say shut up! Let Paul write, or whatever . . .

I'm not ashamed of the *Beatles*! I did start it all! But if some of the *shit* we took to make them so big, I thought we all felt that way in varying degrees, obviously not . . .

Do you really think most of today's *art* came about because of the Beatles? I don't believe you're that insane. Paul, do you believe that? Didn't we always say we were *part* of the movement, not all of it, of course, we changed the world, but try and follow it through. GET OFF YOUR GOLD DISC AND _____! . . .

I left the Beatles, Paul and Klein both spent the day persuading me it was better not to say anything, *asking* me *not* to say anything because it would "*hurt the Beatles*," and "lets just let it peter "out," remember? So get that into your pretty little perversion of a mind. Mrs. McCartney, the cunts *asked* me to keep quiet about it. Of course the *money* angle is important, to all of us, especially after all the pretty shit that came from your insane family in New York and GOD HELP YOU OUT, PAUL, see you in two years, I reckon you'll be out then.

In spite of it all

Love to you both,

John and Yoko

John Lennon
PRESS CONFERENCE
July, 1971

QUESTION: Your recent public statements suggest your views are becoming increasingly radical. When did this happen?

JOHN LENNON: I've always been politically minded and against the status quo. It's pretty basic when you're brought up, like I was, to fear the police as a natural enemy and despise the army as something that takes everybody away and leaves them dead somewhere. It's just a basic working-class thing, though it begins to wear off when you get older, get a family, and are swallowed up by the system. In my case I've never not been political, though religion tended to overshadow it in my acid days, which would be around '65 or '66. And that religion was directly the result of all that superstar shit. Religion was an outlet for my repression. I thought, "Well, there's something else to life, isn't there? This isn't it, surely?" But I was always political in a way, you know. In the two books I wrote, even though they were written in a sort of Joycean gobbledegook, there's many knocks at religion and a play about a worker and a capitalist. I've been satirizing the system since childhood. I used to write magazines in school and hand them around. I was very conscious of class, they would say, with a chip on my shoulder, because I knew what happened to me and I knew about the class repression coming down on us. It was a fucking fact, but in the hurricane Beatle world it got left out—I got farther away from reality for a time. When it comes to the nitty-gritty, they won't let the people have any power, they'll give all the rights to perform and dance for them, but no real power. After the revolution you have the problem of keeping things going, of sorting out all the different views. I don't know what the answer is; obviously Mao is aware of this problem and keeps the ball moving. Once the new power has taken over they have to establish a new status quo just to keep the factories and trains running. We all have bourgeois instincts within us, we all get tired and feel the need to relax. How do you keep everything going and keep up the revolutionary fervor after you've achieved what you set out to achieve? Of course Mao has kept them up to it in China, but what happens after Mao goes? Also, he uses a personality cult. Perhaps that's necessary; everybody seems to need a father figure. But I've been reading *Khrushchev Remembers*, I know he's a bit of a lad himself, but he seemed to think that making a religion out of an individual was bad, that doesn't seem to be part of the basic communist ideal. If we took over Britain, then we'd have a job of cleaning up the bourgeoisie and keeping people in a revolutionary state of mind.

QUESTION: How do you think we can destroy the capitalist system here?

JOHN: Only by making the workers aware of the really unhappy position they are in. They think they are in a wonderful free-speaking country; they've got cars and tellies and they don't want to think there's anything more to life; they are prepared to let the bosses run them, to see their children fucked up in school. They're dreaming someone else's dream. They should realize that the blacks and the Irish are being harassed and repressed and they will be next. As soon as they start being aware of that, we can really begin to do something. The workers can start to take over. Like Marx said, "To each according to his need," I think that would work well here. But we'd also have to infiltrate the army, because they are well trained to kill us all. We've got to start all this from where we ourselves are oppressed. It's false, shallow, to be giving to others when your own need is great. The idea is not to comfort people, but to make them feel worse, to constantly put before them the degradations and humiliations they go through to get what they call a living wage.

John Lennon
SELECTED QUOTATIONS
. . . .

There was a third version of *Revolution* that was just abstract *musicque concrete*, loops and that, people screaming. I thought I was painting in sound a picture of revolution, but I made a mistake, you know. The mistake was that it was anti-revolution.

On the version released as a single I said, "When you talk about destruction you can count me out." I didn't want to get killed. I didn't really know that much about the Maoists, but I just knew they seemed to be so few and yet they painted themselves green and stood in front of the police waiting to get picked off.

I just thought it was unsubtle, you know. I thought the original communist revolutionaries coordinated themselves a bit better and didn't go around shouting about it.

That was how I felt. I was really asking a question. As someone from the working class, I was always interested in Russia and China and everything that related to the working class, even though I was playing the capitalist game.

● ● ●

They knock me for saying, "Power to the people," and say no one section should have power. Crap! The people aren't a section. *The people means everyone.* I think everybody should own everything equally and the people should own part of the factories and they should have some say in who is the boss. It's the same as students being be able to select teachers. It might be like communism, but I don't really know what communism is. There is no real communist state in the world, you must realize that. Russia isn't, it's a fascist state. The socialism I talk about is a British socialism, not where some daft Russian might do it, or the Chinese might do it. That might suit them. Us, we'd have a nice socialism here. A British socialism. I'm not sure how something like a record company would be run, but they would certainly have a piece. The thing at the moment is, it's not mine. If I had my way, it would be different altogether. If the workers ever took it over, they could have it. I said that years ago.

● ● ●

The thing the sixties did was show us the possibility and the responsibility that we all had. It wasn't the answer, it just gave us a glimpse of the possibility, and in the seventies everybody's going nah, nah, nah and possibly in the eighties everyone will say, "Okay, lets project the positive side of life again."

● ● ●

We're either going to live or we're going to die. If we're dead we're going to have to deal with that, if we're alive we're going to have to deal with being alive. So worrying about whether Wall Street, or the Apocalypse is going to come in the form of the Great Beast, is not going to do us any good today.

• • •

But the world is not like the sixties, the whole world's changed. I am going into an unknown future, but I'm still all here. And still, while there's life, there's hope.

• • •

You have to give thanks to God or whatever is up there, the fact that we all survived. We all survived Vietnam or Watergate, the tremendous upheaval of the whole world. It changed. We were the hip ones of the sixties.

CHAPTER FOUR

"Why?" Says the Junk In the Yard/ Paul McCartney

Paul and Linda McCartney
WEDDING PRESS CONFERENCE
London, 1969

QUESTION: When did you decide to get married, Paul?

PAUL MCCARTNEY: About a week ago.

QUESTION: What prompted it?

PAUL: We just decided to do it instead of thinking about it.

QUESTION: How do you feel about it, Linda—you're obviously terribly happy?

LINDA MCCARTNEY: Terribly happy.

QUESTION: You've been described as a New York socialite. Does that mean you will be spending most of your time in New York?

LINDA: No.

QUESTION: Where will you be living?

LINDA: London.

QUESTION: Paul, how do you feel about being the father to a six-year-old?

PAUL: (*Joking with Heather*) It's terrible! I hate it! It's going to be such a burden!

HEATHER MCCARTNEY: You don't mean it!

PAUL: (*Making faces*) I do! It's awful!

Paul McCartney

INTERVIEW

London, 1970

PAUL McCARTNEY: All I want are paid advisers who will do what I want them to. And that's what I've got. If the others want Klein, that's up to them, but I've never signed a contract with him. He doesn't represent me. I'm sure Eastman is better for me. The real breakup of the Beatles was months ago. Ringo left when we were doing the White album, because he said it wasn't fun playing with us anymore. But after two days of us telling him he was the greatest drummer in the world for the Beatles, which I believe, he came back. Then George left when we were making *Abbey Road* because he said he didn't think he had enough say on our records, which was fair enough. After a couple of days he came back. Then last autumn I began to feel the only way we could ever get back to playing good music was to start behaving as a band. But I didn't want to go out and face 200,000 people because I would get nothing from it, so I thought up this idea of playing surprise one-night stands in unlikely places. So one day when we had a meeting and I told the others about my idea, and asked them what they thought of it, John said, "I think you're daft!" I said, "What do you mean?" I mean he is John Lennon, and I'm a bit scared of all that rapier wit we hear about. And he just said, "I think you're daft. I'm leaving the Beatles. I want a divorce." John's in love with Yoko, and he's no longer in love with the three of us. Let's face it, we were in love with the Beatles as much as anyone. We're still like brothers.

Paul McCartney
PARTIAL LEGAL STATEMENT AGAINST THE BEATLES
London, 1970

During the making of the "White Album" Richard Starkey (whom I shall call Ringo) announced he was leaving the group, saying he was "not getting through" to the rest of us. He came back after two days. At this stage none of us wanted the Beatles to finish, but we were becoming musically less compatible and were beginning to drift apart. Each began to look to his own interests rather than those of the group. Musical differences became more marked, particularly between myself and John. He and I had been the principal collaborators in writing the songs. By the time "Abbey Road" was recorded we were openly critical of each other's music, and he was no longer interested in the performance of songs which he had not written himself. . . .

During the early part of 1969 John and Yoko launched various ventures separate from the Beatles, including "Plastic Ono" and other recordings, picture exhibitions, and personal appearances. John told the rest of us, at the end of January 1969, that Allen Klein was to be his new business manager, and suggested we as a group should employ him. At about this time, against the wishes of the other three, I left a meeting which was attended also by Klein. I believe the meeting went on until about 2 A.M. and resulted in some sort of arrangement being made between the other three and Klein. Thereafter, the other three told me they could go ahead without me. George and Ringo also became keen on the idea . . . I distrusted Klein in view of his bad reputation and wanted the New York law firm called Eastman and Eastman to represent me because, quite apart from the fact that John Eastman is my brother-in-law, I trusted him. This was the first time in the history of the Beatles a possible irreconcilable difference had appeared between us. Hitherto we had always decided matters unanimously after appropriate discussion. I was most anxious not to stand out against the wishes of the other three except on proper grounds. I therefore thought it right to take part in discussions concerning the possible appointment of Klein, though I did not in the least want him as my manager . . .

In September 1969, I was still keen the Beatles should continue as a group. I therefore proposed we should get the group together again and play live before small audiences. Ringo agreed with this proposal and George was non-committal. Later at a meeting, John said: "I think you're daft. Look, I might as well tell you, I'm leaving the group. I wasn't going to tell you till after the Capitol deal. When I told Allen (Klein) last night he said I was not to. I've had enough. I want a divorce, like my divorce from Cynthia. It's given me a great feeling of freedom." He then said in effect our recording activities had come full circle, because the photograph on our very first album was almost exactly similar to the photograph then planned for the album called "Get Back." The rest of us were shocked by this announcement: I certainly had not thought along these lines at that stage. But we all agreed it would be best that nobody should know the group was finished . . .

The idea that I should also leave the Beatles gradually formed in my mind during the early part of 1970, when I was making a record of my own. During this period I telephoned John and told him I was leaving the Beatles too, to which he replied, "Good! That makes two of us who have accepted it mentally." I also told him in the same conversation I was handing over all my business arrangements to Eastman and Eastman. My intention was hardened by the treatment I received from Klein in relation to the release date of my own record and the alterations to "Let it Be" hereinafter referred to . . .

At this stage I was disputing the deal which Klein had made in relation to "Let it Be." Ringo told me that if I would agree to the "Let it Be" deal, they would let my album come out. I rejected this suggestion. At this stage, also, Ringo visited me, bringing two letters signed by George and John with which he said he agreed. These letters confirmed that my record was not really ready for release, and I told him that Klein had no release date for "Let it Be" from United Artists. After telling Ringo how furious I was with the other three for impeding the release of my record, I told him to get out. He appeared shaken, and I believe that shortly afterwards Peter Howard telephoned EMI and gave Apple's consent to the record being released on 17th April 1970 as it eventually was.

I received the acetate copy of "Let it Be" in late March or early April 1970, accompanied by a letter from Phil Spector whom Klein had engaged to re-mix the album, saying that if I wanted any alterations I should say so. I found that in the recording of my song "The Long and Winding Road," Spector had not only "mixed" the recording, but had added strings, voices, horns and drums, and had changed the recording of my songs considerably. This had never happened before and I regarded this as an intolerable interference with my work. I therefore telephoned Spector but was unable to contact him. I then telephoned the other three who approved the changes. On 14th April 1970 I wrote a letter to Klein. Although in my opinion there would have been enough time to have made the required alterations, none were in fact made . . .

In August 1970, I wrote a letter to John suggesting we should "let each other out of the trap." He replied with a photograph of himself and Yoko, with a balloon coming out of his mouth in which was written, "How and Why?" I replied by letter saying—

"<u>How</u> by signing a paper which says we hereby dissolve our partnership.

<u>Why</u> because there is no partnership."

John replied on a card which said, "Get well soon. Get the other signatures and I will think about it."

Paul McCartney
SELECTED QUOTATIONS
London, 1973

"I never cared about a career, a future and all that, but I had a bit of a conscience towards me dad. One day he told me to go out and get a job, so I went down to the Labor Exchange in me donkey jacket and jeans. The fellow sent me to an electrical firm called Massey & Coggins. I told the boss I wanted a job. I wasn't particular, I said. I'd sweep the yard if he wanted. He asked where I'd been educated and when I said the Liverpool Institute he started making big plans.

• • •

"They gave me this job of winding coils for about seven pounds a week, big money then. At work they called me Mantovani because of the long hair. Anyway, I was hopeless. Everybody else used to wind fourteen coils a day while I'd get through one and a half and mine were the ones that never worked. After a bit I started getting lunchtime dates playing at the Cavern. I had to whip out of work over the back wall at lunchtime and go in the next day and say I'd been ill. One day I just didn't go in and that was that.

• • •

"I remember I used to walk home from John's house if I didn't have enough for the fare, but I never minded that. I wrote lots of songs on those walks. 'World Without Love' and 'Love of the Loved' included, though John helped me polish them up. I remember those walks home very well. I had to cross this horrible, pitch-black golf course. I'd always be singing, but if ever I came across somebody in the dark, I'd shut up and try to pretend it hadn't been me. Met a copper once. I had a guitar round my neck and was quite cheerfully playing and singing at the top of my voice. I thought he was going to arrest me. But he walked up and asked if I'd give him guitar lessons!"

Anything I do is always compared with something I've already done.

• • •

I generally get up in the morning and go for a run, which I never used to do—I never used to be the least sporty—but I like it now. Jogging begins at forty.

I'll come back and have breakfast, and I might take a train to work—*noooo!* You don't take a *train* to work, surely!—Yes, I do. And I *meet* people. Last time I met the *Sunday Times* racing correspondent. He told me all about horses and I told him about records.

I'll work a pretty normal day. I might meet Linda for lunch, and I'll go home and see the kids at night. That becomes the important thing after a while, to make time for them.

• • •

My daughter went through that phase when all of her friends were really quite gentle, caring people, but they just dressed weird and looked like they were going to hit you.

• • •

The best songs come of their own volition. "Yesterday," I just fell out of bed and it was there. And I thought, well, I must have heard it last night. But I spent three weeks asking all the music people I know, well, what is this song? Where have you heard this before? I couldn't believe I'd written it.

• • •

We like all the Chuck Berry Little Richard Carl Perkins Elvis American stuff, black American especially.

At that age you tend to get cliquey and prefer the B-sides people have never heard of. Much of the early Beatles albums one B-sides of black artists.

• • •

When the kids are home it's okay, but they go to school, they've got their own lives. I'm not the kind of person who can easily sit home and twiddle his thumbs.

I don't know why I'm still hungry. But I'm lucky enough to be in a position where what you do is actually fun, rather than banging rivets in a car on a conveyor belt.

● ● ●

Two of the kids take piano lessons, but I'm not really pushing, because I never got pushed. I hated piano lessons. It was like homework, and I had homework, from school and having another batch was a definite loser.

My playing just developed out of my love for it. So I still can't write music.

● ● ●

I'm not living a legend, you know. I'm not doing the thing that's written about me. I'm really just bringing up a bunch of kids and trying to have a good as life as possible, please. I don't have a special mission.

● ● ●

I feel lucky I'm able to make money cleanly, without exploiting anyone, which is pretty rare.

Exploitation is part of the game in the West. In Nashville recently I saw "the John Lennon whiskey decanter," which is a bit yucky as he didn't even drink it. I prefer to remember him how I knew him, but this is America, folks.

● ● ●

Linda and I met in a club in London called the Bag o'Nails. I was in my little booth and she was in her little booth and we were giving each other the eye, you know.

● ● ●

About a year later, we both knew we wanted to get married. We thought it was a bit crazy at the time, but we also thought it would be a gas.

Linda was a bit dubious because she had been married before and wasn't too set on settling. In a way, she thought it tends to blow up things. Marrying ruins it.

But we both fancied each other enough to do it. And now we're glad we did. It's great. I love it.

At the beginning, to most people, she was just some chick. But I figure she was the main help for me on the albums around that time. She was there every day, helping on harmonies and all that stuff.

● ● ●

I think all this business about getting Linda into the act was just my way of saying: "Listen, I don't care what you think, this is what I think. I'm putting her right up here with me."

Later we thought it might have been cooler not to have introduced her so bluntly. Perhaps a little more show business: "Ladies and gentlemen, I'd like to introduce you to my better half. Isn't she sweet and coy?"

* * *

You can have millions of friends, but when someone asks you how many friends you've got, it depends on how honestly you're going to answer because I don't think I have that many.

No one went against me or anything. I just isolated myself a bit. It's just one of those things.

* * *

I don't think it's difficult for the kids, being my daughters, I mean. I don't think they're going to be crazed kids.

But it's funny sometimes. I remember I was sitting in a field and Heather was leading Mary and little baby Stella on a pony, and Mary said to me: "You're Paul McCartney, aren't you?"

* * *

It's nice we have all girls. If we had a son it might be harder on him, like Frank Sinatra, Jr. Everyone assumes he'll turn out to be his dad.

* * *

I remember Stella shocking us across the generation gap when she pointed to our blue Beatles' tenth anniversary T-shirt at Elton John's Wembley concert last year.

"That's Ringo," she said pointing both to the likeness of Mr. Starkey and Ringo who was standing joking with me. "And that's Daddy. But who's that?"

She was pointing to the picture of John Lennon!

* * *

The kids go with us on all our recording jaunts, which for tax reasons have to be out of Britain. Yet I'm British to the core. So much so that I call Linda, who's American, "honorary British."

I wouldn't leave. So many people are leaving and trying to make it look like they're not leaving.

I'm not ashamed of anything I've done. I kind of like the idea of doing something and if it turns out in a few years to look a bit sloppy I'll say, "Oh well, sloppy, so what?" I think most people dig it.

* * *

In the normal day-to-day life, you don't love everyone you meet, but you try and get on with people. You don't try and put 'em uptight.

Why should I go round slagging people? I really didn't like all that John did.

He came out with all that stuff like I'm like Engelbert Humperdinck. In the press they really wanted me to come out and slam John back, and I used to get cheesed off at the guys coming up to me and saying: "This is the latest thing John said and what's your answer?"

I believe, keep cool and that sort of thing passes over.

At the time I hated it when I read the stuff. I sat down and pored over every little paragraph, every little sentence. "Does he really think that of me?" I thought.

* * *

I like to write with John. I like to write with anyone that's good.

* * *

The Beatles knew we were going to give up playing, but we didn't want to go and make some big announcement. So we just kind of cooled it and didn't go out.

* * *

I am proud of the Beatle thing. I believe that we did bring a real lot of happiness to the times.

* * *

I don't like criticism. I don't think I ever have. Like when my Dad said: "I don't like your trousers."

* * *

For a while after I left the other three, Linda was the only person to bounce my ideas off. Now I mainly bounce them off myself. Call it what you will, maturity?

* * *

If you have a song you want me to write I can manage it. I'm quite proud of the fact I can do that.

* * *

People think it's an incredible gift, but I always maintain it's the same as any gift. It's like someone who can strip a car down, I'd be just as proud of that.

PAUL McCARTNEY: When the Beatles broke up we all had to decide whether or not we should do Beatles material because it might seem like we were harkening back to the old days rather than building our own futures. All of us independently refused to do Beatles stuff. I could never do "Nowhere Man" and "Hey Jude" forever and keep up the old grudge, but twenty years later it's a novel idea to do them because they're so fresh.

QUESTION: Do you hold a grudge against Michael Jackson for buying the Beatles songs?

PAUL: No, Michael bought the songs fair and square. But the way I look at it, I've been working for that company for thirty years and I'm going to ask him for a raise.

QUESTION: There's a Transcendental Meditation Center here. . . .

PAUL: There is, great!

QUESTION: Is that something you're still involved with?

PAUL: I'm not involved with it, but I still think it's a great thing. I had a wonderful time with that experience. I found it very interesting and relaxing. I still believe in it. I think the Maharishi was *not* a rip-off.

QUESTION: Do you try to write a particular style?

PAUL: I try not to have a style because the minute you do it's boring. More often I write the music and then try to write words for it, but it can happen either way. As a kid, I did what everyone else did and went to music lessons, but I couldn't really relate to it.

QUESTION: Tell us about the upcoming Beatles documentary.

PAUL: It's a long-standing project we've been meaning to do with the Beatles to try to get the story right from our point of view. So many people write books and tell you how people like us and Elvis lived so, this would be a good opportunity to say, "That's right and that's wrong." There will be stuff you've never seen before, but I'm not sure we're not that deep into it yet.

QUESTION: What's the story behind the missing note in "Day Tripper"?

PAUL: Your guess is as good as mine, Guv! I haven't even heard the legend, never mind the story. They're normally rubbish, those stories, like me crossing Abbey Road with no shoes on, it was a hot day, honest it was, folks.

QUESTION: You're not dead, then?

PAUL: Not quite.

QUESTION: Are there any tracks you're sick of and never want to hear again?

PAUL: There's a few tracks I'm not that keen on. I was talking to producer Trevor Horn, and was saying I hate the track "Bip Bop" on *Wildlife*. He said, "I like that one, it's my favorite track." So, what can you do?

Paul McCartney

PRESS CONFERENCE
• • • • • • • • • • • • • • • • • • • •

Philadelphia, 1990

QUESTION: Twenty years later you're still using your Hofner bass!

PAUL MCCARTNEY: Yeah, I bought it in Liverpool mainly because it was cheap and so was I! I also bought it because it was symmetrical, I could play it left-handed, turn it upside down and it wouldn't look mad. I used it for a long time, but I gave it up because it's a rather cheap instrument and goes out of tune easily. Lately, though, I've been working with Elvis Costello and he asked me if I would play my Hofner. So, I got it out and started playing it again. It's a nice instrument. It's not as accurate as modern instruments, but it's got a really unique tone.

QUESTION: Now that the Beatles have settled their lawsuit with Capitol this November, there are rumors there is going to be unreleased Beatles stuff coming out.

PAUL: Yeah, I think there is to be some stuff scheduled to be released. There really isn't much left unreleased. We were pretty careful not to leave much rubbish around. We were quite tidy in the studio, because Buddy Holly, Jim Reeves, and groups like that left stuff behind and had producers come and put other groups on it and then re-release it. There are some takes we did for the BBC which will be coming out as an album, they're quite good.

QUESTION: Tell us about the tribute to John in your live show.

PAUL: It felt so good we're going to keep it in. It feels really nice to doff the cap to him because he was a great guy.

QUESTION: What goes through your mind when you hear the old Beatles music?

PAUL: Most often the thought that goes through my mind is how quickly we recorded that stuff. We used to go in one morning and do "Michelle," throw a little mix on it, put it on the shelf, and that's the only version that exists. Later that afternoon we'd knock off "Yesterday," it was really quick. We recorded our first album in a day.

QUESTION: Musically, is Paul McCartney with the Beatles much different than Paul McCartney solo?

PAUL: It was a more intense period with the Beatles. Everything was faster. John and I used to take a week to write an album. They'd say, "You've got seven days, go off and write," and we'd say, "Okay." We didn't realize we could have said, "We want three months." It was all very intense. *Sgt. Pepper* was done in six months, which was like *"Wow!, how can anyone take that long?"* The Beatle period was much more compressed, it was only ten years. Now we have more time for things. It takes even longer to record now with all the latest technological advances. It takes about a week just to turn them on!

Paul McCartney

PRESS CONFERENCE

Tokyo, 1991

QUESTION: What do you like to do when you're not on tour? And what's one thing you've always wanted to, but haven't done yet?

PAUL: I like horse riding. Linda taught me to ride about ten years ago. She's a very good rider. I like to do very simple things. I like to go into the forest and clear a path. Things like that. It's very good therapy for me. After all the high tech I like very low-tech things. Go in the forest, light a little fire. Things like that. It's quite simple stuff I do off tour. A new hobby of mine is painting. So to paint a decent picture is something I haven't done yet.

QUESTION: Is there going to be an exhibit?

PAUL: I don't know. It's a private thing for me at the moment. If I get any good I'll get an exhibition.

QUESTION: People respect you all over the world. You had a problem here ten years ago and I think maybe this is an opportunity to give a message about drugs to the children of the world.

PAUL: What I tell my own children, and I've got four: I advise them the best thing is to be straight, stay natural, and don't use any drugs, stimulants, booze. But it is a difficult world we live in and people get into things like alcohol and drugs. Stay strong, that's my advice. As to whether they'll listen to me, that's another matter.

QUESTION: So you look at the police now with a new eye?

PAUL: I don't have any bad feelings about that. It's just the way it was. It's a section of my life that's over, so I don't really want to talk about it too much. I came here and had that problem, but I haven't had that problem this time. So it's finished.

QUESTION: What can you tell me about Hamish Stewart?

PAUL: He's very good to work with and has a great voice. Our voices blend well together. He's got a very good soul. He used to be with the Average White Band. He's a very good guitar player and if I want to play guitar he can play bass. It's working out well.

QUESTION: How does it compare to working with John Lennon?

PAUL: I think it's a difficult thing for Hamish to follow someone like John because he was so great. But he does a great job and I enjoy working with him. We have fun onstage. I don't know whether or not he's like John, but I like him.

QUESTION: Why do you eat only vegetarian foods?

PAUL: Linda cooks that way. We've been vegetarian for twenty years. She did the book because she's very keen on animals. The reason we're vegetarian is because we don't like to kill animals. That's all. Not even fish. Basically, she [wrote her cookbook] to save animals' lives. We eat dishes out of there. My favorite is the squash and she makes very good sauerkraut, page 141.

QUESTION: I like your Beatles song, "When I'm 64." Could you tell me what you will be doing when you are sixty-four?

PAUL: I don't know really. I wrote that song when I was about sixteen. So sixty-four was a long way off then. Right now it's not so far. I hope I'll just be happy. I'll have a great birthday, "birthday greetings, bottle of wine." And I hope Linda "will feed me and will need me when I'm sixty-four."

QUESTION: You say you advise your children not to drink or whatever, but how do you, yourself, feel? Because you said you'd never do drugs again after the Barbados thing. How do you feel now?

PAUL: I feel fine.

QUESTION: So you still take pot?

PAUL: No!

QUESTION: When did you give up?

PAUL: After Barbados. How about you?

QUESTION: I've never done it.

PAUL: The thing about this, actually, is it's a deep subject and I don't think we've really got time to go into it. I mean, as far as I'm concerned, alcohol is often more dangerous than pot, if you want to get into it. So it's very difficult for me to generalize. People should probably draw up a list of substances that are more dangerous and I think you would probably find there could be some good medical opinion on it, that something like pot is an old substance you find when you go back to the American Indians. And from my experience, it has not been as dangerous to me as alcohol. But alcohol's legal and that's the difference. If I'm talking to anyone about it and they want my advice as to what they should do, I would advise them to stay straight and don't do any drugs, alcohol, or cigarettes because of the chemicals. But it's too deep a subject to just casually toss off in a press conference like this. You need a few hours to go into it. I think medical people should draw up a list for the youth of the world, to explain to them, medically, which are the most dangerous substances available. I don't think pot would be very high on the list, myself.

QUESTION: How would you feel if one of your children came to you and said, "Dad, I've been offered pot. I've tried it and I like it." How would you feel knowing that you, yourself, have tried it for many years?

PAUL: That's a personal matter for me. I'm not going to discuss that now, even for *The Sun*, which is a highly regarded newspaper in Britain. You can draw your own conclusions from that one.

QUESTION: You've given a platform to the Friends of the Earth throughout the tour. Is there a chance you are going to be more actively involved? For instance, through your music, write a song. Is there going to be a song for the earth?

PAUL: I don't know, really. You can't just write songs to order, it's not that easy. If I get inspired to write a song along those lines I'd be very happy to do it. You can't just order it up. It's not really that easy. We have given a platform to the Friends of the Earth mainly because it's an important issue right now. I think when people found out in 1989 that there was a hole in the sky with the sun's harmful rays coming through, most were worried about it. At press conferences like this I usually ask people if anyone doesn't agree with that statement to put their hands up. We're just making publicity for anyone that wants to clean up the planet. I personally think it's a very good idea.

QUESTION: Are you in any other way involved in the environment?

PAUL: Not really. I'm really just involved as a parent. I'd like to think that when we go into the next century we'd be living on a good world. Clean enough to live in with water you can swim in and rain you can walk in without getting acid on your head. It's something I think most people agree with. A difficult question, but I'm very optimistic going into the next century that it will happen. And that people will clean up the planet.

QUESTION: How do you choose what material to include on your tour?

PAUL: Well, originally I just looked at what I thought people might want to hear me sing. So I chose a lot of songs and in the end we settled on about sixteen Beatles songs. I didn't really do any from Wings because it was so close to the Beatles breakup the memories are a bit painful. So much time's gone by now that I think of all those good songs, I don't think of any bad memories. So that explained the Beatles, and the reason certain songs got left out was because we either didn't have enough time in the show or some of them didn't work as well when you're in a live situation, but they worked well as records. When we rehearse we just play the songs that sound like they're working we put in. The *Abbey Road* medley was the keyboard player's suggestion. So we tried it out and a friend of mine, who's the engineer, was recording the thing we were rehearsing. He had to go out of the room, he started crying. I thought, that's a good way to end the show. It's emotional, and I don't mind emotion.

QUESTION: We've noticed you've been dedicating several songs to your colleagues in the Beatles. Could you please comment?

PAUL: Normally on the concerts I've been dedicating "Fool on the Hill" to John, George, and Ringo. It's just my way of thanking them as they were a great help to me. And when I do songs like "Fool on the Hill," "Sgt. Pepper," or "Hey Jude," obviously I think of them. So that's what I do at the end of the show. I just announce I'm dedicating it to three friends of mine, George, Ringo, and John.

Paul McCartney
PRESS CONFERENCE
Las Vegas, 1993

QUESTION: Which do you prefer, recording your music, or getting out and performing?

PAUL McCARTNEY: I like performing, because you get to see your audience, but I also like the creative aspect of writing.

QUESTION: You once said you weren't sure if you could write songs after forty—now that you're perilously close, what are your feelings?

PAUL: That's very diplomatic! I always thought you'd have to finish with rock-'n'roll at twenty-four, but it keeps on going until you're thirty. Then you think, "I'll finish up at forty," and then it's, "I'd *better* finish by fifty." Once you get to fifty, I don't know, I guess you stop thinking. The audiences still seem to enjoy it. As long as I keep seeing smiling faces out there, I'll probably turn up.

QUESTION: How do you feel about playing the bigger venues?

PAUL: I rather like these big places. It means you can put on a big show, a spectacle. That way you give people more for their money. We achieve a certain intimacy, I don't know how, but we still get an intimate thing going. The crew prefer the indoors. It's easier for them, less work.

QUESTION: I understand you're doing a set for Earth Day. How did that come about?

PAUL: Somebody asked me, "Will you do Earth Day?" and I said, "Yeah." It's about the best cause you can get, the earth. You can support all the other causes that support the earth, but without the earth to do it on, we're lost! It's something I've been thinking about for a few years, with Clinton and Gore in there it seems like a more optimistic time. So maybe it's a good year to do Earth Day.

QUESTION: Have you been invited to perform for the President?

PAUL: Yeah, I have, actually.

QUESTION: Are you going to?

PAUL: *Noooo!* Well, of course I am. If you get invited to play for the President, you show up. [*Off the Ground*]

QUESTION: On your new album, most of the music is live to tape instead of doing it track by track. Why?

PAUL: It just felt like a good way to do it. These days there is really two ways of doing it. You can lay it down on tape and get that live feel, or you can do it layer by layer. I thought we could get a freer vibe by actually getting together with the band and just playing the songs.

QUESTION: Knowing you're going in with a band, how does that affect your songs?

PAUL: I don't think it does, really. I put out the same amount of effort whether it's a band or a solo album.

QUESTION: What's the biggest gamble you've ever taken?

PAUL: Probably joining the Beatles, because I had a steady job that paid seven pounds fourteen shillings a week and I gave it all up for this!

QUESTION: You'll be in L.A. later this week at the crucial time of the verdict in the Rodney King beating trial. Do you have a message for the officers?

PAUL: No. It's an American affair. I'm just some British guy showing up. I think people all over the world know what they thought of the videotape, and as an outsider, I know what I think about it. But I don't know enough about the case, although I've read about it extensively. I just hope it all works out okay.

QUESTION: If the verdict comes down and there's some civil disruptions, will you cancel the concert or any other dates?

PAUL: Nope.

QUESTION: In recent years I've heard you speak very affectionately about John. If, heaven forbid, it had happened the other way and you were no longer with us, how do you think John would remember you?

PAUL: Have you got a few hours? John would say it was great writing with me and we had a great time. He'd say the same things I say about him, which is that he was fabulous.

QUESTION: When you told us intimate stories about him and you, would he tell the same about you?

PAUL: Yeah, sure. What they would be, I can't tell you. I can only tell you mine.

QUESTION: Recently you've been handing out a lot of literature at your shows about the ecology.

PAUL: You either come, sing a few songs and leave town, or you give them something to think about besides the music, or that which complements the music. For me, in the free program we give out, we let people like Greenpeace, Friends of the Earth, and PETA present their views, which I most often agree with. It's important to get these views over and I think it does some good. Actually, on the last tour we would hear from kids who would take a program home and go give a talk at school. It's very simple information. It basically says, support people who want to save the planet.

QUESTION: Can you tell us about going on the *Rainbow Warrior*?

PAUL: Well, it wasn't the real *Rainbow Warrior*, because that was sunk by the French, as you recall. This was a new one down in Australia and I was honored because it's become symbolic of the ecological struggle. Groups like Greenpeace probably do more for the planet and our future than most governments. So I feel very honored to go on their ships. I basically just walk around saying, "Keep up the good work."

QUESTION: What's happening with the soundtrack work you've been asked to record with George and Ringo?

PAUL: At the moment they're making a ten-part documentary on the Beatles* and at one point George, Ringo, and myself were asked if we'd like to get involved and do a little background music. I actually suggested it because if we had a montage of sequences of John that [would be] a nice little tribute. It also gives us a perfectly good reason for getting back together rather than Sid Bernstein's famous offer. They're about halfway through, they're on about the fifth show of ten.

QUESTION: On the last tour you had direct involvement in the look of the show. How involved are you this time?

PAUL: Well, we normally look at the other shows going out and try not to look like them. To look completely the opposite. We usually get together a group of people I think are talented, like the guy that painted these backdrops, and just have them come to rehearsal, talk to them and play some music at them. They show me the images they're going to use and I say, "That's marvelous." It's a team effort, each individual artist has a lot of say, but I guess I'm the overall director.

QUESTION: In reference to what you said about the literature you pass out, it seems your music has taken a more serious tone.

PAUL: When we started out with the Beatles the songs were all really, "Thank you, girl," "From me to you, girl," "Hello, girl," it was just young guys trying to pull birds, but now I'm married with four children and it's not allowed. The songs have to change and not be so overtly about trying to pull birds. My interests have

---

* *The Beatles Anthology*

changed to things that concern us all. In my great, venerable age it's my duty not to be frivolous when I have so much attention, so many cameras on me.

QUESTION: You are in the second home of Elvis. . . .

PAUL: Which one?

QUESTION: Vegas.

PAUL: No, which Elvis?

QUESTION: Can you tell us what Presley meant to you?

PAUL: I was in love with Elvis. He was a marvelous man. When I first saw his picture I was blown away by his good looks. I was even more blown away by his voice. I think he was one of the greatest voices of the century.

QUESTION: What was his first record you heard?

PAUL: "Heartbreak Hotel." When the Beatles met him in L.A., it was an evening with Elvis. He was brilliant, a really great guy. It was before he took up residence here so I think he was a little more straight.

QUESTION: Are there any musicians you'd like to play with that you haven't got the chance to yet?

PAUL: I know there are some, but I can't think of them.

QUESTION: Little Richard?

PAUL: I've played with Little Richard and he was great. Chuck Berry, all those guys, I love 'em, bring them up and I'll play with them.

QUESTION: Even though you're a rock star, you have a wide taste in music. Is there anything else in the works like the *Liverpool Oratorio*?

PAUL: I liked doing that classic bit because it was so interesting and a real stretch. I've done things like that in the short form, but never in a long form. I would hope to do something like that again. At the moment I've written a little series of piano pieces, so from the three hundred people it takes to do the *Oratorio*, it's just one person at the piano.

QUESTION: On this tour there will be songs the audience will hear live for the very first time, like "Penny Lane" and "Paperback Writer." Are you anxious to see their reactions?

PAUL: No, we've just got back from Australia, it went down great and I have even more faith in the Americans.

QUESTION: What is the secret to twenty-four years of blissful marriage?

PAUL: I don't know, good sex!

QUESTION: Are there any songs Linda won't let you play?

PAUL: Linda's not that kind of person and she knows I wouldn't listen anyway. She's not the kind of person to tell me what to do, she's a pretty cool chick.

QUESTION: There was a nasty trick played on Linda during the last tour where someone isolated her tambourine and harmonies, what was your reaction?

PAUL: Horror! Then I tried to remind her that the Stones have tapes like that out and that it's pretty easy to isolate someone's harmonies going *"AYYYAYYYA"* which sounds pretty awful, which is what they did for those of you who don't know what the nasty trick was. She had to be pretty strong, because it's not easy to be made that much fun of. She is back singing better than ever, she just doesn't wave her arms around as much.

QUESTION: How did you and Elvis Costello end up coming together?

PAUL: Someone suggested we might get together so we met and found it was quite easy. We enjoyed writing with each other.

QUESTION: Are there any songs you wish you had written?

PAUL: Millions. If I single one out, which I'm going to do because it's a press conference, then it's not going to be right. "Stardust," I wouldn't have minded writing that one, but there are millions. All the old standards and everything since. But I've done okay, I've written one or two, so I'll have to be happy with them.

QUESTION: Paul, what's your favorite sport?

PAUL: Sex! I like track and athletics. I like to watch athletics.

QUESTION: Would you accept an offer to a half-time show during the Super Bowl?

PAUL: No, I couldn't see myself doing a half-time show, it's a real American thing. It's the kind of thing Michael [Jackson] would do.

QUESTION: Would you consider doing something else with Stevie Wonder?

PAUL: I'd love to, he is a magic musician. We only did the one thing, "Ebony and Ivory," and it was magic, but we have nothing planned at the moment.

For Immediate Release
Japanese Legal Loophole Attacked by Paul McCartney

The London offices of MPL Communications Ltd., the company owned by Paul McCartney, today issued a statement strongly attacking the exploitation of a legal loop-hole in Japan which allows early Beatles recordings to be made available through companies other than EMI (the Beatles recording company) and on which no artists' royalties are being paid to them.

Paul McCartney said: "It is ridiculous that in Japan the period of copyright protection for recordings is only 20 years—instead of the 50 or 75 years common in other developed societies—and as a result some companies in Japan have now issued low quality compact discs or early Beatles recordings on which no artists' royalties are being paid."

The CDs issued by EMI with technical advice by George Martin are the only faithful reproduction of these original recordings.

The Veggie Chronicles
PAUL AND LINDA McCARTNEY
1991–1997

For the forest to be green each tree must be green.

—THE MAHARISHI MAHESH YOGI

● ● ●

During the course of a Sunday lunch one afternoon we happened to look out the kitchen window at our young lambs racing happily in the fields. Glancing down at our plates, we suddenly realized we were eating the leg of an animal that had until recently been gambolling in a field itself. We looked at each other and said, "Wait a minute, we love these sheep, they're such gentle creatures, so why are we eating them?" It was the last time we ever did.

LINDA

● ● ●

When I was a boy, I would never have believed it if someone told me one day we'd have a hole in the sky, the ozone layer, there would be acid in our rain, the seas wouldn't be clean enough to swim in and the air not clean enough to breathe. All I am trying to do is make people think about how we're wrecking this world and ask them to challenge their politicians to act.

PAUL

● ● ●

We did consult a nutritionist about our vegetarianism at one point because of our kids. As Paul said, it was one thing for the two of us to expose ourselves to what was, twenty years ago, a bit of a controversial diet, but we wanted to make sure the children wouldn't suffer and that they would get all the protein their growing bodies needed. This doctor, who wasn't vegetarian, told me your daily need of protein can be sustained with just half a cup of baked beans and a glass of skim milk. So rather than discovering that there was any protein deficiency, we learned that we tend to eat far too much protein anyway.

LINDA

● ● ●

Linda is a crazy animal lover. We have lots of pets and as a kid I used to run around with my *Observer Book of Birds* in my pocket. From then on we stuck to eating things where nothing had to lose a life. One Christmas, Linda even managed to make a kind of macaroni turkey: you could cut it into slices just like the real thing. I know it sounds a bit corny, but we really value being vegetarians, and it doesn't seem too daft because our place is a nuthouse anyway!

PAUL

• • •

I like to start the day with a cup of orange pekoe tea. Nothing else unless it's a Sunday, in which case I cook up a big vegetarian breakfast for the family, scrambled eggs, vegetarian "sausages" made of vegetable protein, tomatoes, a great whole-meal bread Paul makes, and freshly-squeezed orange juice.

LINDA

• • •

I'm not an exercise fanatic, but I ride my horse, Lucky Spot, every day.

LINDA

• • •

I meditate every day. I go off in a field or the woods and I sit and try to take in the whole harmony of nature. If we're on tour and I'm completely confined to hotel rooms, airplanes, or whatever, which I really don't care for at all, then I try to have a massage if I possibly can.

LINDA

• • •

PAUL: "Wheel of Fortune" is the only big-name game show that still gives away fur coats as prizes. Help us get them to drop fur by calling Merv Griffin, the show's executive producer.

LINDA: Come on, Merv, you don't really like fur! Give me a break. Thumbs up to Estée Lauder, Clinique, Avon, and Revlon for ending animal tests. Thumbs down to Gillette for refusing to stop poisoning and killing animals.

PAUL: The Sill Spring monkeys are survivors of a lab closed down by police nine years ago. They've been kept in tiny cages by the National Institute of Health ever since the research was arrested. Please call President Bush and ask him to give the word for those poor monkeys to be moved to a sanctuary.

PAUL AND LINDA

• • •

I believe firmly in the advantages of homeopathy. I generally keep as good a check on my health as anyone, I guess. I have a complete yearly checkup. I don't drink alcohol, I avoid coffee and I don't smoke.

LINDA

• • •

So many people dismiss vegetarianism as if it's some mystic cult with no substance, as if veggies are not quite right in the head. In the twenty years and more since Paul and I stopped eating animals, I've been called it all; a crank, a loony, weirdo. . . . Not that I'm complaining. If you strike out against convention with what is seen to be a new idea, you have to expect the catcalls and suspicion, because people enjoy the comfort zone of the status quo and change is always seen as challenging.

We waste sixteen pounds of grain in livestock feed to produce a single pound of beef. We feed 80% of the corn grown in the USA not to people, but livestock.

If we are to address this problem of world hunger—and who else is responsible for it except those of us living here?—we need to effect a massive shift in what we feed the foods of our fields. Instead of feeding grain to livestock, we could feed the world by feeding the grain directly to people.

It occurs to me as you can grow 40,000 pounds of potatoes or 10,000 pounds of beans on an acre of prime land that would produce just 250 pounds of beef, one of these new ways has to be a major shift away from meat-eating.

LINDA

● ● ●

A number of doctors have told me a vegetarian diet is one of the most effective ways of fighting the diseases of modern society. It lessens the risk of heart disease and has also been shown to be an effective weapon against cancer, particularly breast cancer.

LINDA

● ● ●

An Open Letter to the People of Norway
From Paul and Linda McCartney

Dear People of Norway,

On Tuesday, May 21st a small group of your countrymen will once again take up the "tradition" of whaling and will set to hunt down and kill 425 Minke whales. By this action, this minority is going to earn your country the contempt and scorn of the rest of the world and we believe you should realize that.

The whalers say they are doing this because it is a long established Norwegian tradition. You know and we know this is nonsense. The cloak of "tradition" is being used to disguise the fact that, with the price of whale meat at 290 a kilo, this whole bloody exercise is being done for a huge profit.

But who will really profit from this massacre? Probably not the people of Norway. A few whalers will make a lot of money and a few rich businessmen in Japan will be able to grotesquely impress their dinner guests.

But the losers will be you and your country. Just as, years ago, the right-thinking world condemned slavery, so too your beautiful land will be stained and despised on account of the handful of traditionalists who are going to tarnish Norway's name through their actions.

As you know, we have many friends in Norway. When we have toured there, it is one of the best places to be. In our experience, the overwhelming majority of Norwegians, especially young Norwegians, are kind and forward-thinking. They are concerned about ecology and open to new, better ideas like whale watching.

Our friends in Norway have told us most Norwegians don't eat whale meat anyway and, as Greenpeace has alerted, this whole sad and sick exercise is being conducted not to uphold tradition but for greed.

Last year, the Norwegian whalers slaughtered 232 minke whales. This year they intend to double the slaughter. Last year the International Whaling Commission (IWF) called on Norway to "halt immediately all whaling activities."

That's not just men in suits passing a resolution. That IWF ruling is the world calling. The rest of the planet with the exception of the few hypocrites who whale for the "scientific purposes" that don't fool or impress anybody, is imploring Norway to stop or be shamed.

We don't believe the people of Norway want or deserve that shame. We believe you have it within your power to stop this killing. Call on your leaders to write to Mrs. Brundtland, and demand a ban on Norwegian whaling. You could earn the praise and respect of the world.

With love,

Paul & Linda McCartney

• • •

PAUL McCARTNEY
HOW I SCAMMED THE FUR TRADE

Even though Paul McCartney's wife Linda is battling breast cancer, the couple care so deeply about animal rights they've launched a sting on the fur industry.

Linda, 55, was operated on for the cancer last December in Britain and she's now undergoing secret treatments in Los Angeles with Paul at her side.

But her medical crisis didn't stop the couple from taking action when they heard that the October 14th issue of *New Yorker* magazine would include a special section that promoted furs.

They planted a phony ad from "Paul's Furs," telling readers, "Before you buy, let us show you our lively collection of fox, mink and raccoon."

But anyone who calls the listed phone number gets a nasty surprise in the mail—a horrifying tape of animals drowning, being electrocuted and having their necks broken so people can wear fur. The video ends by asking readers to stop buying fur coats.

In an exclusive interview, Paul commented, "At least now, some prospective fur buyers will learn who pays the ultimate price for fur coats—the animals. I urge everyone to join Linda and me in being animal friendly and fur free."

OCTOBER 14, 1996

CHAPTER FIVE

The Road to Mandalay/ George Harrison

George Harrison
SELECTED QUOTATIONS
● ●
London, 1969

Everywhere you go you've got a number of choices. There's a crossroad and you can go left or right, but if you just follow yourself, your natural instincts, you don't have to really decide. You'll naturally go down one of them and there's always choices and many different ways to go, but if you just keep following yourself and what you feel then you automatically go down the right road. It happened with me just through constantly experiencing action, reaction, action, reaction. I got into Indian music, which was very remarkable because the first time I ever heard it was on a Ravi Shankar album, which it had to be really, looking back. I played the music and although it's sort of intellectual, it is technically and spiritually the most amazing music I have ever heard. I listened to the music and even though I didn't really understand it, I felt within myself as though I knew it back to front. It seems so obvious and logical.

● ● ●

Ravi Shankar is probably the person who has influenced my life the most. Maybe he's not that aware of it, but I really love Ravi and he's been like a father figure and spiritual guide to me. Later I realized Indian music was like a steppingstone to the spiritual path because I also had a great desire to know about the yogic path. I always had a feeling for that and the music led me there. I got involved with Hinduism because Ravi was a Hindu and because it just happened it came my way and I went to India.

● ● ●

I got to understand what Christ really was through Hinduism. Down through the ages there has always been the spiritual path, it's been passed on, it always will be, and if anybody ever wants it in any age it's always there. It just so happens India was the place where the seed of it was planted. The Himalayas were very inaccessible, to people, so they always have peace there. The yogis are the only people who can make it out there. It may be something to do with my past lives, but I felt a great connection with it. In this age the West and East are closer and can *all* benefit so much from each other. We can help them with our material attributes and they can help us with their spiritual things.

● ● ●

You need the outer aspect of life as well as the inner because the outer is empty if you don't have any spiritual side to life and vice versa. The Western people needed to go through this material life. Well, they've *been* through it now and we've got so many material things it's got to evolve into the other now. We can give to each other, it's all a part of the evolution, taking the best from both sides. Not only do we have the yogis coming over here, but our business people are going over there.

George Harrison
PRESS CONFERENCE
• • • • • • • • • • • • • • • • • • •

Los Angeles, 1974

QUESTION: Why did you decide to return to America?

GEORGE HARRISON: I've been back many times. This is the first time I've been back to work, and it's the first time I've had a H-1 visa since 1971.

QUESTION: What was the reason for not having the H-1?

GEORGE: I had the same problem as John Lennon. I was busted for marijuana way back in 1967 by Sgt. Norman Pilcher, who was in jail for six years for planting dope on people.

QUESTION: Would you ever consider touring Mexico?

GEORGE: I wouldn't mind, I just believe there's a bunch of loonies down there, I mean, I would go anywhere. This is really a test, I either finish this tour ecstatically happy and I'll want to go on tour everywhere or I'll end up just going back to me cave again for another five years.

QUESTION: Looking back, what do you consider the crowning glory of your career as a musician?

GEORGE: As a musician, I don't think I've achieved that yet. As an individual, just being able to sit here today and be relatively sane. That's probably my biggest accomplishment to date.

QUESTION: What is the possibility that you and the rest of the Beatles will become the Beatles again?

GEORGE: It's a very slim possibility at the moment, everybody's enjoying being individuals, we were boxed together for ten years, and personally, I'm enjoying playing with this band.

QUESTION: You said in your bio in 1964 that meeting the Beatles was the biggest break in your musical life and in '74 leaving the Beatles.

GEORGE: The biggest break in 1963 was meeting the Beatles. The biggest break since then, I mean in retrospect, was getting out of them.

QUESTION: George, could you tell us your feelings and expectations for the upcoming tour?

GEORGE: I think if I had more time I'd be panic-stricken, but I don't really have the time to be worried about it.

QUESTION: Is there any reason why Keltner, Clapton, and Voorman didn't accompany you?

GEORGE: Oh well, I mean Eric's out on his own, Klaus has been living in America so I haven't seen him all year, and during that time I met Andy Numark and Willy Weeks. It's just time for a change.

QUESTION: Why would they perform on an album and not in concert?

GEORGE: They performed on the album because they were there at the time. I didn't meet Willy Weeks and Andy Numark, they're bass and drums, until about July this year.

QUESTION: Are you getting divorced?

GEORGE: No, I mean, that's as silly as marriage.

QUESTION: Allen Klein is suing the Beatles. How is that affecting you?

GEORGE: No. To tell you the truth there's a whole lot of money which is in receivership since Paul McCartney sued us and actually it's fortunate he did sue, because the money's in receivership so at least nobody can spend it. There's millions of dollars from the Beatles partnership and we either give it to the lawyers or give it to the revenue.

QUESTION: How do you see the role of the entertainer as concerned with causes and charities?

GEORGE: I don't think that has any relation to causes and charities. I don't think that's particularly an entertainer's job—I think it's up to each individual to do what he can. I do what I can through music, but I don't think it's particularly just isolated to musicians.

QUESTION: What are your hopes for Dark Horse Records?

GEORGE: I want it to be reasonably small. To tell you the truth, I've been here just over a week and if I signed all the people who gave me tapes I'd be bigger than RCA, but fortunately I don't have time to listen to them.

QUESTION: Does your wife cook for you?

GEORGE: First of all, I don't have a wife anymore, but even when I did, she used to cook sometimes and I learned how to cook myself. I cook vegetarian Indian food. Although I like other food as well, I'm a vegetarian. I don't eat fish, I don't eat chicken, and I don't eat meat. That's why I'm so pale and thin.

QUESTION: Are sales down for the concerts?

GEORGE: Oh, no.

QUESTION: What's your relationship with John and Paul?

GEORGE: It's very good, actually. I haven't seen John because he's been in the States, although I've spoken to him quite a lot on the telephone and he sounds to me like he's in great shape. It's as if we've gone right round the cycle and we're back at the beginning. I just met Paul recently and everybody's really very, very friendly. But it doesn't mean we're going to form a band.

QUESTION: Will the publicity from your tour lead to the re-release of *Raga*, Ravi Shankar documentary?

GEORGE: I'm not sure if it ever even got released. It may do, it depends on people's interest. The problem is the people who distribute movies. It's very difficult to get a look in there. The film industry, this is my personal opinion, needs a kick in the behind because it's too controlled by people who own the theaters, who own the distribution networks. It's like if you don't work on Maggie's farm you don't get your movie on.

QUESTION: Do you still meditate?

GEORGE: I must say there's a state of consciousness which is the goal of everybody. I haven't sat down and done meditation for some time but at the same time I constantly think of the Lord in one fashion or another. My thing is just to remember and to try to see him within all of you and that feeling itself is a meditation.

QUESTION: Can you foresee a time when you'll give up your musical objectives?

GEORGE: I can see a time when I'd give up this sort of madness, but music, I mean everything is based upon music. I'll never stop my music.

QUESTION: There's a paradox there between lifestyles.

GEORGE: It is difficult, yeah, but the point is it's also like good practice in a way. As they say "to be in the world, but not *of* the world." You can go to the Himalayas and miss it completely, and you can be stuck in the middle of New York and be very spiritual. I mean, I noticed in certain places, like New York, it brings out a certain thing in myself. If I go to some place like Switzerland I find a lot of uptight people because they're living amongst so much beauty there's no urgency in trying to find the beauty within themselves. If you're stuck in New York you have to somehow look within yourself—otherwise you'd go crackers. So, in a way, it's good to be able to go in and out of both situations. Most people think when the world gets itself together we'll all be okay. I don't see that situation arriving. I think one by one, we all free ourselves from the chains we have chained ourselves *to*. But I don't think that suddenly some magic happens and the whole lot of us will all be liberated in one throw.

QUESTION: What direction is your music going now?

GEORGE: Haven't got a clue. I mean it's getting a bit funkier, especially with Willy Weeks and all them.

QUESTION: Do you pay much attention to what critics say?

GEORGE: I cancelled all my newspapers five years ago, to tell you the truth, so I don't really know what people say. If I do see a review of an album I'll read it, although it doesn't really make too much difference what they say because I am what I am whether they like it or not.

QUESTION: Are you ever amazed by how much the Beatles still mean to people?

GEORGE: Not really. I realize the Beatles did fill a space in the sixties, but all of the people they meant something to are all grown up now. It's like anything you grow up with, you get attached to it. That's one of the problems in our lives, becoming attached to things. I can understand the Beatles, in many ways, did nice things and it's appreciated people still like them. The problem comes when they want to live in the past and hold on to something. People are afraid of change.

QUESTION: Would you ever want to live permanently in India?

GEORGE: Yes. When I get through with all this madness. There's a word called karma and it means that whatever we are now we cause by our previous actions. Whatever is going to be in the future is what we cause by our actions now. I'd like to be able to cause my actions to lead me to end up sometime in India.

QUESTION: Who are some of the contemporary artists you admire?

GEORGE: There's so many. Smokey Robinson I am madly in love with. Smokey is my favorite, but I like Dicky Betts. There's a lot of guitar players—Ry Cooder I think is sensational.

QUESTION: What about big groups like the Rolling Stones?

GEORGE: The Stones, yeah, they're fine, you know, they're nice. I like the Stones. Variety's the spice of life.

QUESTION: Are you involved in any serious negotiations to get the Beatles back together for one night?

GEORGE: No, you've been reading *Rolling Stone*. I thought the fifty million for one shot . . . after reading that I was a bit disappointed at Bill Graham saying he could make us four million, especially as Crosby, Stills, Nash, and Young made eight! I mean, sure, we could make more than that. The point is, it's all a fantasy, the idea of putting the Beatles together again. If we ever do that, the reason will be that everybody's broke! And even then, to play with the Beatles, I'd rather have Willy Weeks on bass than Paul McCartney. That's the truth, with all respect to Paul. The Beatles were like being in a box, it's taken years to get to play with other musicians because we were so isolated. It became very difficult playing the same old tunes day in, day out. Since I made *All Things Must Pass*, it was so nice for me to be able to play with other musicians. I don't think the Beatles are that good. I mean, they're fine. Ringo's got the best backbeat I've ever heard and he'll play a great twenty-four-hours-a-day. He hated drum solos. Paul is a fine bass player, he's a little overpowering at times. And John has gone through his scene, but it feels to me like he's come around. To tell you the truth, I'd join a band with John Lennon any day, but I couldn't join a band with Paul McCartney, and that's nothing personal. It's just from a musical point of view.

QUESTION: What do you think of Lennon's solo material?

GEORGE: His new record I think is lovely.

QUESTION: How is it you don't want to do personal interviews?

GEORGE: There's nothing to say, really. I'm a musician, not a talker. I mean, if you just get my album, it's like *Peyton Place*, it'll tell you exactly what I've been doing.

QUESTION: Did you do a musical rebuttal to "Layla" on that album?

GEORGE: What you do mean, rebuttal? That sounds nasty, doesn't it? I'd like to sort that one out. I love Eric Clapton, he's been a close friend for years, and I'm very happy about it. I'm very friendly with them. Sure.

QUESTION: Why are you *happy* about it?

GEORGE: Because he's great. I'd rather Pattie was with him than some dope.

QUESTION: Is it conceivable you could get together the Beatles to generate some money for charity?

GEORGE: Well, if you're a promoter I'd say no, but I wouldn't rule anything out in life. People think we plan, but we don't plan anything. It's all at the mercy of the Lord and I'm sorry to keep talking about the Lord to y'all, but he's there, I have experienced something in my life, and I know he's there. . . .

QUESTION: What's your attitude about drugs now?

GEORGE: What drugs? Aspirin, or what are you talking about? I think it's awful when it ruins people. What do you define as a drug and what isn't? I don't want to advocate it all because it's so difficult to get into America, you know.

QUESTION: You said you had an experience which made you believe in the Lord. Was this a specific experience?

GEORGE: Just certain things happened in my life which left me thinking, "What's it all about, Alfie?" and I remembered Jesus said somewhere "Knock and the door shall be opened" and I said, "(Knock, knock) Hellooo!" It's very difficult. From the Hindu point of view each soul is potentially divine, the goal is to manifest the divinity. The word yoga means union and the union is supposedly between the mind, the body, and the spirit, and yoga isn't lying on nails or standing on your head. I mean, there's various forms of yoga and they're all branches on one big tree. The Lord, or God, has got a million names, whatever you want to call him, it doesn't matter as long as you call him, Jesus is on the mainline, tell him what you want. Going back to self-realization, one guru said he found no separation between man and God saving man's spiritual unadventurousness, and that's the catch, everybody's so unadventurous. We're all conditioned, our consciousness has been so polluted by the material energy it's hard to try and pull it all away in order to really discover at our true nature. Everyone of us has within us a drop of that ocean and we have the same qualities as God, just like a drop of the ocean has the same qualities as the whole ocean. Everybody's looking for something and we are it. We don't have to look anywhere—it's right there within ourselves.

George Harrison and His Divine Grace A.C. Bhaktivedanta Swami Prabhupada

BHAKTIVEDANTA MANOR, LETCHMORE HEATH, OUTSIDE LONDON

July, 1974

GEORGE HARRISON: I seem to keep going around in circles. Maybe it has something to do with me being a Pisces, one fish going this way and one going that way. I have periods where I can't stop chanting Hare Krishna, and other times where I turn into a demon and forget to chant.

A.C. BHAKTIVEDANTA SWAMI PRABHUPADA: You are not a demon, you are a demigod! Somehow or other you were attracted to Krishna, so let Him help you.

GEORGE: I'm reading your Gita. I read it over and over.

SRILA PRABHUPADA: All the instructions are there. So, this is your duty now. By the grace of Krishna you are a very great personality. You are a young man, but Krishna has blessed you with such a high position, there are many young men who follow you.

GEORGE: In a way, when you really commit yourself to something it's like putting your head on the chopping block. Someone can turn around and chop it off, or if you're lucky, it doesn't get chopped off. I find the more commitment I make, even though it's a small one, I find it provokes bad reactions.

SRILA PRABHUPADA: There is a saying, "If one is foolish and you give him good instruction, he will become angry." Has it happened like that?

GEORGE: I feel a little animosity from people. In some ways the more committed you are, and the stronger you are in what you do, the stronger the animosity. Sometimes I get the feeling there's one person to whom it means something real and ten it doesn't mean a thing to. I'm not sure how it all balances out.

DEVOTEE: If you reach one person it's worth it.

GEORGE: But what if you don't reach anyone? If you only reach one person and by reaching that one twenty people are annoyed.

SRILA PRABHUPADA: Yes, preaching is very difficult. When one preaches, he must tell the truth. Just like Jesus Christ, people didn't like his preaching but he did not stop. In preaching there is always the possibility of creating animosity. By the way, I have heard your new album, *Living in the Material World*, is being appreciated by many people.

97

GEORGE: There is one song in particular which was a direct result of a conversation we had when you came to my home and we talked about fame and fortune.

SRILA PRABHUPADA: People are seeking spiritual enlightenment. Especially in the Western World, that is a fact. Sometimes though people become angry. We have no reason to make enemies, we are simply teaching love.

GEORGE: There is one problem I've found when chanting, I start beginning to relate less and less to the people I know. I suddenly found myself on such a different level where it's really hard to relate. It feels as though I'm at a point where I should slow down or pull back towards those people in order to take them with me. The building up of the mantra and its effect is so subtle. There's a point where I can't relate to anyone anymore. Maybe you don't have that experience.

DEVOTEE: George is saying that when he chants he becomes spiritualized so it's difficult for him to relate to his business associates.

GEORGE: Not even that, my friends, *anybody*! What happens is if I'm not into it too deeply, I'll come down to begin the day and be quite nice and off we go. The periods where I'm so deeply into chanting all the time I'll come down and I'm like Ravana.* I'm not smiling, and I'm not particularly happy. It's like there's more urgency involved. Perhaps it's the realization that everybody's wasting their time doing mundane things.

DEVOTEE: But while you were chanting you wrote these beautiful songs and it's proven by everyone purchasing them that they want to hear them.

GEORGE: The problem is where to find the balance, because obviously I know where I benefit from doing that. However, I'm benefiting so much that suddenly I'm out on a limb and it's hard to pull those people along with you. There's a point where suddenly I'm not going to know them anymore.

DEVOTEE: George says it's difficult when you become spiritualized by chanting. He feels it's a dangerous position because he will be cut off from his audience, the ordinary people. He's afraid they will not understand him and he will not be able to take them with him to that point.

SRILA PRABHUPADA: Yes, keep your balance. Don't spoil your position. Regarding your talent, it is not ordinary. You are getting money. It is not that you should refuse it. Our policy is not that you don't touch money. Krishna instructs we should do so many things and money allows one to do so.

GEORGE: We've just been making some music in California and one of the songs (it's Ravi Shankar's music) is based on the ten incarnations of Vishnu. It's

---

* Ravana is the ten-headed demon king from the Indian epic *The Ramayana*.

a beautiful song. But I was wondering why there isn't anything in the lyrics concerning Krishna?

SRILA PRABHUPADA: Krishna is not an incarnation, rather, Krishna is the origin of all incarnations. His incarnations are called "avatar," but He is "avatari." Therefore the song is a prayer to Krishna. It was composed by a great Vaishnava poet.

GEORGE: There is one song, it is so simple and beautiful. It's in English and only has three lines. "I am missing you, Krishna, where are you? Though I can't see you I hear you flute all the while. Please come wipe my tears and make me smile." It's so sweet I'm sure it's going to be very popular.

SRILA PRABHUPADA: When I entered this room I said, "All glories to George Harrison!" You have given us this center* and Krishna will surely give you shelter at his lotus feet. You are very nice and sincere.

GEORGE: The Krishna Consciousness movement is getting so big there's going to be a point where it's going to need such fantastic management. . . . At the moment we have Prabhupada who is the figurehead which everyone can draw energy from. Sooner or later though, everybody's going to be out there on their own and carry out what they've learned.

DEVOTEE: We'll always rely on our spiritual master, even if he is no longer with us. We'll always take our strength from him.

GEORGE: I must go but I'll be back very quickly.

SRILA PRABHUPADA: You are going alone or is someone going with you?

GEORGE: I go alone. . . . Well, a little bit of *you* will certainly be with me!

SRILA PRABHUPADA: My sincere blessings to your wife. Thank you very much for your kindness.

* Bhaktivedanta Manor, ISKCON's European headquarters near the village of Radlett outside London.

I find myself torn between two extremes. I'm very, very serious about things which I personally feel are serious. But most worldly things I'm very *un*serious about, I take it all with a pinch of salt.

● ● ●

Monty Python was completely outrageous and off the wall, but to me it was the only "real" thing on the BBC. The show was totally crackers, and when they finished and the *real* guy came on the tube and said, "Well now, we'd like to continue with the next program for tonight," I'd just fall over because how can you treat *anything* seriously after "Monty Python's Flying Circus"? Seeing their show, I'd realize that I'm completely comical, I like craziness. I had to be, in order to be in the Beatles.

● ● ●

"Some times are good/some times are bad/it's all a part of life/and standing in between them all/I met a Mr. Grief." Mr. Grief isn't just to rhyme with *life*, as most people would think. There is a real person, and I met him in Southern France a few months ago. He was talking to me and the way he was talking really struck me. So I told him, "I don't know if this is an insult or not, but you remind me of Lord Buckley. He's my favorite comedian." He's dead now, but he was the first of the real "hip" comics. And this guy nearly fell over. He said, "Hey, I managed him for eighteen years!" So we were talking about Lord Buckley and Mr. Grief said he lived in a little shack which he called "Crackerbox Palace." Because everything with Buckley was "my lords, my ladies, and gentlemen of the royal court," so beautiful and "up."

I loved the way "Crackerbox Palace" sounded, I loved the whole idea of it, so I wrote the song and turned it from that shack into a phrase for the physical world. "I was so young when I was born/my eyes could not yet see/and by the time of my first dawn/somebody holding me . . . they said/we welcome you to Crackerbox Palace/we've been expecting you." I wrote those lyrics because, again, the world is very serious and at times a very sad place. But, at the same time, it's such a joke. It's *all* Crackerbox Palace.

● ● ●

I try to lay down more basic tracks than I actually need. Sometimes you'll lay down a track and it sounds real good, but when you get into overdubbing certain things change. There can be a world of difference between a basic track and a finished mix. Usually they evolve and reveal themselves as the ones that will be on the album. For *Thirty-three & 1/3* I cut twelve tracks, but I decided not to even bother overdubbing on two of the cuts because I was more than satisfied with the other ten. So those two songs will go into my backlog of material, and maybe they'll be on the next album I do.

• • •

Thirty-three & 1/3, the title was so simple really. I thought that somebody must have used it before, but apparently they haven't. When the Beatles were still together we used to travel along on tour in the car when we had a new album and just think of album titles for hours and hours. I remember specifically on the *Revolver* album we were happy with the title, because it suggested the record going round and round. It's almost surprising we never came up with *Thirty-three & 1/3*—then again, maybe somewhere down the line we thought of it. Every time we'd have a new album we must have gone through thousands of titles, some of them ridiculous and some of them had potential. We'd just keep throwing out titles until one of them would stick.

• • •

Something can be important to one person and it can be of no importance what-soever to somebody else. It's really a matter of values and that's what I deal with in [the song] "It's What You Value." This thought came about, and the song fol-lowed, because of a friend of mine. We did this tour and everybody got paid really well on it. And there was this friend of mine and I was trying to get him to play and after I bugged him to death he finally said he would do it. He agreed to play but he said, "I don't want you to pay me. However, I'm sick of driving that old Volkswagen bus." So I said, "Okay, I'll get you a car." So we got him a car, a Mercedes 450. Then some of the other people later on were saying, "Well, how come *he* got a motor car when I only got money?"

So that's how the lyrics of the song came about: "Someone's driving a 450/And his friends are so wild/They're still in their stick shifts/But they feel they have much more style/But I've found . . . It's all up to what you value." To one person the Mercedes was a big deal, but to somebody else it was just a throwaway thing.

• • •

Ravi Shankar's nephew [Kumar] reminded me of [the song "See Yourself"], so I pulled it out and we put down the basic tracks. As we overdubbed more things on it, I began to like it more and more. The original idea in the first verse came about in the sixties when this thing happened with Paul McCartney. Everyone who remembers that period will know that there was a big story in the press where somehow they'd heard Paul had taken the dreaded LSD. They hounded him, saying, "Okay, have you taken LSD?" And he said, "Well, look, whatever I say, I'm going to tell the truth and it's you, the media, who are going to spread it around." And they said, "Did you take it?" And he said, "Yeah." And they took it and put it in all the papers. Then other reporters came around, asking, "Did *you* take it?" And we said, "Sure, we had it years ago." But then there was an outcry from people who said, "You should have said you didn't take it." The effect of that was, "You should have told a lie." They had put the responsibility on Paul, saying he was going to influence other people to take it and he'd already said up front, "It's going to be your responsibility." So I put in "See Yourself": "It's easier to tell a lie than it is to tell the truth/it's easier to criticize somebody else/than to see yourself." Because people won't accept responsibility for themselves and it's very often that we all, myself included, point fingers at people and pass judgement on others when first what we should do is see ourselves.

George Harrison
PRESS CONFERENCE
Los Angeles, 1979

QUESTION: What are your feelings about your new LP, *George Harrison*?

GEORGE HARRISON: I feel happy about it. The response is really nice. I mean, sometimes you do something and it's like swimming against the tide. No matter what you do, it just doesn't have that natural flavor, whereas with this the timing, the songs, are all being supported by positive reaction which is very nice.

QUESTION: How have the changes you've gone through with your last LP-33 1/3 affected the new record?

GEORGE: What happened between this album and the last is that *everything* has been happening nice for me. My life is getting better all the time, I'm happy, and I think that it's reflected in the music. Also, it became really difficult making these records because if you're writing the tunes, you're singing on them, you produce them and mix them, you know you go crazy, or I do. I don't know if everybody does. In a group situation you have a few people who all pull together and bounce off ideas together, whereas in my situation I have musicians who come in to do the basic tracks then they all split and so all the decisions are mine and there's a point where you can be at a loss so I decided I would work with somebody else. So I prayed to the Lord to send me a co-producer and I got a co-producer. That helped a lot, just having somebody else even before the record was started. It helps to have some other opinions so that at least when you know you're going crackers you got somebody to tell you.

QUESTION: How did you wind up losing your voice on the *Dark Horse* album?

GEORGE: There was only the one cut called *Dark Horse* which I was singing with a hoarse voice. That was because at the time I was rehearsing to go on the road, I was losing my voice very quickly and I hadn't completed the studio version of *Dark Horse*. I had almost finished so I decided, 'Well, as I'm gonna do this live with the band we'll just do it like a live take and use that as the album cut, but I just listened to it the other day and I think it's great. I love it. I wish I could sing like that more often . . . like Louis Armstrong!

QUESTION: You've been accused of lacking a sense of humor in your work. How do you respond?

GEORGE: Well, it depends on which side of your face you smile, really. That's been a problem for awhile. People always felt I was the "serious one," but people don't get concepts about people or put a tag on somebody and no matter what you do, they seem to think that's what you are. But if you go back through all those albums, or even with the Beatles, it's tongue in cheek. If you crack a joke and you don't smile, it doesn't mean it's not a joke, but on this album, for example, *Not Guilty*, the whole lyric is that is kind of comedy.

QUESTION: Is that song specifically written about Paul McCartney?

GEORGE: No, it's just about that period in 1968. It's a *complete* joke, the lyrics, in fact, if you go back on all the records, there's a lot of comedy. You just have to look for it.

QUESTION: What was your opinion of the *Sgt. Pepper* film?

GEORGE: Well, that got a bit out of hand. On a TV interview in England they asked me, "What do you think of *Sgt. Pepper*, the Stigwood film?" I said, "Well, I don't know. Everybody tells me it's awful, but I haven't seen it." Then they said, "Are they allowed to do that?" Referring to the Beatles and people who do these stage productions. And I said, "I don't think so. There are certain laws that protect individuals' rights or name and likeness. The problem is that the Beatles were all so spaced out and over the last few years nobody would ever get together again. But finally it's all been unraveled and we've agreed that what we'd do is, have a company in America and it would be their job to license if there's any merchandising. It would be that company's job so they don't have to bother us all the time. At the same time, if anybody is doing anything illegally, it'd be the company's job to go out and get them. So that's what I said, but the *Daily Mail* turned it into, "Oh, George is suing Robert Stigwood . . ." He's cool. I'm sure they made up the script. It's their own and they paid their performance rights so it's okay.

QUESTION: Do you plan on seeing it [the film]?

GEORGE: Not tonight. I mean, sure, I'm going to have to see it. I'll probably catch it on an airplane somewhere. Everyone keeps telling me it's awful, so why do you want me to see it? I'd rather see the Fab Four.

QUESTION: What do you think about Allen Klein's tax trial in New York?

GEORGE: I didn't even know he was still in New York. I feel sorry for the man, really . . . he looks miserable always. But maybe for him he likes it. For me, it's miserable if you're always in court.

QUESTION: How much do you think John Belushi's takeoff in *The Rutles* resembles Allen Klein?

GEORGE: Quite a lot, actually. I mean that line was wonderful. "You ask me where the money is. I don't know where the money is. But if you want some, I'll give it to you." I mean, that sort of summed it up.

QUESTION: How do you select your material?

GEORGE: It was a great help to have someone to work with as another objective point of view. A lot of musicians say, "Well, I like that." Generally they play on whatever tunes you give them. And they don't have that much involvement, whereas if you're in a band, it's a livelihood, or if you have a coproducer, that way you get much more of an idea if you're going off the rails. So in that respect, I wanted a coproducer, somebody to give me a hand for years. I'm sure a lot of people would come and produce me, but you have to live with someone for a long time. It's important not only that musically you see eye-to-eye, but as personalities you get on.

QUESTION: Why don't you collaborate more with people like Gary Wright?

GEORGE: One of my problems as a songwriter has been that John and Paul were always the songwriters and they started out writing together. It always printed "Lennon/McCartney." But with two people, again, you can bounce off each other. I've always written on my own except in situations where I've been forced into writing with somebody else. For example, I wrote some tunes with Ringo because he started the songs and then got stuck so I had to come and help him finish them. I also did some with Doris Troy because I was producing her album and we got to the session and she didn't have any tunes so we had to make them up on the spot. But generally there's been very few cases where I've sat with somebody and tried to write. I'd love to do it if I could get over the initial problem. If you don't already have a relationship with somebody and just to go into a room and sit with them and say, "Hello, jinga, jinga, jinga," it's not too wise. I'm sure that will happen maybe for an hour, or a few weeks, or something and then once you get into some sort of communication there, it may work out. Or you may end up with a load of rubbish wishing you'd just stayed on your own. I don't know, but I'd like to do that.

QUESTION: Do you have any plans to tour again?

GEORGE: I don't know. This continual question is always asked. The answer to it honestly at this moment is, no. But there's always a fifty/fifty chance. There's a part of me that enjoys that once you get through all the barriers and all this and that. There's always great moments when you want to do less of a thing. But basically, I'm not into touring like Eric Clapton. He's always on the road. It becomes a sacred thing, "Hey, man, I'm on the road!" But the road for a lot of musicians is a way out. It's a way of escaping from the income tax, the bill collectors, the telephone, your mother-in-law. And in another way, it is good, too. It's entertainment and people need entertainment, but at the same time it becomes, like being an alcoholic, being on the road. It's like a workaholic. It has its problems, too. So I'm not a great fan of touring although at the same time, to try to think of a way to do it, controlled, sanely, because you find the madness overpowers you until it sucks you in and until in the end, you just become like a demon on this rolling, mad tour while everybody else is sitting around crackers and you got pulled into it. Like in '74, I was ready for the broom closet after that.

QUESTION: Have you entered a new phase in your musical evolution?

GEORGE: I'm always entering new phases each day as far as trying to enjoy the moment now. Just to experience the experience *deeper*. That's the main thing. Is just to remember that we're all here now and we're all happy and if we're not, try and be happier. That's the most important thing, no matter what you're doing. I don't think you get happy by going on tour, or coming off tour. I don't see it as this phase, or that phase. The phase is to try to manifest love in your life. And that's all, that's really all I can try and do.

QUESTION: Are there deeper meanings in your music?

GEORGE: I think there has always been that element. But it's the same with art. There are paintings for you to sit and enjoy as well as to go into deeply and understand the meaning. I think there's a time when you do this and a time when you don't. In the early 1970s, or 1960s, the Beatles had a lot to say and me too as a solo artist in the early 1970s and now it's a recurring thing, but what I'm trying to say is *be happier*, that's all. If you push "My Sweet Lord" down people's throats too much, they jump back and try to bite you. "Your Love is Forever," on the new album, is really just the same old story. It's, "My Sweet Lord," really. It's just done in a way which maybe is less offensive to people, or through me getting older. And you know just being a bit more laid back.

QUESTION: Have you heard of "Come Back Beatles," by the People on Zebra Records?

GEORGE: Nope. The last thing I heard was some guy in San Francisco who had this project to reunite John, Paul, George, and Ringo. I wrote to him, I don't know what the others did, because he said, "If I don't hear from any of you by such and such a date, I'll take it that it's okay to go ahead with it." He already had all the stationery and all I could say to that was, "Look, that was then." There is this thing that says one of the main problems in life comes from everybody encroaching upon other people's lives. And that's true. You see one country suddenly jump on another country's territory and you have a big war. When somebody starts out, "Hey, you, I'm coming into your life now to tell you what you should do." Well, the answer to that is, this guy is on a trip about the Beatles. He's built up this big fantasy about how the Beatles are the only thing that can save the world. And that is complete rubbish. The Beatles can't save the world. We'll be lucky if we can save ourselves. Do you think a big new group can escape the tag of being "The New Beatles"? Somebody who is the New

Beatles, or the New Bob Dylan, or the New Elvis Presley will be whoever he is. It's all the people who don't quite fulfill the public's demands, desires, or hopes. They're the ones who get tagged with, "They're not the New Beatles, or the New Bob Dylan." Bob Dylan is Bob Dylan and the Beatles are the Beatles and when the new one comes along, they'll be whoever they are and you'll never have to ask the question, "When are they coming?" Because the Beatles came when they came. You knew it. The same with Bob Dylan. They'll answer the question just by being there.

QUESTION: Do you think music has stagnated, thus sparking an interest in a return to the Sixties?

GEORGE: Yeah, although I hope the 1980s would turn into, or at least have the spirit the 1960s created, because it was that desire musically to have more intrigue, deeper meaning, generate more love. And we went out of our way. That whole generation. That period. I was very disappointed when it got to like 1969 and suddenly everybody starts kicking each other and stabbing each other in the back again, after the whole love generation. Where did they go? Where are you? Suddenly it becomes all this hate and deceit, so I hope the 1980s, because the 1970s was a bit stagnant and a bit lost in direction and it was this fad, that was chopping and changing and I don't know what's in store, but I hope there is possibly that desire again to have some positive music.

QUESTION: Did the Beatles lead the media in the Sixties?

GEORGE: You are the media and you all know how you will decide and go after a certain thing and also to the extent of how much you make a thing news value. That happened with the Beatles and it happens with anything. There is a point where they think, "Good, that's a new tip for the papers," or "That's something new and different to write about." And they go after it and it gets to the point where, "Okay, now what can we do, we've said everything about it. The only thing we can do is knock it," that's what happened to the Beatles, because although everybody talks about the Beatles as being loved, we were loved one minute and then they hated our guts, then they loved us again, then they hated us. That was one reason we all went into meditation, because as Maharishi Mahesh Yogi said, "It's like being a ship on the ocean at the mercy of whatever chopping and changing occurs unless you're anchored to the bottom." And that's what was happening to us. So the point is we learned you can't rely upon this *external* change that's happening, you have to then find some real point. I think things have a snowballing effect. It's like what happened to Pete Frampton in the early '70s, or Fleetwood Mac, or the Bee Gees. You can struggle to sell maybe half a million records, or a million. You get to a point where if you get over that normal sales thing until suddenly they are selling six million. I just wish the Beatles had been selling records in the Seventies.

QUESTION: Were you distraught when the Beatles broke up like Paul says he was?

GEORGE: No. I thought, "Thank God!" Not completely. I understand what he means. It was the same when our business manager, Brian Epstein, died. It was suddenly being faced with the realization that nobody thought we haven't got that side covered. "What are we going to do?" The idea of the Beatles being like a job, getting off at five and then the factory burns down! For me, I was sort of glad we burned it down. It became too stifling. If any of you've got brothers and sisters and you're all forty-years-old and still haven't moved out. It was like that. *You need your space.* We had to try to help break that Beatle madness in order to have space to breathe, to become sort of human.

QUESTION: Would you ever consider a Beatles reunion?

GEORGE: It's just that it wasn't as much fun for us in the end as it was for all of you. I've said a hundred times what was happening was that we were relatively four sane people going on in the world and everybody else was going crackers. They were using us as an excuse to go mad. Here come the Beatles. Crash! Let's smash up some windows. Rip up limousines. Just let's have fun and go mad! And we were in the middle of it all getting the blame.

QUESTION: Does it bother you people want a Beatles reunion?

GEORGE: I don't know. I did resent it for awhile, but not anymore. Now I face it. I must admit, it was a privilege to have that experience, to have been one of the Fab Four, because there were only four of us who had that experience. I don't resent it. I look on it like Laurel and Hardy, or the Marx Brothers. But it was that time, *that period in history.* It'll always be there. You can always go and look at the Marx Brothers movies. You can get fed up with it, but at least now I can deal with it on a happier level. There was a period of years when it drove me crackers. I would say, "Why don't you shut up asking those dumb questions about the Beatles?"

QUESTION: Do you ever forsee a time when the Beatles will actually reunite?

GEORGE: Just a cup of tea together? To get the four people together and just put them in a room and have tea and satellite it all over the world and charge $20 each to watch it. We could make a fortune! What we could do is just sit there. "Well, John, what have you been doing? Well, Ringo, I think . . ." But that would be just as difficult, because everybody's left home and they're living their own lives. I haven't seen John for two or three years.

QUESTION: Are you past all the bad feelings?

GEORGE: Oh, sure, everybody's cool now. We could all hang out together and have a great time, but the only thing that would spoil it would be all of you with the cameras and microphones.

QUESTION: Will it ever happen?

GEORGE: I doubt it, and if it does, we won't tell you!

QUESTION: On a hypothetical level, what would a reunion album be like? Would it consist of a bunch of songs by each member?

GEORGE: There's a good chance of that. It's all day dreams. Until it ever happens, if it did, and I'm telling you it won't, then you'll never know what it would be like. If it did happen, there's no way we'd do a mediocre album. It would be very, *very* good. Maybe that's what people want. Maybe people want them to all get together and they all fall over and everyone can say, "Yeah, well, I told you they would."

QUESTION: Are you irritated by constantly being asked Beatle reunion questions?

GEORGE: There's a limit to how many times you ought to answer the question. It doesn't bother me once every blue moon, or once every time I put an album out, we go through it all again. That's not bad. If it was everyday though, it would drive me crazy.

George Harrison

QUESTION: What is it about chanting the Hare Krishna mantra that brings about this feeling of peace and happiness in you?

GEORGE HARRISON: The word "Hare" calls upon the energy of the Lord. If you chant the mantra enough, you build up an identification with God. God's all happiness, all bliss, and by chanting His names we connect with Him. So it's really a process of actually having God realization, which becomes clear with the expanded state of consciousness that develops when you chant. Like I said in the introduction I wrote for Prabhupada's* *Krishna* book some years ago, "If there's a God, I want to see Him. It's pointless to believe in something without proof. Krishna consciousness and meditation are methods whereby you can actually obtain God perception."

QUESTION: The Vedas inform us that because God is absolute there is no difference between God the person and His holy name; *the name is God*. When you first started chanting, could you perceive that?

GEORGE: It takes time and faith to accept there is no difference between Him and His name, to get to the point where you're no longer mystified by where He is. You know, like, "Is He around here?" You realize after some time, "Here He is, right here!" It's a matter of practice. So when I say "I see God," I don't necessarily mean to say that when I chant I'm seeing Krishna in His original form when He came five thousand years ago, dancing across the water playing His flute. Of course, that would be nice and it's quite possible. When you become real pure by chanting, you can actually see God like that, personally. But no doubt you can feel His presence and know that He's there when you're chanting. It's really the same thing as meditation, but it has a quicker effect. I mean even if you put your beads down, you can still sing the mantra without actually keeping track on your beads. One of the main differences between silent meditation and chanting is that silent meditation is rather dependent on concentration with God. Chanting Hare Krishna is a type of meditation that can be practiced even if the mind is turbulent. You can even be doing other things at the same time. In my life there's been many times the mantra brought things around. It keeps me in tune with reality. The more you sit in

---

* His Divine Grace A.C. Bhaktivedanta Swami Prabhupada, founder–acarya (spiritual master) of the Hare Krishna Movement.

one place and chant, the more incense you offer to Krishna in the same room, the more you purify the vibrations.

QUESTION: What else helps you fix your mind on God?

GEORGE: Well, just having as many things around me that will remind me of Him, such as incense and pictures. Just the other day I was looking at a small picture on the wall of my studio of Guru Dasa and Syamasundara.* Just seeing all the old devotees made me think of Krishna. I guess that's the business of devotees, to make you think of God.

QUESTION: You once asked Srila Prabhupada about a particular verse he quoted from the Vedas in which it's said that when one chants the holy name of Krishna, He dances on the tongue and one wishes one had thousands of ears and mouths with which to better appreciate the holy names.

GEORGE: Yes. I think he was talking about the realization that there is no difference between Him standing before you and His being present in His name. That's the real beauty of chanting, you directly connect with God. I have no doubt that by saying Krishna over and over again He can come and dance on the tongue. The main thing, though, is to keep in touch with God.

QUESTION: Some people say that if everyone on the planet chanted Hare Krishna, they wouldn't be able to keep their minds on what they were doing. They wonder if people would stop working in factories, for example.

GEORGE: No. Chanting doesn't stop you from being creative or productive. It actually helps you concentrate. I think this would make a great sketch for television: imagine all the workers on the Ford assembly line in Detroit chanting "Hare Krishna" while bolting on the wheels. Now that would be wonderful. It might help out the auto industry and there would probably be more decent cars too!

QUESTION: We've talked a lot about japa, or personalized chanting on beads, which most chanters engage in. But there's another type, called kirtana, when one chants congregationally in a temple or on the streets with a group of devotees.

GEORGE: Yes, going to a temple or chanting with a group of other people, the vibration is that much stronger. Of course, for some people it's easy just to start chanting on their beads in the middle of a crowd, while other people are more comfortable chanting in the temple. But part of Krishna consciousness is trying to tune the senses of all the people, to experience God through all the senses, not just by experiencing Him on Sunday by kneeling on some hard wooden kneeler in the church. If you visit a temple, you can see pictures of God, you

---

* Two of George's devotee pals from the Radha Krishna Temple, Apple's token spiritual recording group.

can see the Deity form of the Lord. And it makes it that much more appealing, seeing the pictures, hearing the mantra, smelling the incense, flowers, and so on. It incorporates everything: chanting, dancing, and philosophy. The music and dancing is a serious part of the process, too. It's not just something to burn off excess energy. I wrote in the *Krishna** book, "Everybody is looking for Krishna. Some don't realize that they are, but they are. Krishna Is God and by chanting His Holy Names, the devotee quickly develops God-consciousness."

QUESTION: Srila Prabhupada often said that after a large number of temples were established, most people would simply begin to take up the chanting of Hare Krishna within their homes. And we're seeing more and more that this is what's happening.

GEORGE: I think it's better it's spreading into the homes now. There are a lot of "closet Krishnas," you know. There's a lot of people out there who are just waiting. And if it's not today, it will be tomorrow, next week, or next year. Back in the sixties, whatever we were into we tended to broadcast as loud as we could. I had certain realizations and went through a period where I was so thrilled about my realizations I wanted to shout and tell it to everybody. But there's a time to shout and a time not to. A lot of people went underground with their spiritual life in little nooks and crannies in the countryside. People who look and dress straight, insurance salesman types, but they're really meditators and chanters, closet devotees. Prabhupada's movement is doing pretty well. It's growing like wildfire, really. How long will it take until we get to a Golden Age where everybody's perfectly in tune with God's will? I don't know; but because of Prabhupada, Krishna consciousness has certainly spread more in the last sixteen years than it has since the sixteenth century, since the time of Lord Chaitanya.† The maha mantra has spread more quickly and the movement's gotten bigger and bigger. It would be great if everyone chanted. No matter how much money you've got, it doesn't necessarily make you happy. You have to find your happiness with the problems you have, not worry too much about them, and chant Hare Krishna, Hare Krishna, Krishna Krishna, Hare Hare, Hare Rama, Hare Rama, Rama Rama, Hare Hare.

QUESTION: What effect do you think that tune, "The Hare Krishna Mantra," having reached millions and millions of people, has had on the cosmic consciousness of the world?

GEORGE: I'd like to think it had some effect. After all, the sound is God.

---

* Prabhupada's 1970 book culled from the tenth canto of the ancient Srimad Bhagavatam.

† Lord Chaitanya Mahaprabhu, the Golden Avatar of West Bengal, India. The great saint and incarnation of Krishna who popularized the chanting of Hare Krishna and founded the modern day Hare Krishna Movement.

QUESTION: When your recording company, Apple, called a press conference to promote "The Hare Krishna Mantra," the record media seemed shocked to hear you speak about the soul and God as being so important.

GEORGE: I felt it was important to try and be precise, to let them know. Because once you realize something, you can't pretend you don't know it anymore. I figured this is the space age, with airplanes and everything. If everyone can go around the world on their holidays, there's no reason why a mantra can't travel a few miles as well. After I got Apple Records committed and the record released, and after our big promotion, we saw it was going to become a hit. You know I used to sing the mantra long before I met any of the devotees or Prabhupada, because I had his first record for at least two years. When you're open to something it's like being a beacon, you attract it. From the first time I heard the chanting, it was like a door opened somewhere in my subconscious, maybe from some previous life. The first time I met Syamasundara, I liked him. He was my pal. I'd read about Prabhupada coming from India to Boston on the back of his record, and I knew Syamasundara and all of you were in my age group. The only difference, really, was that you'd already joined and I hadn't. I was in a rock band, but I didn't have any fear, because I had seen saffron dhotis* and shaved heads in India. Krishna consciousness was especially good for me because I didn't get the feeling I'd have to shave my head, move into a temple and do it full time. So it was a spiritual thing that just fit in with my lifestyle. I could still be a musician, but I just changed my consciousness, that's all.

QUESTION: The Tudor mansion and estate you gave us outside London has become one of our largest international centers. How do you feel about the Bhaktivedanta Manor's† success in spreading Krishna consciousness?

GEORGE: Oh, it's great. Actually, it gives me pleasure, the idea that I was fortunate enough to be able to help at that time. All those songs with spiritual themes were like little plugs, "My Sweet Lord" and others. And now I know that people are much more respectful and accepting when it comes to seeing the devotees in the streets. It's no longer something that's coming from left field. I've given a lot of Prabhupada's books to many people and whether I ever hear from them again or not, it's good to know they've gotten them and if they read them their lives may be changed.

QUESTION: When you come across people who are spiritually inclined but don't have much knowledge, what kind of advice do you give them?

---

* Indian robes for men.

† Bhaktivedanta Manor, a seventeen-acre estate outside London, was purchased by George in 1973 and donated to ISKCON for use as a temple. For years this property was in great danger of being closed down altogether by the village's conservative neighbors, but after an extensive legal battle, the devotee's won the right to continue worshipping at Harrison's elegant country ashram.

GEORGE: I try to tell them what my experience is and give them a choice of things to read and places to go. Like, you know, "Go to the temple, try chanting."

QUESTION: When you did the *Material World* album, you used a photo showing Krishna and His friend and disciple, Arjuna. Why?

GEORGE: It was a promo for the devotees, of course. I wanted to give everyone a chance to see Krishna, to know about Him. I mean, that's the whole idea, isn't it?

QUESTION: You and John Lennon met Srila Prabhupada together when he stayed at John's home in September of 1969.

GEORGE: Yes, but when I met him at first, I underestimated him. I didn't realize it then, but I see now that because of him the mantra has spread so far in the last sixteen years, more than it has in the last five centuries. That's pretty amazing, because he was getting older and older, yet he was writing his books all the time. I realized later he was much more incredible than you could see on the surface.

QUESTION: What about him stands out the most in your mind?

GEORGE: His saying, "I am the servant of the servant of the servant." I like that. A lot of people say, "I'm *it*. I'm the divine incarnation. I'm here and let me hip you." But Prabhupada was never like that. I like Prabhupada's humbleness. The servant of the servant of the servant is really what it is, you know. None of us are God, just His servants. He just made me feel so comfortable. I felt he was a good friend. Even though he was seventy-nine years old, working practically all through the night, day after day, with very little sleep, he still didn't come through as though he was a very highly intellectual being, because he had a sort of childlike simplicity. Even though he was the greatest Sanskrit scholar and a saint, I appreciated the fact he never made me feel uncomfortable. In fact, he always went out of his way to make me feel comfortable. I always thought of him a lovely friend, really, and now he's still a lovely friend.

QUESTION: In one of his books Prabhupada said your sincere service was better than some people who had delved more deeply into Krishna consciousness but could not maintain that level of commitment. How did you feel about this?

GEORGE: Wonderful, really. It gave me hope because, as they say, even one moment in the company of Krishna's pure devotee can help a tremendous amount. I think Prabhupada was really pleased at the idea that somebody from outside the temple was helping get the album made.* Just the fact he was pleased was encouraging to me. I knew he liked the song "Govinda."

Prabhupada's accomplishments are very significant. Even compared to someone like William Shakespeare, the amount of literature Prabhupada produced is

---

* The Radha Krishna Temple LP issued on Apple Records in 1970.

The savage young Beatles outside the Cavern Club, Matthew Street, Liverpool, 1962.

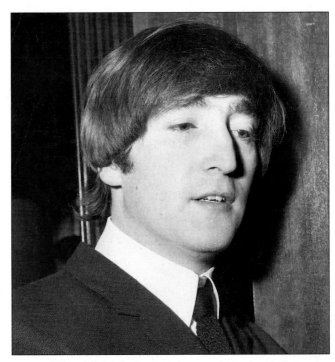

John at a press conference at the Kilburn Cinema in London, October, 1964.

The Beatles rehearse for an appearance on American television.

Enduring yet another moronic photo op, 1964.

On stage in Liverpool, 1962.

The Beatles meet the press in Memphis, August 19, 1966.

John barnstorming America, 1965.

A sober-looking Lennon, 1970.

John in London, 1967.

George on-stage with the Beatles, 1966.

Starr relaxing in the drawing room of Brian Epstein's fashionable Belgravia, London home, May 20, 1967.

Lennon and McCartney, New York, 1968.

George Martin and Ringo accept a Grammy award on behalf of the group.

Relaxing at Ronnie Hawkin's Mississauga, Ontario, farm, winter 1969.

Ringo signing an autograph outside Apple, 1969.

His Divine Grace A.C. Bhaktivedanta Swami Prabhupada, Pattie, George, and Dhananjaya Dasa on the grounds of Friar Park.

John and Yoko, Montreal, 1969.

George in 1974 during the height of his much misunderstood Krishna Consciousness phase.

*Denny, Linda, and Paul accept yet Wings more gold records
following the release of their* Speed of Sound *LP, London.*

Paul in St. John's Wood, 1977.

Paul on the streets of Soho, London, 1989.

George with Eric Clapton in Japan, 1992.

Ringo on-stage during his All Stars tour.

truly amazing. It boggles the mind. He sometimes went for days with only a few hours' sleep. Even a youthful, athletic young person couldn't keep the pace he kept himself at seventy-nine years of age. Srila Prabhupada has already had an amazing effect or the world. There's no way of measuring it. One day I realized, "God, this man is amazing!" He would sit up all night translating Sanskrit into English, putting in glossaries to make sure everyone understood it and yet never came off as someone above you. He always had that childlike simplicity. What's most amazing is the fact he did all this translating in such a relatively short time, just a few years. Without having anything more than his own Krishna conscious-ness, he rounded up all these thousands of devotees, set the whole movement in motion, which became something so strong it went on even after he left. And it's still escalating even now at an incredible rate. The more people wake up spiritu-ally, the more they'll begin to realize the depth of what Prabhupada was saying and how much he gave.

QUESTION: What do you think is the goal of human life?

GEORGE: Each individual has to burn out his own karma and escape the chains of maya (illusion), reincarnation and all that. The best thing anyone can give to humanity is God consciousness. But first you have to concentrate on your own spiritual advancement; so in a sense we have to become selfish to become selfless.

QUESTION: What about trying to solve the problems of life without employing the spiritual process?

GEORGE: Life is like a piece of string with a lot of knots tied in it. The knots are the karma you're born with from your past lives and the object of human life is to try and undo all those knots. That's what chanting and meditation can do. Otherwise you simply tie another ten knots each time you try to undo one. I mean, we're now the results of our past actions and in the future we'll be the results of the actions we're performing now. A little understanding of "As you sow, so shall you reap" is important because then you can't blame the condition you're in on anyone else. It's your own actions that relieve or bind you.

QUESTION: What would you say is the difference between the Christian view of God, and Krishna as represented in the *Bhagavad-Gita*?*

GEORGE: When I first came to this house it was occupied by nuns. I brought in this poster of Vishnu†. You just see His head and shoulders and four arms hold-ing a conch shell and various other symbols, and it has a big "om" written above it. He has a nice aura around Him. I left it by the fireplace and went out into

---

* The Bhagavad-gita, or the Song of God, is the 5,000-year-old Vedic text accepted as divine by orthodox Hindus.

† The preserver or sustainer of Hindu belief.

the garden. When we came back in the house they all pounced on me, saying, "Who is that? What is it?" as if it were some pagan god. So I said, "Well, if God is unlimited, then He can appear in any form, whichever way He likes. That's one way. He's called Vishnu." It sort of freaked them out. But the point is, why should God be limited? Even if you get Him as Krishna, He is not limited to that picture of Krishna. He can be the baby form, He can be Govinda and manifest in so many other well-known forms. You can see Krishna as a little boy, which is how I like to see Him. It's a joyful relationship. There's this morbid side to the way many represent Christianity today, where you don't smile, because it's too serious, and you can't expect to see God, that kind of stuff. If there is God, we *must* see Him. I don't believe in the idea you find in most churches, where they say, "No, you're not going to see Him. He's way up above you. Just believe what we tell you and shut up!" I mean, the knowledge that's given in Prabhupada's books are the world's oldest scriptures. They say that man can become purified and with divine vision he can see God.

QUESTION: You wrote in your book: "Most of the world is fooling about, especially the people who think they control the world and the community. The presidents, politicians, military, etc., are all jerking about, acting as if they are Lord over their own domains. That's basically Problem One on the planet."

GEORGE: Unless you're doing some kind of God conscious thing and you know He's the one who's really in charge, you're just building up a lot of karma and not really helping yourself or anybody else. There's a point in me where it's beyond sad, seeing the hate in the world today. It's terrible, and it will be getting worse and worse. More concrete everywhere, more pollution, more radioactivity. There's no wilderness left, no pure air. They're chopping the forests down. They're polluting all the oceans. In one sense, I'm pessimistic about the future of the planet. These big guys don't realize for everything they do there's a reaction. You have to pay. That's karma.

QUESTION: Do you think there's any hope?

GEORGE: Yes, one by one, everybody's got to escape maya. Everybody has to burn out his karma and escape reincarnation and all that. Stop thinking that if Britain, America or Russia or the West becomes superior then we'll beat them and we'll all live happily ever after. That doesn't work. The best thing you can give is God consciousness. Manifest your own divinity first. The truth is there. It's right within us all. Understand what you are. If people would just wake up to what's real, there would be no misery in the world. I guess chanting's a pretty good place to start.

QUESTION: I've been looking forward to a new George Harrison album ever since *Gone Troppo*.

GEORGE HARRISON: This one [*Cloud Nine*] is really good, actually. The layoff I took really helped and the music business is in a much better position than it was at that time. Everybody was getting a bit weird, you know, saying, "Well, hits should be like this" or whatever. It's good because this album I've done the way I wanted to, and fortunately, the record company really likes it, too. It's not like they're saying, "Well, it's good, but you should have done something else." They're *really* pleased with it.

QUESTION: So was it actually the state of the recording industry that was responsible for you not putting out an album for five years?

GEORGE: Well, remember, there was the recession and the oil crisis and everything went weird. The record companies were getting rid of artists and radio stations weren't sure what they were playing. I don't know whether you remember that song from the *Somewhere in England* album called "Blood from a Clone," but that was my reaction to what was happening on the radio and with the record companies.

QUESTION: It seems like the record industry had gotten very conservative.

GEORGE: I think there was just a general confusion. People were frightened because they felt a lot of companies were losing money and the radio stations were being dictated to by their sponsors and the record company executives were being very, very conservative and doubly paranoid about what should be released. Quite honestly, after doing it for twenty-five years, it's not the kind of thing I enjoyed hearing, "Well, we don't really want to put your record on the radio because of one reason or another." So I just decided after *Gone Troppo* had been out that I'm just going to get out of here for a bit. I thought when I do this next album I want it not to be so hard, mentally, for myself. Because [it's difficult] if you write the tunes, produce them, and do everything yourself. I just thought, "I've got to get a producer I can work with." Fortunately, I remembered of Jeff Lynne, the guy from Electric Light Orchestra. I though if we could meet and get on well, he would be just the sort of guy for me.

QUESTION: How did you meet him?

GEORGE: I had to make a point of finding out where he lived, so I mentioned it to Dave Edmunds. Dave lives near me and we see each other quite a bit. So a couple of months later, Dave phoned me saying, "Well, Jeff's gonna come down to London, so should we all get together?" And I said, "Yeah, come over to our house, have dinner and stuff." So we kept in touch and got to know each other a bit more. Jeff worked with an attitude which was really nice, just being my friend, hanging out and helping me make this record. We got to know each other and I think it worked out really well. What he's done is, of course, a great contribution, but at the same time, it's *my* record. It sounds like me *now*. It doesn't sound like I've been covered up in layers of technology or even the Electric Light Orchestra. I'm sure when you hear it you'll know what I'm talking about. It's really worked out nicely.

QUESTION: You mentioned the period of time two years ago. Would that have coincided with your participation in the Carl Perkins cable TV special, "Blue Suede Shoes: A Rockabilly Session"?

GEORGE: It was around that time or just before. You see, I've never actually stopped writing. I've got a studio in my house and from time to time, I'll write a tune and put it on the twenty-four track. Not properly, not with an engineer or anything. Just on my own. I've got loads of demos lying around, so as I was getting to know Jeff I played him very rough demos to get an idea of which songs we wanted to record. The Carl Perkins show was really for me. It was done because I like Carl and I thought I ought to do something. Otherwise I'd get so out of it I might never want to do that kind of thing again. It's hard just to step back out after you've not done any shows. So I did it thinking, "Well, Carl Perkins' music is so enjoyable and such fun that it's the kind of thing I should be able to do without too much worry."

QUESTION: I was reminded of the days when you called yourself Carl Harrison.

GEORGE: Yeah! Well, that's really going back before the Beatles. It was when we got our first semi-professional job backing this singer in England called Johnny Gentle. We really didn't have any money for outfits, so we bought these real cheap white shoes and black shirts. We thought we should have stage names, so we all made up silly ones. But "*Carl*," to me, always seemed so cool. Apart from his tunes, which are so good, Carl Perkins is just such a nice man. That's the main reason why that show came across so well. I mean, everybody's out there with their egos, but at the same time, it's all concentrated for the love of Carl. I thought that really came across. And it was nicely presented. Did you hear what he said? "Look at you guys, all in your nice, clean shirts and your little guitars." He was so blown away. I mean, there was one point where he was almost in tears saying, "It's been thirty years since I wrote this tune and I've never enjoyed it so much as with my rockabilly buddies." He's so sweet.

QUESTION: What about playing live, though?

GEORGE: Well, obviously I haven't really played live. It's very difficult. I mean, I do enjoy it. Once you get to do it, it's really enjoyable. There's nothing nicer than being in a band when it's all rocking, but to actually get to that stage. It's the sort of thing you must do permanently, I think. Even Eric Clapton said to me, "God, I'm getting so I can't play. My fingers are jamming up and all that." It's the kind of thing you've got to do all the time and he takes gigs in between his own albums and tours. He plays on everybody's stuff and plays in everybody else's bands. And I admire that because he's never lost his touch by stopping. Yet, at the same time, to just go on stage after not doing it is very hard. I did two nights of the Prince's Trust Concerts this year and I was so nervous. On the actual record, it didn't sound bad. I liked the show on TV except that I really don't like watching myself. It was very nerve-racking.

QUESTION: So it's hard coming back and playing live again.

GEORGE: It is, unless you're gonna rehearse for a long time. And having done that, there's no point in just doing three or four shows.

QUESTION: Well, you'd have to be on the road with people you'd really like being with.

GEORGE: Yeah, but even then, it's one thing, just say, with travel. I mean, I enjoy being in different places but hate that bit of going from one place to another. Don't forget you're only on stage for a couple of hours and the rest of the time you're stuck in weird, little motels and airplanes. You're away from your family and all the things that make your life pleasant. I can see it when you're younger. Although for people like B. B. King who keep touring all the time, that's become their life. But for me, the point when we stopped touring because it just became too difficult, we really lost our touch for doing it and the desire to do it again.

QUESTION: Someone told me that you were reportedly recording a whole batch of old rock'n'roll classics for a possible album, rather like John's *Rock'n'Roll* LP.

GEORGE: No, it's not true, actually. But I've tried to write those kinds of tunes because years ago, Leon Russell always used to say to me, "That's the kind of record you should make, a rockabilly album." Because that's the kind of music I'm good at playing. The night before we did that show Carl came over to my house with Dave Edmunds and a couple of the guys from the band. We had dinner and a couple of bottles of wine and started playing guitars. I said to Dave and Carl, "It's a pity that these days there's not the kind of songs that are so simple and yet really classic." So Carl started playing some of the new songs he'd written and they were just killers. I mean, if they could be recorded like his Sun records, just done really nicely, up-to-date but with that sound, I mean those songs are as good as his original hits. He did one new tune, "I Was There When They Invented Rock'n'Roll," and it talks about the Beatles, the Stones and all that kind of stuff.

QUESTION: So you're not sure whether or not you're going to tour in support of *Cloud Nine*.

GEORGE: I don't think so. I haven't got any plans at this stage to get a band together and go out to tour this album.

QUESTION: What about doing something like what Dylan did with Tom Petty and the Heartbreakers?

GEORGE: Yeah, but that's much easier for Dylan because he's got all of these tunes which he can either play on his own or just have a small group backing him. So basically, there's not a great deal of rehearsal to do. I know what you mean, though, I just step into someone else's band.

QUESTION: Sure. Front their band.

GEORGE: Yeah. Well, I suppose that's a possibility. Although I hear from Eric Clapton that Elton John's gonna form a band for over forty-year-olds and apparently I'm in it. So I won't discount the possibility of doing some things like that, but I must admit I don't have it all lined up at the moment.

QUESTION: Let's talk about *Cloud Nine*. I was intrigued by one of the song titles, "When We Was Fab." Is that what I think it's about?

GEORGE: It is, yeah. It was written by Jeff Lynne and myself. I thought that it would be nice to write a song just like one of those Fab Four late'67–68 kind of tunes.

QUESTION: Like "Old Brown Shoe"?

GEORGE: No, it's got the cellos on it. It's more in the vein of a John song like "Walrus" or something. But at the same time, it has this nostalgic sound. And maybe lyrically as well there's a little bit of that. It's still a new song, but it's made with that in mind. Like the first thought I had before I wrote it was that I heard Ringo in my head counting in the song going, "one-two-dadada-dadada-dant!" And I took it from there. It's a bit like one of those songs you would expect John to write, but having said that, it hasn't got really loony lyrics like "Walrus." I'll tell you the words: "Back then long time ago/When grass was green/Woke up in a daze/Arrived like strangers in the night." And then the chorus goes: "Fab/When we was fab/Fab/Long time ago/When we was fab/Fab/When income tax was all we had." It's really a tongue-in-cheek sort of joke. But we've got little hints of sounds from that period like phasing some of the backup voices and a little bit of backwards stuff and it ends with the sitar going off into the ether.

QUESTION: Sitar? Great! Are you still playing sitar?

GEORGE: I just play it for my own amusement. It's such a great instrument with such a wonderful sound. But this song is like a montage, in a way, of those moods or feelings from that period.

QUESTION: Are you nostalgic about those days?

GEORGE: I'm able now to really see the fun that it was and I think more about the good things that happened. As opposed to maybe ten years ago, it was just thinking about all of the lawsuits and all the negative stuff. A lot of that has just gone away with time. It's quite enjoyable now to think about the things we did and the things that happened.

QUESTION: How do you like the CD versions of the old albums?

GEORGE: Well, I know there's a big controversy over whether they're any good or not. I know that the first batch of CDs, as George Martin said in Billboard, they were only made in mono, so you can't really make them sound like brand-new digital things. That's it, they were mono. But some of the others, like *Sgt. Pepper*, I was frankly a bit disappointed. I don't know exactly what happened. For instance, I hear this sound like a real tinny tambourine that keeps coming out of the right-hand speaker. And something's happened where the mix itself . . . you know, the balance we had . . . because everything is really down to a mix. It becomes one thing in the mix, but on this CD, somehow you can see behind it and you hear things sticking out too much.

QUESTION: I'm sure you can hear a lot more things we don't hear as well.

GEORGE: To me, it just sounds like a rough mix. It seems that some of the hard work we did to get them to sound like they sounded has been undone. I don't know if that's just the result of the digitalizing of these songs or not. You have to remember that most of them were either done on two- or four-track machines and now we're getting into the later ones. I think that *Abbey Road*, our last album, was an eight-track. I also heard a strange story that Geoff Emerick had done the CD mixes and somebody at EMI had a cassette copy of them and the copy was faulty and they listened to it and said, "Oh, these are terrible." So somebody went in and re-did them, but actually, Geoff Emerick's mixes were good. But I'm as out of touch now with the old Beatle stuff as everybody because we no longer have that deal with Capitol-EMI. They no longer really consult us about anything and so we just know what we read and hear.

QUESTION: What about all the reports that there are lots of unreleased Beatles recordings still in the vaults?

GEORGE: It's not true; there were only ever a couple of songs I can remember that weren't put out. Like there was a song I did with John and Yoko called "What's the New Mary Jane?"

QUESTION: That's on the *Sessions* bootleg.

GEORGE: There are some things which people may regard as being performances, but they're really not and shouldn't have been released. I know there's a version of "While My Guitar Gently Weeps" with just me and acoustic guitar.

QUESTION: That's on that *Sessions* album, too.

GEORGE: I haven't even heard that. Someone I talked to yesterday has put it on a cassette for me.

QUESTION: That album also has Paul's demo of "I'm Looking Through You." It's really nice and simple, so it has a certain value.

GEORGE: Like now I've got a demo of a song that's on my new album, they're not really interested in that. They'd rather get the proper version. But if in twenty-nine years, that surfaces, then they'll all want to hear it because it's rough and not quite the same. It's funny how people see this stuff.

QUESTION: Are you still interested in Formula One racing?

GEORGE: Yeah, I am, actually. I follow the world championship. In fact, I got to my hotel last night and I was really tired. And I was going to have an early night and I was just going through the TV channels and heard Jackie Stewart's voice. It began with the Portuguese Grand Prix from last Sunday. So I ended up sitting up until 2:30 in the morning watching all that.

QUESTION: What originally interested you in racing?

GEORGE: When I was a kid, they used to have races at a place in Liverpool called Aintree and I used to go and watch the motorbike racing and the car racing. There was a World Championship Grand Prix there, I think, in 1954, won by Manuel Fangio, who was one of the greatest racers of all time. I was always into watching racing.

QUESTION: What did you think of all of the nostalgia surrounding the summer of 1967? I mean, you personally seemed to be in the eye of the hurricane of that whole thing.

GEORGE: I don't suppose you got to see the TV show that was made about the summer of 1967. It's quite interesting as a historical piece. I suppose it was to be expected because nostalgia is a big part of our lives. Ever since I can remember they're always showing Hitler on television in England. I think it becomes more romanticized as time goes by.

QUESTION: Do you look at that period and say, "Boy, we were young and stupid?"

GEORGE: Yeah, we were a bit. But at the same time, I think there was a lot of good came out of it, too. Although people considered us to be the leaders, we were just as much caught up with what was happening as the rest of the people. Although I suppose we were being more innovative, a bit more so than others. I don't know. There was a lot of energy in those days.

QUESTION: You were once quoted as saying you'd had enough fame for one lifetime. Do you still feel that way?

GEORGE: Yeah, I do, really. This is the conflict I have: I like making records and writing songs; when you do that and go to all that trouble, it's nice to get people to hear them. It's such a huge business now that, unless I make a video, unless I do interviews, the public just don't know it exists. So somewhere you have to make a compromise. I would really prefer just to make records and put them out. I don't really enjoy the self-glorification, or whatever you call it, because I had my fill of ego fulfillment during all those years. Although now, it's easier because I think I'm more mellow. I can handle that and I enjoy doing it. But sometimes it gets too crazy when you're talking about yourself and your past all the time.

George Harrison
SELECTED QUOTATIONS
London, 1988

We came up with a lot of different titles for this album [*Cloud Nine*]. For awhile we were going to call it *Fab*, which everyone liked because they got the joke. But in the end I had to pick, so I took a cue from the clouds on the album cover. Of course, judging from the picture it might just as well have been called *Spot The Loony*, but I don't think the record company would have gone for that.

• • •

The guitar on the cover was the first really good American one I ever owned, back when the Beatles first started out and we were still in our leather gear. I bought it for seventy-five pounds off a sailor in Liverpool. Eventually I gave it to Klaus Voorman and he took it to L.A. when he moved. Using that particular guitar on the cover seemed like a good idea because we set out to do a record that was of today, but also echoed that late-sixties feel. We used real guitars, real keyboards, real drums, and real people, playing real songs.

• • •

"Got My Mind Set on You" is the first single, and it's also the only one that Jeff [Lynn] and I didn't write for the album. Rudy Clark wrote it back in the late fifties and the tune's been stuck in my head for twenty-odd years, although this version is quite different from the original. It rocks along quite nicely, I think.

• • •

There are some Beatle-y type songs also, but that's quite natural, I think. Jeff is a big Beatles fan and, of course, was part of that whole scene himself. He knew how to approach it from both an old and new angle and it was a great balance working with him. I think together we've brought back some sounds people haven't heard in a bit.

• • •

There's one song I particularly like on the album, called "Just for Today." It was written three years ago after I had some alcoholic friends over to the house. One of them gave me a brochure from AA from which I borrowed the title. It was trying to tell people relax, to not try and deal with everything all at once, which I think is good advice for everyone. You don't need to be an alcoholic to be reminded to stay cool just for today.

• • •

Elton played on three of the tracks, Gary Wright on two, and Jeff took over keyboards on whatever was left. Elton is a really funny fellow and a great rock'n'roll piano player. When he found out I was doing the record he sent a message

124

through Ray Cooper, volunteering to help, so I said, "You're on. Come by at two o'clock." Which he did.

＊ ＊ ＊

Eric Clapton also played on "Devil's Radio," "Cloud Nine," and "The Wreck of the Hesperus." We've been friends for years and probably always will be. After all, we shared the same wife. And, of course, Ringo is on drums. I don't need to tell him what to do. He just hears the song and plugs in with that rock-steady beat. He's got the feel and we're actually quite alike in that we hardly ever practice. We just pick up our instruments when we need them . . . very naughty boys.

＊ ＊ ＊

I'm always playing with someone or other. There's lots of guys in my neighborhood who are guitarists: Ian and Jon from Deep Purple; Mick Ralphs from Bad Company; David Gilmour from Pink Floyd, as well as Alvin Lee, Gary Moore and a very famous Cockney guitarist from the early sixties named Joe Brown. There's always guitars goin

＊ ＊ ＊

I'm very happy to be making records again. People think in terms of a comeback, but I really haven't been anywhere. I've been here the whole time. This record is very much the music I wanted to make. I don't think it's right to try and mold what you do to the current market. It's like the old song says, "Take me as I am or let me go." This is me, I hope I fit in but I'm not going to lose any sleep over it.

I really have no concept of myself, no image that I'm trying to get across. As far as my work with Handmade Films is concerned, I consider myself as much a filmmaker as I do an ex–pop star. I say "ex" because to me pop stars are teenagers, and I'm not that, for sure. I play a little guitar, write some songs, and make a few movies. I even do a little gardening, but none of those things are the real me. The real me is something else entirely, just like the real you.

＊ ＊ ＊

I love playing on stage, but I'm not so sure I'll be touring this time around. On the last tour I'd get up in front of all these people and after awhile it was obvious that half of them were there to see me and the other half because it was what was happening in town that night. I wasn't sure I even really liked all these people. I'd rather play for twenty friends who really care than a stadium full of yobbos. We'll see.

＊ ＊ ＊

I guess it all has to do with getting older and more experienced. When I was a Beatle, one day was like ten years. We met everyone in the world and never had a moment's peace. It made me realize that being rich and famous was a load of rubbish. So you go on and try to figure out what really matters. It's part of the process of being happy in your heart. I've got the gist of it finally. Now it's just a question of experiencing it more deeply.

GEORGE HARRISON: Mark Lewisson thinks he is a big expert. He has written a book recently which, I have to admit, is very thorough, because he has tried to go back even to the years before the Beatles were famous and establish every dance hall and little club we played in.

In a way, he had done a lot of work on that, but everybody holds him as being the foremost authority, because he got access into EMI and listened to all the tapes, and I don't really agree with that. For instance, this book that everybody is acclaiming, I got a copy, and I opened it, again, randomly, near the front, and I looked at the dates, and I saw straightaway three things which were wrong.

As far as I am concerned, you know, you got to have been there. That is what it was about. It was doing that and being there. And if you weren't there, it is speculation, no matter how good your recollection is; no matter how good your source. It is surmising.

You know, even if he got a large element of facts right, it is still, you know, who is interested in, I am not interested in what *other people* say happened. I did it. I lived it, and to me, it is all just people looking to make some money out of the name of the Beatles.

CHAPTER SIX

Don't Pass Me By/ Ringo Starr and Pete Best

Ringo Starr
PRESS CONFERENCE
1978

QUESTION: What was it that was so special about the Beatles?

RINGO: The four boys. The four of us were just magic. I think that came across to the audience. There was something about the four of us that was just dynamite. In addition to John and Paul writing a bunch of hits, there was a chemistry and honesty that went out from us to the people and back to us from them.

QUESTION: Do you think it had anything to do with the time, or the era?

RINGO: Who can tell! At the time, the music industry wasn't in a very good state. It didn't have anything very strong, and we just happened to come out and be quite strong.

QUESTION: Do you think it could happen again?

RINGO: Yes, of course, it can. Not with us, but with someone else.

QUESTION: The Beatles are still very much a part of popular culture. Look at all the merchandising.

RINGO: We don't get any part of that. People think we make a fortune, but the stuff they sell, we don't get anything from that, people just do it. So we don't support it, or I don't support it.

QUESTION: What about the show *Beatlemania*, on national tour with the fab four look-alikes?

RINGO: They have nothing to do with us. There's only one real look-alike, I believe—I've never seen the show. It's called *Beatlemania*, but from what I've heard from the people that have seen it is that it deals with the sixties and not just us. They should call it the *1960s Show*, but, of course, we're bigger than the sixties.

QUESTION: The fact that you are not making music any more as the Beatles, and the fact that people still go to these conventions and still buy the albums every time Capitol re-releases the package, is incredible!

RINGO: They re-release them because people want them. We're back in the charts again with *Sgt. Pepper,* and it was eleven years ago that we made it. That's why I can sit in Hollywood Hills.

QUESTION: Doesn't the fact that you are so popular again give incentive for you four to get back together again?

RINGO: The Beatles will go on, as George said, "With us, or without us." It just goes on anyway, that's no reason to get back together.

QUESTION: How did the Beatles come apart?

RINGO: At the seams? A lot of reasons. We were all married at the time, I had the children, I didn't want to go out on the road. People were splitting up with their wives, there were thousands of reasons. It was just the time to end it.

QUESTION: Did you feel it was time to end it?

RINGO: I think we all did. We were all waiting for someone to say, "Let's get out of here."

QUESTION: Who finally said it?

RINGO: Truth be known, it was probably John, but it was so long ago.

QUESTION: What's he doing?

RINGO: He was baking bread and looking after the baby last time I spoke to him.

QUESTION: Do you keep in touch with the other Beatles?

RINGO: Yes, I do. When I'm in England I'll see who's ever there and I spoke to John about three days ago on the phone wherever he was, Japan, that's it. We keep in contact. It's not like everybody believes in this big split.

QUESTION: We hear so much about how awful it was and how everybody was fighting.

RINGO: We were fighting. I was very annoyed when Paul sued me.

QUESTION: Why?

RINGO: Because he was a spoiled brat.

QUESTION: No, what was his claim?

RINGO: It was all over the Allen Klein deal. Sorry, Allen, but this is life. He was our manager, at that time, of the Stones, the Kinks, and the Beatles. Things weren't going so well so Paul decided to sue the other owners of the company, which were George, John, and I. But that's enough of that.

QUESTION: I was a big fan of your acting in *That Will Be the Day* and, of course, you did *Candy* as the Mexican gardener.

RINGO: I did *The Magic Christian* and one that has never been seen in America called *Blind Man*.

QUESTION: Any plans for acting in the future?

RINGO: Nothing right now. I'm in between engagements.

QUESTION: What's the hardest part of divorce?

RINGO: Through my divorce the hardest part was the children. I was an only child and my father left when I was three. Maureen was an only child, too, so we quickly had three kids.

QUESTION: How long have you been divorced?

RINGO: Three years now.

QUESTION: How do you handle the depression of having your children leave you?

RINGO: I ended up on a lot of barroom floors. I don't know anyone that has been through it straight.

QUESTION: Why was it so difficult?

RINGO: You can't try to be married like you can't try to be in love. Either you are, or you're not. Then you say, "Let's try it for the children," but they know what's going on. And then it gets so polite and apologetic, it's madness. Then you try separate bedrooms, this will do it! It's silly, but you go through these separate stages. Now Maureen and I have a relationship where we can finally deal with each other. At first it was very difficult. It could be Tuesday and we'd be at each other's throats and then Wednesday it would be fine. It's better now, but it takes a couple of years.

QUESTION: Do you think it had anything to do with the fact that you are Ringo Starr, superstar?

RINGO: No. It never bothered us in the middle of all the hype. We divorced in 1975 and it was well over by then. We went through the mania together. It was not the fame, because we'd already been through the height of it. That was when Maureen would get beat up because she knew me.

QUESTION: She'd get beat up!

RINGO: Yeah, kids would try and attack her. Then we got married and it was fine, except they'd try and steal the baby to put in the scrapbook. You'd see someone's autograph and then this poor little thing pinned in the book!

QUESTION: How do the kids feel being the children of Ringo Starr?

RINGO: Well, Lee was the coolest. She went to school and they said, "Your daddy's Ringo Starr!" and she said, "No, he's not, he's Daddy." Zak, he's the oldest, went through a scene where kids and photographers would be hiding in the bushes and he'd be there posing, but now he's calm. He's old enough now that he doesn't like the band. He says, "You had a few good records." He loves the Who!

QUESTION: If your kids said, "Dad, we want to be in show business," what would you tell them?

RINGO: Well, I think Zak will be in show business, he's a fine drummer. They're all musical. They all take piano, and Jason takes violin. Lee plays piano and takes ballet, you know, kiddie ballet where they are all just fairies in the wind.

QUESTION: What about their Daddy—does he still practice his drums every day?

RINGO: I never did. One time I practiced. It was in Liverpool in this little back room and all I kept hearing was, "Keep that noise down." I never practiced after that and joined a band one month later. I've made all my mistakes on stage, I've learned with bands.

QUESTION: Do you think you're a pretty good drummer?

RINGO: I'm the finest rock'n'roll drummer around.

Ringo Starr and Barbara Bach*
PRESS CONFERENCE
1984

QUESTION: Are you in love?

RINGO STARR: Yes. Do you know how amazing that is?

QUESTION: Obviously you two have a very special love affair.

RINGO: Being in love is totally different than loving someone. Love caused a bond between us. It's like I love Barbara and I'm *in love* with Barbara.

QUESTION: Ringo, how did you start off?

RINGO: It was a natural progression with me in music. I started in local bands taking any job I could get and worked my way through from band to band in Liverpool because the aim of the game is to be in the best band as a musician.

QUESTION: Did the fame that came from being one of the Beatles take its toll? I read that at a concert it got to the point where you were playing out of tune.

RINGO: Yes, we were playing out of tune and we were doing the same songs over and over again. To keep myself entertained I'd play some of the songs like a rumba and no one would notice. It was bad for us and me personally because I was ending up a bad player. So we decided to stop the tours because we were touring constantly. We decided it was more important to go into the studio and explore all those avenues.

QUESTION: Considering John Lennon's death, is there a risk inherent with fame?

BARBARA BACH: I'm only afraid of getting hurt in crowd situations. It's new to me and it does frightens me. Ritchie's quite used to it. I'm only really that it will become overwhelming and they'll hurt him. Other than that I'm thrilled that people love Ritchie.

QUESTION: How did the two of you become involved?

RINGO: I always liked Barbara. I always fancied her. We were together and she said to me, "Do you know what I want to do now?" And I said, "Yes," and we've been living together ever since.

QUESTION: Was there another woman in your life before the movie?

---

* Barbara Bach is Ringo Starr's second wife. The onetime Bond girl has since all but given up her film career to be Mrs. Richard Starkey.

RINGO: Yes. I phoned her up and said I was in love with Barbara, good night. Not that cruel, but I did ring her up, I was so excited.

QUESTION: Barbara, right now you're living every woman's dream: a rich, famous, sexy man has fallen in love with you.

BARBARA: More than rich and sexy, a warm, kind-hearted, generous, human being.

RINGO: Here's another dollar, dear.

Ringo Starr
PRESS CONFERENCE
May 25, 1995

QUESTION: How did you choose the musicians for your new tour?

RINGO STARR: The process always goes in if they've had hits from this century, 1960s, 1970s and 1980s. . . . That's the criteria we start from and that they're good musicians and they're free. . . . This year we started with Felix Cavaliere, he was free and he's got a new record out and he has all those hits from the Sixties. Then it was Billy Preston. I thought this year we would have a keyboard group because last time it was mainly guitar. Then I thought of Randy Bachman, let's give it an edge, he's a tough rocking dude and he has great numbers. You have to have numbers, that is the fact. We got him and then John Entwistle, because we really need Boris The Spider. But it's very hard to find bass players that have any numbers . . . He and Zak get on real well and that's always a good combination, the drummer and the bass player so we had him. I needed one more guitarist and you just go through your memories. Grand Funk Railroad, what is happening? Where is Mark Farner? We found him and he was free for the summer so we asked him to come along and that's how it worked.

QUESTION: How is touring different for you today from the Sixties?

RINGO: It's more fun and it's quieter. The pace is not like it was in the Sixties. When you were touring every minute was taken up with doing stuff. Here you can relax. I love it now. The pressure's not half as much. Not even a quarter.

QUESTION: This is the 30th anniversary of "Yesterday," the most played song of all time. Your reaction when you first heard it?

RINGO: No. I remember it was "Scrambled Eggs." That's my earliest memory and then it just turned into a cloud. We're not even on it. If a song called for this attitude then that was what was done to it. We didn't all sit there saying, "We're not on the record." So anyway, happy birthday "Yesterday." The most recorded song in history, I didn't know that.

QUESTION: On the last tour you mixed in songs from your new album.

RINGO: Well it was because I had a new album to plug, that's why . . . I think people really come to have a good time. They come to see the combination. "What, him with him?" Wow, what's that gonna be like? In general though, I think they're coming to have a good time. I don't think they're coming to really listen. It's not one of those audiences. I couldn't deal with that.

QUESTION: What about all the people like this that you didn't get to play with on a tour like this. People like Keith Moon and Harry Nilsson?

RINGO: Well, Harry actually got up with us in Vegas on the last tour and that was great, because he was my best pal. He was just actually getting in the mood for going live. He was talking about it more and more and, of course, he didn't quite make it.

QUESTION: Tell me about the new Beatles track, "Free As a Bird."

RINGO: It's done, ready, mixed. Sounds just like 'em. No, it does because they're on it. I mean, it's always hard for me to say, because I'm on it and so are the others, but it's a really cool track.

QUESTION: Will this sound like a Beatles' track, or John, Paul, George, and Ringo twenty years on?

RINGO: It really sounds like a Beatles' track. You could say they could have made this in 1967. It was weird for me and I'm on it. I was listening to it. There's so much distance that's gone down from those days, twenty-odd-years. It was just amazing, because I was playing the track and I thought, "Sounds just like them." But just really the light went on.

QUESTION: Did you record it all at the same time or was it overdubbed?

RINGO: We had to overdub, because we started off with a cassette Yoko gave us and a cassette is not the greatest thing for keeping time, so we couldn't really play with it. Also the cassette wasn't in the greatest condition and didn't have the greatest clarity. So with modern science we can really work on the tape. Jeff Lynne did a great job putting it in time and cleaning it up so that we could work on it.

QUESTION: Were you in the studio together?

RINGO: Yeah. We were all there hanging out together, but we didn't do it like we used to in the old days. Like the four of us would just kick in and get the backing track. We couldn't do that.

QUESTION: Didn't you record more than one song together?

RINGO: Yeah, we did "Real Love."

QUESTION: Paul McCartney said you did more than that.

RINGO: Such a blabbermouth that McCartney! We did do three tracks, but we could only finish two. One of them is just sort of left half-finished.

QUESTION: How difficult was it to record the new tracks with Paul and George without John physically being there?

RINGO: At the beginning it was very hard listening to the tape knowing that we were going in there to do this track with him. It was pretty emotional. I loved John . . . We had to sort of feel that he's only gone for a cup of tea. He's gone on holiday, but he's still there. That's the only way I could get through it. If you asked the others I think that's the same . . . Maybe the best thing about recording together was that this was a joyous experience in the face of the bitterness of the Beatles breakup. There were a lot of bad feelings. We'd been in and out with each other for the last twenty years. But doing this project, it sort of brought us together. Once we got the bullshit behind us we all end up doing what we do best, which is making music. That goes out the window and we were having a lot of fun, a lot of laughing.

QUESTION: I understand you, Paul, and George did some jamming at George's house for the *Anthology*. What was that like?

RINGO: It was just acoustic. Two acoustic guitars and me on brushes . . . It was like an *Unplugged*.

QUESTION: How much involvement did you, Paul, and George have in the production of the TV series *Anthology*?

RINGO: Well, we look at it all. I've seen every frame actually and the edits. We sit in the editing room with the director and the producer and say, "We'd like that changed, we want that lengthened," or, "We want that cut out." We are totally involved with this thing. We've spent hours, which the good part about that is, that we've hung out together so it's got rid of all the dog dirt we were sort of involved with each other. . . . We've always had dinner but working together sort of brought out the more loving aspect of all of this. Once you're working that's what you're doing, the rest, throw it out the window . . . It's a musical documentary because we were a music band. As that's going on, when it hit certain points so far I've been interviewed separately, so has George and so has Paul and we've used John from anywhere we could find him, audio tapes and interviews he'd done that relates to a specific incident. You know like say coming to America, or the Cavern, or getting our first record deal. Or playing Shea, *"Ed Sullivan."* . . . We're very good at bouncing off of each other and that's what was happening. Then it was becoming fun. Then it got to "Well, why don't we do some music?" We took the easy route, "Why don't we do some incidental music, because what can we do? There's four Beatles and there's three of us left." And then this idea about Yoko finding tapes came. It was just a natural thing. It just started evolving and we were getting more involved and that's what happened.

QUESTION: What are your recollections of those days where you had quite a few hits with your solo career?

RINGO: Oh, great, the solo career. The seventies, my career after the Beatles, suddenly I had to pick myself up, dust myself off and do something. Of course I took the easy way with George Martin doing the *Sentimental Journey* album which I didn't play on. Then I did the Nashville album* which I didn't play on. I was just trying to find myself. Suddenly I was on my own. Then it got to the *Ringo* album with Richard Perry and, of course, who else is on there, but John, Paul, and George. I was drumming again and I was really on a roll.

QUESTION: Tell us about the duet you did with Stevie Nicks for the Harry Nilsson tribute album.

RINGO: Harry was my dear friend and he was really preparing himself for an album, always writing songs. He gave me this song, "Lay Down Your Arms," four or five years ago. And I always thought I wanted to do this song one day if he doesn't do it on an album. So when they came around to doing the album, *For The Love Of Harry*, everyone did songs already done by Harry. And I had this song that nobody had done, but he had written it. It was real emotional for me because I was doing it for Harry and it was "Lay Down Your Arms," about the gun laws and everything else. I just called Don Was. I said, "Have you got a couple of hours?" Everyone was sort of doing it at home, it wasn't a big production record. And he had a studio so I said, "I've got this idea for this track. I'll bring it over and see what we think, what we can do with it." We pressed the buttons. He put a line down on piano, we had the keypad for the drums. I did a bit of that and got some rhythm section going. Did the vocals. And he said, "Let's see if so and so is in?" Some guy came over and played guitar and then Stevie Nicks was down the road, "Give her a call." And she came over with her girls and they did the vocals. We did it in a night. It was like good old records, where you're not suffering for years. You just got it together and people were just popping in. It was like a little conveyor belt in a way. If people would come in and do the guitar. "Okay, thank you, we need the room." Because it was just in a house room. I'd bring in someone else and it was just great. We started around about six at night and it was mixed by three in the morning.

QUESTION: The New York drum community has been asking for years if the rumors are true that Bernard Purdie played on any Beatles tracks.

RINGO: That's the biggest bullshit I've ever heard. Every couple of years Bernard comes out, "I did it all!" He's not in one photo, I might say. It's just crap. I hate to use words like that, but it's crap. Max Weinberg has offered him two hundred and fifty thousand dollars if he can prove it.

QUESTION: Were there any myths that you wanted once and for all to clear up in the *Anthology*?

RINGO: Well, I don't know if there's one thing we can pick. You'll see it, like the Bernard Purdie thing, is that what really happened? So there's not really one I could explain.

---

* *Nashville Skyline*, released on Apple Records in the early seventies.

Pete Best*
INTERVIEW
. . . .
New York, 1965

QUESTION: Could you tell me a little about your early life?

PETE BEST: I was born in Madras, India. I came to Liverpool when I was four years old. The transportation was a troop steamer. On board were dozens of wounded soldiers. During the war my father was involved in the Great Bombay Explosion. More than thirteen hundred tons of raw explosives went up that day, turning the ship they were stored in (plus twelve others) into a useless pile of scrap metal. The tragedy claimed hundreds of lives and flattened three hundred acres of the Bombay Docks. A tidal wave caused by it was so gigantic it lifted a four thousand–ton ship nearly fifty feet into the air and literally threw the vessel onto the roof of a nearby shed. My father was one of many men who helped rescue the wounded and those buried under mountains of debris.

QUESTION: What were your first impressions of your new home?

PETE: When we arrived at Liverpool, the first thing I remember is seeing snow. Of course, there was never any snow in India and to me, picking up a handful and playing with it was quite an experience! The next few years were uneventful. I did well in athletics, judo, boxing, etc., representing my class in active competition with other schools.

QUESTION: How did you come to be associated with the Beatles?

PETE: The first time I met John, Paul, and George, was when my mother was opening a club called the Casbah in the cellar of our home. I was seventeen years old. We had booked the Les Stewart Quartet and the day the Casbah was scheduled to open, Les broke up with the other guys. John and Paul approached us at about the same time and Mum got hold of George Harrison who was playing in another club two hundred yards down the street. They rehearsed for two and a half hours and Mum liked them very much. They signed on under the name the Quarrymen and played the club for several months. Then they went to Scotland for another engagement. By that time, I had formed my own group and we took over the spotlight in Mum's club. Eventually, all of us broke up and went our separate ways.

---

* Pete Best was the Beatles' first real drummer, playing with the group from '60 to '62. He was ultimately sacked on the very eve of the group's phenomenal success.

QUESTION: What about actually signing up as a full-fledged Beatle?

PETE: One day, unexpectedly, I received a phone call from Paul. The group had an offer to go to Germany, but they needed a drummer and he was wondering if I could help them out. Paul said that he and the others had talked over the matter and they wanted me to audition for them. Stu Sutcliffe had joined them on bass with George was on lead and John and Paul on rhythm guitar. I auditioned and they kicked things around. Within thirty-six hours we were on the way to Hamburg, to play the Indra Club. At that time, we were all pretty young and reckless, really living it up. We were staying in back of the club and the surroundings weren't, shall we say, very elaborate. But the kids were beginning to dig us. Later, we moved down the street into a bigger club. We were performing for a solid eight hours every night.

QUESTION: Didn't you continue to play your mother's club after returning from Germany?

PETE: Sure. Our first date was in December, just before Christmas. More than five hundred kids were there and gave us a great homecoming reception. The news of our Hamburg success apparently spread throughout Liverpool. Virtually overnight, we were the number one group. We stayed there for about eight months and then returned to Hamburg for a period of ninety days or so. Of course, Paul and I had earlier been deported from Germany, in August of 1960. George was also sent home because he was considered too young to get proper working papers. Paul and I had a big argument with the club owner over several matters, most important being the fact that he'd paid for five musicians in the group and wanted to reduce our pay after George left. It turned into a fight. We weren't about to pay any fine, so we got the boot. But our deportation came later. There were no electric lights where we'd been living and we couldn't see a damn thing to pack. Finally, we managed to get our things together. We went out to buy some cigarettes, John and I. By the time we'd returned, the living quarters were ablaze. Paul had accidentally knocked over a candle which set some torn pieces of tapestry ablaze. Both he and Stu were arrested. The manager claimed we had tried to burn down his club in order to get back at him. So we were deported!

QUESTION: How did you feel after being ousted from the Beatles?

PETE: I'm much too quiet. I don't like to fight or argue. I was raised to be well mannered and respectful and never to lose my temper. So I just stayed in my room at home, didn't come out. I thought I was really finished. I would stare into space and do nothing, not eat or drink or anything. Pretty soon, the incident got around and my friends came and tried to make me snap out of my depression. Girls were sleeping in our back garden, waiting for me to pass by a window so they could shout how they still liked me despite the fact that I was no longer with the Beatles. I became a hermit, literally living alone and sealed off from the world around me. I was living in a world of my own. Then my parents got hold of me and told me how foolish I was acting. They urged me to go out and be with people. After ten days, I managed to bring myself back to reality.

QUESTION: Was that the end of your show-business career?

PETE: Under Mum's management, I formed a group called the All Stars which included myself, Tommy McGuirk, Wayne Bickerton, and Tony Waddington. We split up because Tony felt he wanted a normal life instead of the chaotic one we were living. Then the rest of us changed the sound of the group, and added two saxists, Bill Burton and Trev Barker. We became the Pete Best Combo, went to Germany and did very well, played one of the clubs I'd been at with the Beatles. We felt we were on the verge of breaking into the big time, but then our popularity tapered off. In September, we went on a tour of Canada and I signed two new managers, David Rolnick and Bob Gallo, of Savage Records in New York City. They rushed out an album, *Best of the Beatles*.

Pete Best
SELECTED QUOTATIONS
New York, 1990

Let's put it this way. We were seventeen-, eighteen-, and nineteen-year-olds in Hamburg, Germany, "Sin City" of the world, and were put there by ourselves. We had conquered the German audience. The birds were there, the booze was there. Everything was at our fingertips. We used to perform wild antics on stage, we used to jump off stage. John used to split his jeans, there were mock fights, we'd jump off stage and dance with the audience, you name it. In a way it was a release for us. The faster the music, the more the German crowd went wild.

• • •

Maybe you've seen it in movies, but this is what happened. We finished playing on stage and we'd been warned before it was a rough place to play, but we weren't too worried about it because we could handle our own. We could stick up for ourselves. But on this particular night as Stu was coming through the stage door a gang of what we used to call teddy boys grabbed Stu and pushed him back through the stage door and started beating him up. John and I had seen what was going on and jumped in and sorted the problem out, beat the other guys up and threw them out the band room. But Stu had taken quite a beating. He took a few blows around the head and to his body. We had to make sure we got him out of the band room in one piece. We put Stu in our van and made sure he got home as fast as he could. A lot of people say it was that particular fight which might have led to the fact that Stu died of a brain hemorrhage. No one, as far as we're concerned, can say it was that particular incident, but in a way it may have started something, who knows. That's actually what happened.

I heard of Stu's death when we had gone over to open the Star Club in April of '62. This was the first time we'd flown over and we were expecting Stu and Astrid to meet us at the airport. When we got off the plane we saw Astrid and it was a case of, "Where's Stu?" If you saw Astrid then you expected Stu to be there, too. She didn't keep it back or anything. She just said that Stu had died a couple of days before we had actually gotten into Hamburg. It upset us because we all had a lot of respect for the guy regardless of the fact he had left the band and had gone back to working in Hamburg. It was the first time I had seen John actually physically break down and cry in front of someone. I think this indicates the total admiration John had for Stu as a friend. It was a very upsetting scene. It upset John tremendously.

• • •

From my point of view, the guy I was closest to in the band was John. I had known him for a couple of years before actually joining the band. I admired him as a person, I admired him as a friend, as a musician, a clown, a fighter, a lover, anything. He was my forte in the band. We got along really great together. We had great times. To ask "Who did you least get on with?" Most probably at that time, Paul would have been the most difficult to get through to. He was very different from the rest of us in that he wanted to attract all the attention. By that, I mean, he wanted to be in the limelight all the time, where the rest of us would go out and just enjoy ourselves and have a lot of fun.

* * *

You realize talent when you see it, and John had great talent, it was as simple as that. To say it was a result of him taking drugs which led to him becoming the John Lennon we all know today, I really can't answer that question simply because I wasn't there. I don't know what pressures were going on, or whether he relied on drugs to come up with further material. All I can say is that in the early days when I was associated with him, it was true talent that came out and was not drug oriented. Each particular member of the band had their own charisma—Paul had a good delivery, John had good delivery. But there was something there which was raw, uninhibited and I think it was that which he later took and developed many years afterwards into the type of music and charisma John had.

* * *

One particular night we had gone on and gotten really blathered, you know, absolutely non compos mentis. We got back to the flat which was just over the road from the Star Club. We had all just gone to bed and George was sleeping on the other side of the room. In the early hours of the morning we heard, "Bleeaahh!" It was George, he'd rolled off the side of his bed and puked. He was so drunk, he let it stay there. Normally we'd have cleaned it up. We took one look at it and said, "Ugh! Leave it, we'll take care of it in the morning." So the morning came and George woke up and he's looking at this horrible mess splat-tered all over the floor and we're looking at it as well. We said, "Hey, George, are you going to clean it up?" He said, "I'm not bloody well cleaning it up!" We said, "Well, we're not going to clean it up either!" So it stayed there. The cleaner came in and she wouldn't touch it. It got to the stage where George was terrified of going to bed, because every time he'd tried to climb up over into bed "Thing" would try to have a go at him.

Mootsy went and got Horst, who was the only guy who could get us to do any-thing in those days. So Horst came around and said, "Hey, George, you've got to get rid of this horrible mess on the floor." So George turned around and said, "Sorry, Horst, that's our pet." The rest of the guys said, "You can't do that! You can't get rid of 'Thing'!" Horst disappears and we say, "I think we've won." The following morning he comes back with a bloody big shovel and gets straight under old "Thingy" and pulls it up. He goes over the road to a bin outside the Star Club. All the rest of the Beatles are walking out like a death parade with our head down coming out to see "Thing" go to his final resting place. He put the bin lid down and said, "That's the last bloody time 'Thing' is going to be seen in Hamburg!"

* * *

I had known Ringo through playing in my mother's bar, the Casbah, when he was with Rory Storm and the Hurricanes. I met him again in Germany, because he was out there on the same tour. When we came back to Liverpool, he came round the scene again with Rory Storm. We buddied up and became great friends. But that fateful day in August 1962 it happened that Ringo was the guy who replaced me. Even though he took over my particular role in life, or what was destined, I have no hatred for him.

* * *

Initially, when we went out to Hamburg it was seven or eight hours a night, seven days a week, with about fifteen or twenty minutes off. So, it gets around two o'clock in the morning, once we've played and blasted steam and done whatever we had to do, it was a case of going out and enjoying ourselves. Normally we'd go out after the show to Harold's Cafe. If Horst was with us, and nine times out of ten he was, it would be a case of going out to a few clubs, wandering around, act the goat, get drunk, and then head back. Day in and day out we did that. The more drunk we became, the more fun we had.

CHAPTER SEVEN

Newspaper Taxis/
The Media

NEWSPAPER REPORTAGE
1960–1997

DANCE CLUB IN HOUSE CELLAR

LIVERPOOL—Four young men making a name for themselves in the world of skiffle and "pop" music are the Quarrymen, who played for many teenagers to dance at the opening of West Derby's "Kasbah" Club on Saturday evening.

The club where teenagers can meet their friends, dance and drink coffee, has been opened in the cellars of a house in Hayman's Green, West Derby. The Quarrymen, complete with a varied repertoire and their electric guitars, will play at the club each Saturday in the future.

They are John Lennon, 251 Menlove Avenue, Woolton; Paul McCartney, 20 Forthlin Road, Allerton; George Harrison, 25 Upton Green, Speke; and Kenny Brown, 148 Storrington Avenue, Norris Green.

1960

● ● ●

BOILING BEATLES BLAST COPY CATS "Even Our Hair Styles Are Aped"

LONDON—The Beatles launched a blistering attack on their "copyists" this week.

John Lennon, twenty-two-year-old Beatles rhythm guitarist and the group's spokesman said:

"Certain groups are doing exactly the same thing as us. I wouldn't have brought the matter up, but some guys are having digs at us.

"Look, we copied nobody. I'm not a Negro so I can't copy a Negro singer, can I? We've got our own style, our group.

Bandwagon

"But some other groups around are climbing on this rhythm-and-blues bandwagon they're talking about and pinching our arrangements. And down to the last note, at that."

Lennon claimed that fellow-Liverpudlian hit paraders Gerry and the Pacemakers also suffered "terrible copying," too.

John continued: "It annoys me a lot. And to crown it all, some groups coming up are getting on the wagon by doing stuff we were playing two years ago.

"Why can't these copyists make their own styles like we did?"

And in a final blast, an angry Lennon said: "It happens in hair styles, as well. I see players in some groups even have the same length hair as us.

"Digs at Us"

"It's no good them saying they're students and they just happen to have long hair. We were students, as well, before we came to London and we didn't have these styles then, did we?"

Lennon added: "I suppose people might say it's an honor to be copied, and I wouldn't have bothered to have hit back really. But when they have digs at us, we're going to have a go.

"I've wanted to say this for a long time . . ."

AUGUST 3, 1963

• • •

BEATLES AND BILLY J. FOR PALLADIUM TV

LONDON—The Beatles and Billy J. Kramer with the Dakotas are the first of the Liverpool hit parade groups to be signed for *Sunday Night at the London Palladium*! The Beatles will headline the show on October 13, for which Brook Benton has already been set. Billy J. Kramer and the Dakotas have been booked for October 27.

Billy J. Kramer is canceling a date the previous evening at the Frodsham Merseyview in order to be fresh for his Palladium debut. A new date has been set for this same venue for December 14.

In addition to their Palladium show, the Beatles will visit Sweden for five days. In addition to concerts, they will guest on Swedish television, in a programme titled "Drop In". They leave on October 25.

1964

• • •

BEATLES HAVE TAKEN OVER ELVIS' THRONE

We Must Reply to Miss Anne Thurgood and Everyone Else Who So Stupidly Criticize the Beatles.

Elvis is no longer the King; although we do agree he once was. His popularity was waning for some time before the Beatles came on the scene.

Elvis vacated his throne and the Beatles took it over.

Why can't they face it, Elvis has had his day!

We admit the Beatles cannot remain teenage idols forever but they certainly have the talent and personality to carry on and be remembered, long after the group scene has diminished. Surely their first film has proved this.

The Beatles' first film gives a picture of them as they really are, (which is very interesting and unusual) rather than a lavish highly colored improbable fairy story, with a song a minute thrown in for fair measure.

Please, let Elvis die a natural death, as we accept that one day in the very distant future the Beatles will also have to.

MISS.S.BUTTERFIELD AND MISS.L.HILL,
ARCHERY TERRACE, LEEDS
1964

• • •

BEATLES BAD NEWS FOR ONE REPORTER

"A plague has swept the land, but we have been left whole" was the way one writer reviewed the first invasion of the Beatles, England's mop haired rock'n'roll sensation. Like most, the writer felt the idols were a fad among teenagers which would pass as quickly as it arrived. How wrong he was!

The Beatles returned in August, stronger than ever. Motel owners found their doors denuded of knobs because adolescent girls believed "the

Beatles had touched them." An attendant found himself driving an ambulance through seething streets, and hidden in the back were the Beatles. "If those kids had caught them, they'd really have needed an ambulance," he said. Some fans did require medical aid, one burst blood vessels in her neck, she screamed so hard; another fell and was used as a vantage point by spike-heeled fellow fans.

Some people profited, such as the entrepreneur who bought sheets from the Beatles' hotel beds and sold them at $1 per square inch!

How did the Beatles take to America? "Can't say," Ringo admitted. "Didn't see much. Luv-ed the money, though." He was referring to the $2,112,000 the Beatles took home with them.

1964

• • •

3,000 GIRLS SCREAM AS BEATLES HIT N.Y.

NEW YORK—Though they arrived in the dead of night, the Beatles were met by 3,000 very-much-alive teenagers at Kennedy Airport early today.

It was 2:55 a.m. when the Beatles arrived from Cincinnati, where they were virtually drowned out by 13,000 screaming teenagers during a thirty minute performance Thursday night.

When the Beatles arrived at a Park Avenue Hotel in Manhattan, scores of fans broke through police barricades and surged against the four

entertainers, who squired away and ran into the hotel.

In the crush outside, Beatle Ringo Starr's shirt was ripped and someone yanked a St. Christopher medal from a chain around his neck.

WABC Radio disk jockey Bruce Morrow was broadcasting from inside the hotel, and Starr went on the air with the message:

"Cousin Brucie, somebody took my medallion. It means more to me than almost anything. I've had it since I was ten-years-old."

Anybody who returned the medal of St. Christopher, patron saint of travelers was promised a meeting with Ringo and his fellow Beatles, John Lennon, Paul McCartney and George Harrison.

The broadcast was picked up on transistor radios in the crowd outside the hotel, mostly teenage girls.

WABC said 155 girls telephoned the studio, each saying she had the medallion.

A girl who identified herself as Angie McGowan, fifteen, a high school student in Manhattan, turned up at the studio shortly and handed the medallion to Morrow, WABC said. How she got the medal was not stated. She was promised a meeting with the four lads from Liverpool this afternoon.

1964

• • •

BEATLES SELECT GIFTS IN PRIVATE

LONDON—Harrods, the London store where Queen Elizabeth II goes shopping, allowed the Beatles to do their Christmas shopping after hours behind locked doors Thursday night.

That privilege has never before been granted not even to the Queen, Jacqueline Kennedy or visiting royalty and nobility. They all had to jostle with Harrods regular customers.

Queen Elizabeth Friday spent two hours picking out presents, but other shoppers were there at the time.

The management feared that mob scenes might erupt if they allowed the Beatles to shop during normal opening hours.

1964

• • •

THREE TEENAGERS ARRESTED

MEMPHIS—Three teenagers were arrested Wednesday in connection with the theft of a stereophonic record player, plus fifteen record albums and a box of 45 r.p.m. singles—all by the Beatles.

1964

• • •

BEATLES ARE ANNOYED BY JELLY BABY BARRAGE
Ringo: "They All Hit Me"

SYNDEY—Liverpool's usually cheerful Beatles are feeling annoyed today with Sydney fans.

Despite all the appeals they've made to the huge audiences not to throw jelly-babies during performances because of the danger to their eyes, girls are persisting in flinging handfuls of these sweets at John,

Paul, George and Ringo as the stage in the center of the enormous Sydney Stadium revolves slowly making each of them targets in turn to each section of the audience.

Paul McCartney said bitterly, 'I keep asking them not to chuck those damned things, but they don't seem to have the sense to realize we hate being the target for sweets coming like bullets from all directions.

Ducking

"How can we do our jobs on stage when we are having all the time to keep ducking to avoid sweets, streamers and the other stuff they keep throwing at us?"

John Lennon said, "It's ridiculous. They even throw miniature koala bears and gift wrapped packages while we are going round on the revolving stage. We haven't a chance to get out of the way."

Twice during the show, Paul McCartney has stopped singing in the middle number and said to the audience:

"Please don't throw those sweets at us. They get in our eyes."

Each time his request has been greeted by screams and another shower of sweets, so Paul has finally shrugged his shoulders and said, "Well, I asked you, anyway."

Nonsense

This nonsense about the Beatles liking jelly-beans began many months ago, with a much-regretted publicity yarn saying these were their favorite sweets.

"Wherever we've been since, America, Europe and now Australia, that stupid story has gone ahead with the result that we get jelly-babies chucked at us until we're really fed up," said George Harrison.

Ringo Starr chipped in to say, "It's all right for you lot, you can jump aside and dodge them, but I'm stuck at the drums and can't move, so they all seem to hit me."

Said young George, "We can't hear ourselves singing, so how can they hear us? There's never a pause in their screaming, they're great."

Sydney Stadium has never known anything like it. More than 10,000 fans at every performance, have, according to official statements by an acoustics expert of New South Wales University Mrs. Anita Lawrence, made more noise than a Boeing 707 jet in full screaming flight.

Said Mrs. Lawrence, whom last night took a sound level meter with her to check the pitch of audience noise, "Normally, noise reaching the ground from a Boeing jet plane is up between ninety and 100 decibels.

"When the Beatles appeared, the pure screams alone showed 112 decibels on the recording apparatus. For the next half hour the needle never fell below 100 and many times leapt higher."

The decibel meter showed Paul McCartney the most popular member of the Beatles. Whenever he bobbed his head and grinned, the needle shot up as high at 114 decibels, which is more than the noise given out by an electric saw three feet away from your ears.

Hysteria

During the last couple of nights here, more than a hundred young girls received first aid ambulance treatment after collapsing during the Beatles' performance.

Most of the these were cases of hysteria and nobody was injured.

"Tonight's two shows end our Sydney visit," commented bassist McCartney. "Tomorrow morning we leave Australia for a week in New Zealand, where they tell us excitement has been building up for months in anticipation of our arrival."

1964

• • •

BEATLES "ESCAPE" IN AN ARMORED CAR

LOS ANGELES—The Beatles fled in an armored car from thousands of screaming fans after their concert in the Dodgers baseball stadium at Los Angeles last night.

As the quartet tried to leave by the main gates scores of delirious teenagers climbed all over the limousine and it was forced to turn back.

The Beatles then fled to offices under the grandstand as crowds charged the 151 foot high entrance gates. Time and again, police were forced to hit out with their clubs, to keep the fans off the gates. Youths then charged the gates with wooden barricades which had been set up to keep the crowds back.

They hurled sticks and bottles at police until they were finally turned away with a shoulder to shoulder charge by officers who cleared a sort of no-man's-land between the crowds and the exit gate.

1964

• • •

Newest Thing, Beatle Wallpaper

BELLAIRE—President Lincoln's famous quotation, paraphrased roughly that "for a person who likes that sort of thing, that is the sort of a thing they would like," applies aptly to a wallpaper display at the Sherwin-Williams Co. store at 3394 Belmont St. in Bellaire.

George Rykoskey, store manager, has learned that there are people, mostly young and female, who "like that sort of thing," and there are people, mostly old and male, who "don't like that sort of thing." There seems to be no middle ground.

The wallpaper is a new item manufactured in England and containing, of all things, pictures of the "Beatles" in "living color" and their autographs.

The most pithy comment on the display was by a man who said that its only redeeming feature is that at least the wallpaper doesn't sing.

Rykoskey put a roll of the paper in the window Thursday afternoon at 12:20 p.m., ten minutes before classes resumed at Bellaire High School about a block away. Which may explain why some of the students may have been late for fifth period classes.

Within the space of seconds some fifteen or twenty teenagers had gathered in front of the window, the girls approv-ingly and the boys disapprovingly. Three girls were counting their combined funds to see if they had enough to buy a whole roll, twenty-seven inches wide and thirty-six feet long.

"Can't you see what this wallpaper will do for a young person's bedroom?," he asked. "Why, it will add a whole new dimension to listening to Beatle records. Imagine being surrounded by Beatles!"

Rykoskey paused briefly, then added with a thoughtful look, "Yeah, just imagine!"

A Sherwin-Williams outlet in Cleveland sold 500 rolls, enough to paper 100 average-size rooms, within a week, Rykoskey said. Some smart operator promoting a benefit dance in that city struck a good financial blow for the Crippled Children's Society by buying three rolls, cutting them into twenty-one inch swatches, and selling them for ninety-six cents at the dance. He sold out completely.

1964

• • •

Beatle Who Missed the Boat in Liverpool

LIVERPOOL—You could hardly blame Peter Best if he cried a lot.

He is in the finest tradition of history's wrong guessers, such as Napoleon who sold Louisiana thinking it nothing more than a swamp, your grandfather who sold his Ford stock because he thought the automobile was a passing fancy, Roy Riegels who ran the wrong way in the Rose Bowl.

Best had a career decision to make two years ago. He was a member of a singing group in England. They were stalemated after a successful engagement in Germany and there was trouble with the management.

Best decided the time had come to strike out on his own, and form his own vocal group.

So he left the Beatles, to be replaced by a lad called Ringo Starr. His old group will make about $15 million in 1964.

1964

• • •

BEATLES BURGLED

LONDON—Two of the Beatles were burgled Sunday night.

Thieves broke into the west end apartment of George Harrison and Ringo Starr while the two were at a show, and escaped with cash, cufflinks and souvenirs worth $500.

1964

• • •

"SWING, MAN . . ."

After viewing the Beatles on *The Ed Sullivan Show,* I must conclude that Mr. Sullivan is finally beginning to "Swing, Man, Swing!"

MRS. JACKIE G. MOSLEY
MOBILE, ALA.
1964

• • •

Never before has Sullivan stooped so low to obtain so high a rating.

TOM STORCH
LONG BEACH, N.Y.
1964

• • •

SULLIVAN RIDING A FAD

NEW YORK—The end of television's "Beatle" infestation is not in sight. Ed Sullivan, whose CBS variety hour seems to be a wholesale importer of Liverpool singing groups, has signed Jerry and the Pace Makers for a second appearance Sunday and taped a third turn.

Still another group, Billy J. Kramer and the Dakotas will appear on the show next month.

Elderly (i.e., over twenty-one years of age) television viewers may be comforted by a statement of Robert Precht, Sullivan's son-in-law, who is the show's producer.

"In our minds, this British thing is something of a phenomenon which has been occurring in the past three or four months," he said. 'They are extraordinarily attractive with the younger viewers and we felt we should go along with it.'

Precht said it is has always been the policy of the show to present singers whose record sales were near the top of popularity lists—which is where "the Beatles" and their British brethren are perched.

1964

• • •

THE BEATLES SAY NO TO £7,000
MADISON SQUARE OFFER REFUSED

LONDON—The Beatles have turned down a £7,000 offer to appear at Madison Square Garden during their New York tour.

Their manager, Brian Epstein, told a reporter in London last night that it would take the edge off of the Carnegie Hall concert the group are giving on the same night, February 12.

"It would be a risky business and I don't want to over-expose the boys nor over-work them," he said.

The promoters had already said they could fill the 19,000 capacity Madison Square Garden with forty-eight hours of opening bookings, but Mr. Epstein felt another factor was whether satisfactory sound could be achieved in a hall of that size.

FEBRUARY 1964

• • •

BEATLES RUSHING TO COMPLETE
SCREENING OF FIRST MOVIE

HOLLYWOOD—*Beatlemania* will be rushed into release, just in case the mania for the Beatles fizzles too soon. The bushy boys are currently filming their first movie at top speed in their hometown of Liverpool.

MARCH 6, 1964

• • •

RECORD REPORT
Vinton New Threat to Beatles

NEW YORK—Bobby Vinton is the man who broke up the Beatles' strangle hold on the top four places. However, as he edges closer with "My Heart Belongs to Only You," the new Beatles offering, "Can't Buy Me Love," leaps into the No. 10 place. Can no one topple the Beatles from the top spot?

Now that we have gotten the required Beatles news out of the way, let's cast an eye on good old Chubby Checker, who with a folk-oriented effort, "Hey Bobba Needle," is about to assault Mt. Beatle.

APRIL 4, 1964

• • •

BEATLES RECEIVE MILD
RECEPTION IN CHICAGO

CHICAGO—the Beatles arrived here from London Thursday with their guards up to avoid screaming fans, but there weren't many fans, and they didn't scream much.

There were perhaps 200 of the curious clustered at a barrier. Only twenty-five to thirty of these looked like teenage girls.

The Beatles, who had a much more rousing welcome in Boston where they changed planes at Logan International Airport, were discharged from their plane at the Pan American Airways hangar in a special stop, before the ship taxied to it's regular slip at the customs and immigration passenger terminal.

Immigration and customs inspectors met the four long-hairs in the hangar and formalities took about five minutes.

Newsmen and fans were kept at a more than discreet distance by policemen as the quartet left the hangar and hoarded a limousine for downtown.

A much larger contingent of fans waited at the Astor Hotel, leaping and screaming as the black limousine drew into it's garage.

About twenty policemen held back several hundred boys and girls but were unable to keep them from swarming all over the car. Several boys hung from the rafters of the garage.

One chubby teenager with her hair in rollers successfully eluded three policemen to rub her handkerchief on the inside of the car on which the Beatles had ridden.

Her feat was greeted with loud yells and hugs from her companions.

AUGUST 11, 1964

• • •

BEATLES ACCUSED OF BEING RUDE

LONDON—London spokesmen for the Beatles were cautious about a British press attack on the pop-singing group accusing them of rudeness to bystanders.

"If they have been, it can only have happened in Nassau, because they have never been rude to anyone here," a spokesman in London said.

He commented on an article in the *London Daily Express*, sent from Nassau where the Beatles are making their second film, which spoke of "tedious temperaments over photographers, tantrums over requests for autographs, bad language with matching manners."

"Rarely have I seen any star behave with such hard case rudeness to the public as the Beatles sometimes do now," the writer declared.

1965

• • •

YANK WHO MAKES BEATLE FILMS FUNNY IS SOLD ON THE BOYS AS INDIVIDUALS

NEW YORK—The Beatles are being exploited by Walter Shenson, but they don't mind a bit.

Mr. Shenson, an American ex-film publicist, produced the Liverpudlians' first and very successful movie, *A Hard Day's Night*, and their second, *Help!* which deserves equal success. His exploitation of the Beatles consists in making their films as funny as possible.

"In Hollywood," Mr. Shenson said, "there is a tendency to say goodbye to actors when filming is done, I exploit the Beatles to the fullest, and they are willing because we all care.

"After a picture is finished, we find places where we can add 20 percent or more humor to it. So we dub dialog to fit.

"With both pictures, we have brought the boys to the studio and shown them a rough assemblage of the film.

"Then we'll find a spot where something is needed and say: 'How about something funny?' They go up to an open mike and start building something right there. They are very quick, sharp boys."

"They are so bright and perceptive. After their first picture was so well-received, they came to my office with their manager Brian Epstein. I asked them if there was anything they wanted for the second picture."

"They said, 'Well, we know what we don't want,' They decided *A Hard*

Day's Night was in black and white, their next should be color.

"The last picture had a lot of screaming fans, so they didn't want any in this. The last picture showed them singing before audiences, and this time they didn't want that.

"The Beatles are not a four-headed monster, they are individuals who dig each other. These boys really love each other.

"There is absolutely no competition among them, no desire to top each other. If one boy makes a joke, the others fall down laughing.

"But despite their difference in personality, there are a lot of adjectives that describe them all. They are witty, outrageous, bright, terribly talented, rude. They are scary because they have all this and are still in their early twenties.

"Yet when you are a generation older, as I am, and you are with them, you become their age, they are so compelling.

"They are so close they have developed a shorthand language so that they can be talking about you in your presence and you won't know it.

"Unlike you and me, they can't go out shopping or to a movie. They love movies, so I would give them private screening of all the latest. Now each one has his own projector and I lend them prints.

"They can't really go out without being recognized. Paul says he can occasionally, if he sticks his hair under a cap and dresses casually.'

"We had one scene for *Help!* in which the boys run into a store. We decided to film it on location, using a good Bond St. store. We picked a Sunday and the boys did their scene.

"While the crew was changing camera locations to shoot the scene again, the boys stayed in the store. John took one look around, he is furnishing a new house, and said, 'I'll take that and that and that.'

"In the seven minutes it took for the new setup, John bought a desk, a grandmother's clock he was very proud that it was a grandmother's and not grandfather's clock and leather-bound sets of George Bernard Shaw and A.A. Milne.

"The deal the Beatles and I have with United Artists calls for three pictures. It's always a challenge to find something new to do for these boys.

"I don't want to sound pompous, but I feel a great obligation not to louse them up. We'll have a meeting as soon as they get back from their American tour, to discuss their next film.

"They have bought a book by Dick Condon called *A Talent for Loving*. It's a Western satire, and that may be the next picture. They have already asked me if I can find someone to teach them the 'fast draw.'

"This is part of kids' loving Westerns, and they are kids. Ringo has also announced to me that he wants to wear all black.

"The Beatles come to my house. I have two little boys and they die because they can't call their friends and tell them who is visiting. Ringo even taught my older boy, who is twelve, how to play the drums.

"My older boy is a classical music bug, but he has pictures of the Beatles all over his walls. However, in one corner, as his rebellion, he has a picture of Beethoven.

"You know what I like about the Beatles? After they finished both pictures, each one came up to me, after seeing the finished product, and said, 'Don't worry. No matter what the critics or public say about the picture, we love it.

"Maybe security comes with success, but most successful performers don't say things like that to the producer. That, incident sums up the warmth and niceness of these boys."

1965

• • •

He Was Against the Beatles

SAN FRANCISCO—Team of girls upsets youth who was carrying a "Beat it Beatles" sign in front of the Hilton Hotel in San Francisco. The girls overpowered the youth and took away his sign. The Beatles appeared before a sell-out crowd at the Cow Palace.

1965

• • •

Rolling Stones Succeed
Beatles Top Pops No More

LONDON—the Beatles, winners of the 1964 Top of the Pops championship, dropped to third place in the 1965 competition.

The championship table is computed by the *New Musical Express*

which awards thirty points for a top spot in the weekly charts down to one point for an entry at number thirty.

Although the Beatles occupied the top spot in the charts for fifteen of the fifty-two weeks of 1965 the Rolling Stones lingered longer at lower positions to clinch the 1965 honors.

The Rolling Stones collected 836 points, followed by the Seekers with 813 and the Beatles coming in third with 760.

Sandie Shaw in fifth place was the only girl in the top ten. Most popular Americans were Bob Dylan and Gene Pitney at eleven and twelve. Elvis Presley crept in at eighteen.

The record of the year was *Tears*, a 1920s ballad, by comedian Ken Dodd which sold more than a million copies in Britain and has been in the parade for eighteen weeks.

1965

• • •

Beatles Picks New Title

LONDON—The new Beatles motion picture will be called *8 Arms to Hold You*, a title invented by the four singers themselves. The picture, currently shooting on location in the Austrian Alps, had been previously known as *Beatles Two*.

Walter Shenson is the producer and Richard Lester the director, the same team responsible for the Beatles first movie, *A Hard Day's Night*, which also owed its unique title to the quartet.

Their second film, *8 Arms to Hold You*, will introduce half a dozen or more new songs written by Beatles John Lennon and Paul McCartney and will be sung and played by the Liverpool four, including Ringo Starr and George Harrison.

Others in the cast are Eleanor Bron, Leo McKern and Victor Spinetti.

APRIL 11, 1965

• • •

BEATLES SELL OUT

LOS ANGELES—Hollywood has never been stunned as by the fabulous impact of the Beatles. Every ticket for their Hollywood Bowl concert (May 30) was sold within three hours! What is really stunning blase Hollywood are the countless classified ads in the Los Angeles papers, almost daily, begging to pay as high as $40 for $4 seats.

The Beatles sing a song from their new movie on *The Ed Sullivan Show* Sunday.

MAY 1965

• • •

BEATLES MAY CALL IT QUITS TO HONE INDIVIDUAL MERITS

LONDON—They're calling it the end of an era, the Beatles' era.

Oddly enough, it was the Beatles' fans who called attention to the rash of speculation about their heroes' collective future.

Last Sunday night, about 200 picketed the London home of Beatle manager Brian Epstein, demanding to see more of their idols. The foursome has not toured Britain this year and there are no plans for personal appearances so their followers can see them, the angry fans said. They were right.

Somebody suddenly realized the possible significance of Epstein's strangely worded refusal of an invitation for the Beatles to appear in a two hour television spectacular to aid victims of the Welsh coal avalanche disaster.

Although show business personalities ranging from the Rolling Stones to Richard Burton and Elizabeth Taylor readily volunteered, Epstein declined, saying, "I know without consulting them the boys would feel unable to make an appearance of this sort for too many reasons to enumerate."

To which Epstein added another ambiguous statement Tuesday: "The Beatles have changed their thoughts as their career has been altered by their attitudes in the past. Naturally this pattern will continue. I'd be a fool to forecast exactly how it will be."

Epstein denied a newspaper report that quoted him as saying he would be meeting the group shortly to discuss the future. "That's silly," said a press spokesman, "he sees them all the time. He doesn't need to have a special meeting to discuss their future."

Epstein may have seen them individually, but he would have had difficulty in recent months trying to sit down with all four at once. John Lennon has been making his first film in Spain and Germany without the other three. George Harrison went off to India for lessons on the sitar, his favorite instrument. Ringo Starr took his pretty wife Maureen and baby Zak abroad for a holiday.

They are all back in England now, according to Beatles headquarters, but the only bachelor Beatle Paul McCartney, who has been composing the musical score for the Hayley Mills film*, is now abroad on vacation.

The obvious conclusion, supported by their words and actions in the past months, is that they are bored with being the Beatles.

They are no longer "boys," though that is how everyone still refers to them. They range in age from twenty-three to twenty-six. George and Paul have grown moustaches, John had his Beatle mop cropped for his role in *How I Won The War*.

They are all wealthy young men, able to support themselves in the manner to which they have become accustomed.

With their success, they have gained a certain sophistication. Their last album, *Revolver,* was musically far ahead of their efforts at the height of their popularity and they are well aware of the fact.

"Songs like 'Eight Days a Week' and 'She Loves You' sound like right drags to me now," John told an interviewer recently. "I turn the radio off if they're on."

They want a chance to grow up and develop. George, the most talented musician in the group, wants to study seriously. Ringo has shown a natural flair for comedy. John, whose second book has just been published, wants to try his hand at scripts.

And Paul says, "I can see myself as a silver-haired songwriter but not as a silver-haired old Beatle."

1966

• • •

BEATLE CRITIC DUMPS 12 MEDALS

LONDON—A colonel set a record for anti-Beatleism today by sending twelve medals back to Queen Elizabeth II.

Col. Frederick Wagg, seventy-four, veteran of two world wars, joined the protest movement against the award of the MBE, Member of the Order of the British Empire, to the long-haired pop quartet.

He also resigned from Prime Minister Harold Wilson's Labor party and canceled a $33,600 bequest to it.

"Decorating the Beatles," said the colonel, "has made a mockery of everything this country stands for!

"I've heard them sing and play and I think they're terrible."

MBE holders have mailed their heavy silver cross back to Buckingham Palace.

Wagg's jester dwarfed them all. Along with protests to the queen, the Queen Mother and Prime Minister Wilson he sent:

The Mons Star, the General Service Medal and the Victory Medal

---

* *The Family Way*

from World War I; The North West Frontier medal from Indian Army service between the wars; The 1939-40 Star, Battle of the Atlantic Star, North Africa Star, Defense Medal and Victory Medal from World War II; and the Belgian Order of Leopold and the French Croix de Guerre and Croix de Resistance.

He said he sent back the foreign decorations because they were granted with royal approval. Britons may not accept foreign medals without royal permission.

The only medal he is keeping he said, is the Croix de Lorraine which Gen. Charles de Gaulle handed to him personally after World War II.

Hundreds of letters about the Beatles award cascaded into the Prime Minister's office at No. 10 Downing Street and Buckingham Palace, officials said, but some of the opposition came from supporters of rival pop groups.

1966

• • •

Epstein Check on U.S. "Holy War" Against Beatles

NEW YORK—Beatles' manager, Mr. Brian Epstein, today weighed the prospects of a U.S. tour by his mop-topped quartet in the face of a "holy war" against them in America.

The furor was caused by Beatles John Lennon's reported remark that the Beatles are more popular than Jesus Christ.

As a result, fans in several U.S. cities have been urged to make bonfires of their Beatle records, and radio stations across the nation have banned their records.

Mr. Epstein, who cut short a holiday to fly to New York last night from London, said he hoped that the Beatles' four-week tour would go ahead. It was to start on August 12.

He said no decision would be made until he had talked with the General Artists' Corporation, the agency which book the Beatles for their 14-city tour.

• • •

Misinterpreted

The "holy war" against the Beatles started in America's "Bible Belt" and quickly spread across the nation.

In Mississippi an imperial wizard of the Klu Klux Klan group said he believed the Beatles had been "brainwashed by the Communist Party."

On arrival in New York Mr. Epstein was asked whether he thought the Beatles were more popular than Christianity. "Of course not," he said.

He said, "John Lennon's views have been misinterpreted," but he declined to say whether he meant that he had been misreported.

"The whole thing," he added, "is a typical Beatles furor."

Mr. Epstein, who has managed the Beatles since their earliest days, will be keeping a close watch on the pop record charts for any reaction by the buying public.

A radio station which has never played the Beatles before played one every thirty minutes last night, preceding the records with a statement denouncing the "hypocrisy" of banning the group's music.

Station WSAC said in a commentary: "This is the best way we can think of to show our contempt for hypocrisy personified."

Some of the stations which have banned the Beatles records play records that are, "the most pornographic melodies since Elizabethan times," the station said.

"Perhaps the Beatles could become more popular than Jesus," as Beatle John Lennon allegedly said.

"Perhaps that is what is wrong with society, and there they are dear friend. You made them think so, not Jesus, not John Lennon and not the Beatles."

WSAC plans to continue broadcasting the commentary and playing Beatles records indefinitely, a spokesman said.

1966

• • •

The Holes in Our Roads*

LANCASHIRE—There are 4,000 holes in the road in Blackburn, Lancashire, or one twenty-sixth of a hole per person, according to a council survey. If Blackburn is typical there are two million holes in Britain's roads and 300,000 in London.

1967

• • •

The Beatles Sample Our Fish and Chips

TAUNTON—Mrs. Amy Smedley, who, with her husband, James, runs a fish and chip shop in Roman Road, Taunton, served four VIC's (Very Important Customers) last Friday.

For that was the day that the Beatles popped in for a meal. And it all came about as a result of a chat Mrs. Smedley had with the famous four in Newquay. Mrs. Smedley was on holiday there when she took part as an extra in the television film the Beatles are making.

In the course of chatting with them, she mentioned she and her husband had a fish and chip shop in Taunton. On Friday morning, she had a telephone call to say the Beatles would be arriving later.

"They got here at lunch time and shot some film outside our shop," said Mrs. Smedley. Then all four of them came inside to have some fish and chips, which they ate in the shop.

"It was marvelous. The Beatles are really very nice people. They chatted away to my husband and I like old friends," she added.

"I still can't really believe they actually ate my fish and chips!"

1967

• • •

---

* This article was John Lennon's inspiration behind a portion of the lyrics for the classic, "A Day in the Life of Sgt. Pepper."

BEATLES MAGIC TV SHOW
Mystery Coach to Devon and Cornwall

LONDON—A sixty-seater yellow and blue coach carrying the Beatles and a film crew, and with the words *Magical Mystery Tour* emblazoned on the side, will leave London on Monday heading for Devon and Cornwall. The Beatles plan unscheduled stops on the route to gather location material for a one-hour color TV special. The program would be completed by November, and there is a possibility it could be a Christmas highlight of the new BBC-2 color service. A follow-up single to "All You Need is Love" is expected in November while the Beatles are in India, it may be "Magical Mystery Tour," which will be the title and theme number of the spectacular. Next month marks the fifth anniversary of the Beatles first hit "Love Me Do."

1967

• • •

A MEDITATION CELEBRATION!
Meditating with the Maharishi Had Its Lighter Side for the Beatles

You'd be forgiven for thinking that everyday's a birthday for the Beatles, but no Beatle has ever had quite such a birthday party as George Harrison's twenty-fifth, which he celebrated during his mediational sessions in India.

Ringo, on his return, described the mediational center as being "a bit like Butlin's"—which, from all accounts, seems a fair description!

Apparently George hadn't given much thought to his birthday, probably thinking it would be spent in meditation. But the Maharishi, a quiet expert in the showmanship field, had some surprises up his sleeve! He had the assembly hall decked with everything colorful that could be found; flags, curtains, yards of silk, so that it looked more like a theater setting than a scene for a party.

The timing of the affair was beautiful. When everyone was seated, the Maharishi entered with his priests and sat crosslegged on a deerskin rug beneath the portrait of his Guru. A real Rishikesh rave-up followed, with the chanting of hymns and the waving of a burning oil lamp!

Fashion note for would-be meditators; the shoeless Beatles and their girls were resplendent in rajah coats, saris and silk trousers, all looking very tanned and dressed up for the occasion.

A sort of "say-it-with-flowers" ceremony followed. Firstly, the Maharishi garlanded George, then George returned the gesture. Then the whole audience garlanded both George and Pattie with floral sprays of yellow marigolds—yellow apparently being an auspicious color for the event. George carried on from there by garlanding the necks of his fellow Beatles and their wives.

When it came to the turn of Mal Evans, one of the Beatles' personal assistants, chaos developed! The garland around Mal's neck caught on one of George's leaving them twisting and wriggling around the stage to free themselves, while the whole place roared with laughter!

Mike Love, leader of the Beach Boys, who was in the audience, was then asked up on stage to speak about meditation.

Finally the Maharishi gave George his birthday present. It was a plastic globe of the world. A simple present, but actually full of meaning. The globe had been fitted so that the map of the world was upside down.

"This is what the world is like today—upside down," the Maharishi announced solemnly. "It is rotating in tension and agony. The world waits for its release and to be put right. Transcendental meditation can do so. George, this globe I am giving you symbolizes the world today. I hope you will help us all in the task of putting it right."

Accepting the globe from the Maharishi, George immediately turned it over so that the map was the right way up.

"I've done it!" he shouted, and was applauded with laughter for his quick wit.

Finally everyone moved outside for a fireworks display, and as the Maharishi left, the Beatles bowed and folded their hands, murmuring "Namaste"—good-bye.

* * *

BEATLE GEORGE AND APPLE MAN PLAN TO WRITE A STAGE MUSICAL
February 25, 1967

LONDON—George Harrison and Beatles friend and press officer Derek Taylor are to write a stage musical together.

The musical, based on the daily life of Apple, the Beatles HQ, is planned first to be shown to American audiences this autumn. Possible staging will be at the famous New York Schubert Theatre.

Taylor told *Disc* on Monday:

"George has already written an outline and some of the music, I'm in charge of ideas and lyrics. We started last Wednesday after Mike Connor, who is in charge of Apple offices in Los Angeles, suggested we get together on a musical."

By basing the show round Apple, with its colorful assortment of staff, George and Derek hope to overcome stage musicals biggest headache, how to get people to burst into song as a natural progression to the story line.

"For everyone life is a mixture of fact and fiction, often this office is like *Alice In Wonderland*," said Taylor. "And since Apple is constantly surrounded and involved in music, it seemed a natural subject to base a musical around."

This will be Harrison's first major musical undertaking since he completed the film score for *Wonderwall* last year.

This week the Beatles were rehearsing their TV spectacular at Twickenham Studios. The spectacular, before an invited audience, will have the Beatles playing live for the first time in six months (the last being when they taped "Hey Jude"). They will do fourteen specially written new numbers for the show which will later be released as a complete album.

"They aren't going to do anything revolutionary on stage," said Taylor. "They just want to get in front of an audience and play and sing, nothing adventurous."

Paul McCartney is writing a song for Judy Garland, the famous American singer.

Miss Garland announced the news when she appeared at the National Film Theatre in London on Saturday to answer audience questions. Asked if she was to make a new record, she conferred with her business manager before answering: "Yes, Paul McCartney is writing a song for me."

Beatles press officer Derek Taylor said: "She's a great singer and her advisers have been in touch with Apple so this is probably what it was all about."

Miss Garland is currently appearing at London's Talk Of The Town.

1968

• • •

ARE THE BEATLES BORED, OR BORING?

LONDON—For six years the Beatles have soared above the entertainment world as millionaires with the Midas touch in music, but now the rocket is beginning to descend and four unhappy young men are learning for the first time how fickle is the public.

The transition from doing everything right in the eyes of their fans to doing almost everything wrong has been painful. Some British commentators have predicted this could be the final phase of their meteoric career.

"Is this the end?" the headlines ask.

The answer is that the Beatles are still the most exciting group in the pop field, in the forefront of the development of the modern song, musically and lyrically. In the recording studios they still have the old magic.

It is in the world outside that they now realize how much they miss their discoverer and manager, Brian Epstein, who died just a year ago. It was Epstein who protected their image, cushioned them against the shocks of too much fame and money too soon.

And when they did sometimes escape his vigilance, as when John Lennon said the Beatles were more popular than Christ, it was Epstein who expertly repaired the public relations damage. Since that uproar two years ago Beatles fans (and stockholders in their music company) have had a lot to think about.

There was the time they talked of taking LSD, their flight to the Himalayan foothills for transcendental meditation, the failure of their self-made film, *Magical Mystery Tour* for mass television audiences.

In recent weeks there have been such image-marring things as their extravagant giveaway of clothes to close their boutique named Apple, Paul McCartney's break from his faithful girlfriend, actress Jane Asher, and Lennon's break from his wife to take up with the Japanese Yoko Ono and her strange art world.

The shop came under the Beatles' Umbrella company Apple Corps which combines their interests in music, movies, electronics and new talent. The company had a stake in the eighty-five minute cartoon of *Yellow Submarine* which contains their music but was produced by someone else.

The Rank Organization, which owns some 400 of Britain's movie houses, caused a stir by saying it had withdrawn the cartoon from thirteen of its London movie houses and would show it at only half their provincial ones because box office receipts had not come up to expectations.

Boredom is a two-way street. The question really is: Are the Beatles also bored with it all?

George Harrison declares, "We are not asking anyone to love us or hate us . . . who was it said we were the goody-goody fab four moptops? Not us. We're not. We're four young people going through life just like anybody else, learning all the time and parts of us are lousy and rotten . . ."

Lennon, twenty-seven, married six years with a five-year-old son, has announced he loves Yoko Ono, who is seven years his senior and also married.

The Beatles closed down the Apple shop after nine months by giv-

ing away $48,000 worth of stock in a free-for-all that police had a struggle to control, they said, "of course we've lost a great deal of money by doing it this way but that's what we wanted."

August 25, 1968

• • •

BEATLES DO A DEAL WITH TRIUMPH

LONDON—A somersault by Triumph Investment Trust and a turnaround by the Beatles and settlement is reached over assets in dispute in NEMs Enterprises (now Nemperor Holding).

There are three main assets in Nems, the late Brian Epstein's show-business management agency:

A contract entitling Nems to collect the Beatles' gross royalty income on record sales from Electric and Musical Industries, quarter by quarter, until 1976, and to retain a 25 p.c. managerial cut;

A 4.5 p.c. equity stake in Northern Songs; and

A 23 p.c. holding in Subafilms which collects royalties on the Beatles' major films.

Triumph's managing director, Mr. Leonard Richenberg, and Allen Klein, the Beatles' business manager, have settled their differences out of court. Triumph will not press its entitlement to the royalties. Instead, it accepts £750,000 in cash now (three years' guaranteed payment on royalties).

From 1972–6 Triumph will receive 5 p.c. of the gross royalty revenue, Mr Klein's favorite figure: Mr. Richenberg would have preferred 10 p.c. Triumph will also get 25 p.c. of the royalties now frozen in court, accounting for 1968's payment.

The Beatles will buy Nems' 23 p.c. stake in Subafilms for some £50,000 cash. They will also have an option on the 237,000 (around 4.5 p.c.) Northern Songs shares so jealously guarded by Triumph throughout the bid battle for the company. The option is for a year and the call price is 30s a share, 10s a share cheaper than the price originally negotiated by Mr. Richenberg some weeks ago.

If exercised, the option will bring the Beatles' stake in Northern Songs almost to a par with that held by Sir Lew Grade's Associated Television Corporation. Although Sir Lew has a one-year "alliance" with a consortium of brokers owning 14 p.c., and thus currently enjoys effective control of NS—with four ATV representatives and five votes on a six-man board, the consortium may now feel drawn to the Beatles. An appendix to the Northern Songs saga may be imminent.

Triumph will also buy the 10 p.c. in Nems it does not already own from the Beatles for 266,000 of its own shares, last night valued at £422.275.

"Triumph is pleased to welcome the Beatles among its shareholders," said Mr. Richenberg yesterday.

"I'm happy with the deal, the boys will make a good profit out of it," said Mr. Klein.

"No comment," said Sir Lew Grade.

1969

• • •

BEATLE RETURNS DECORATION

LONDON—Beatle John Lennon and his wife Yoko Ono displayed a letter from John to British Prime Minister Harold Wilson at the Beatles' London headquarters of their Apple recording company last Tuesday. Lennon's letter explained his reasons for returning his Order of the British Empire medal, awarded by Queen Elizabeth II to all the Beatles in 1965. Lennon said he was protesting British support for the United States in Vietnam and his nation's "Involvement in the Nigeria-Biafra thing."

1969

• • •

DETROIT'S DETECTIVES VIEW BEATLE'S LOVE LIFE ART

DETROIT—An exhibit of lithographs by Beatle John Lennon opened in Detroit yesterday, and two city police detectives were on hand to view the fourteen prints depicting the love life of Lennon and his wife, Yoko Ono.

Eugene Schuster, owner of the London Arts Gallery, said the two detectives from the police censor bureau "took notes and photographs and were supposed to report back to their superiors."

Schuster said the detectives told him "an injunction possibly might be obtained to stop the showing of the lithographs."

Schuster was arrested in London last week when his gallery there unveiled the Lennon prints.

London police seized eight of the prints, which were selling for $960 a set but now are being offered for $1,320 each.

Following the police raid, the exhibition reopened with the remaining six lithographs.

Schuster said he had no trouble getting the prints cleared by U.S. Customs and the entire set, was in the exhibit when it opened in Detroit.

One observer said a large crowd had been attracted by the exhibit but there was no estimate given. Schuster said between 500 and 700 persons had visited his gallery between 10 a.m. and noon.

1969

• • •

SOLO PROJECTS INDICATE BEATLE BREAKUP COMING

LONDON—Beatle Paul McCartney announced yesterday a series of independent projects which close friends say would almost certainly mean the end of the Beatles as a group.

The announcement, issued through McCartney's attorney and brother-in-law John Eastman of New York, said the private ventures will keep McCartney from directly working with the remainder of the Beatle quartet indefinitely.

"It is now highly unlikely they will ever even record together again," one business source said.

The announcement said the first solo venture for McCartney would be the release this month of an album, *McCartney*, Eastman said McCartney wrote all fourteen songs, played all the instruments, sang all the vocals, produced the record and collaborated on the cover design with his wife.

McCartney, also announced he has acquired all rights to a British cartoon bear, *Rupert*.

The pop singer plans to make a full-length film of Rupert, a project which will take several months, the announcement said.

McCartney's plans to branch out on his own came in the wake of reported squabbles among the group and disagreement about their legal and business representation.

Sources close to the group's firm said McCartney has not spoken to fellow Beatle John Lennon since last August. He has not been in a recording studio with the others for several months.

Friends said McCartney was not responsible for the breakup, but was following the example of the three other members of the group.

Lennon and his wife have formed their own band, Ringo Starr has recently devoted much of his time to films, and George Harrison has been involved in song writing and record production.

"You can't expect McCartney, the writer of such great Beatle hits as 'Hey Jude,' 'Yesterday,' and 'Michelle' to just sit around and wait," said one friend.

1969

• • •

BUSINESSMAN KLEIN STEPS IN

LONDON—The Beatles have asked Mr. Allen Klein of New York to look into all their affairs and he has agreed to do so, it was announced from their headquarters at Apple, 3 Savile Row, London W1, today.

FEBRUARY 3, 1969

• • •

BEATLE PAUL TO MARRY

LONDON—Paul McCartney, aged twenty-six, is to marry Miss Linda Eastman today at Marylebone Register Office W1. They first met two years ago when Eastman, a professional photographer, took photographs of the Beatles in America.

Mr. McCartney is the only unmarried member of the Beatles group. Miss Eastman, who is twenty-seven is a member of the Eastman Kodak family. She has a daughter, Heather, by her first marriage.

Last night a group of teenage girls waited outside Mr. McCartney's home at 7 Cavendish Avenue N.W. When he arrived in his car three police cars accompanied him. A policeman said they had been asked to clear the pavement but there was no trouble.

MARCH 12, 1969

• • •

KING OF FUH

LONDON—Apple Records announces that their next single release, The King of Fuh, turned down by EMI as unsuitable for distribution under the terms of their deal with Apple, is now to be released by Apple themselves on May 16. Apple plans to market the single, written, sung and produced in New York by Brute Force, a twenty-year-old discovery of George Harrison, through certain specially selected record stores in London and the provinces and review copies have already been sent to the BBC. Mr. Jack Oliver, head of production, says, "We plan to use mail-order outlets to distribute The King of Fuh. We have a comprehensive system to ensure that we do not have to submit to yesterday's means to achieve today's ends."

MAY 1969

• • •

ON NORTHERN SONGS

LONDON—On behalf of the Beatles and their company, Apple Corps, their business manager Allen Klein of ABKCO Industries after discussion with the Beatles announced in New York today that all negotiations between the Beatles, Associated Television and Northern Songs have been terminated by the Beatles. All of the Beatles and their companies intend to sell all their shares in Northern Songs to Associated Television at a price in accordance with the terms laid down by the takeover panel. John Lennon and Paul McCartney have no intention of involving themselves in any further relationship with Northern Songs or Associated Television beyond the fulfillment of their song writing contract to February 1973. The Beatles intend to keep all their rights within their own company, Apple, which has divisions in records, music publishing, motion pictures and television. After discussions with the Beatles' solicitors and after taking advice of counsel, the writ served upon Northern Songs by the Beatles own Maclen Company will not be withdrawn and a statement of claim will be served within the next few days.

1970

• • •

THREE BEATLES ABANDON THEIR APPEAL

LONDON—Three members of the Beatles pop group yesterday abandoned their appeal against a High Court order putting the affairs of their company, Apple, in the hands of a receiver. John Lennon, George Harrison and Ringo Starr now face a bill for legal costs estimated at £100,000.

The order had been made by Mr. Justice Stamp on March 12 on an application by Paul McCartney, pending trial of his action to dissolve the partnership.

Mr. Morris Finer, Q.C., for the three Beatles and Apple, said in the Court of Appeal yesterday that his clients considered it to be in the common interest to explore means whereby Mr. McCartney could disengage himself from the partnership by agreement. They felt that continuance of the appeal would be inimical to such negotiations. The order appointing Mr. James Douglas Spooner as

receiver and manager of the group's business pending trial of the action will take effect immediately.

Lord Justice Russell said: "I can only express the court's hope that the parties will come to some amicable and sensible arrangement."

1970

• • •

GROUP "NO LONGER THOUGHT OF AS THE BEATLES"

LONDON—Since the Beatles stopped making group recordings they had stopped thinking of themselves as Beatles, Mr. Paul McCartney stated in the High Court yesterday.

He was answering evidence filed by Mr. John Lennon, Mr. George Harrison and Mr. Ringo Starr, the other three Beatles, in opposition to his claim for the appointment of a receiver of the group's assets pending trail of his action to have the group legally broken up.

Mr. Lennon had stated in his evidence: "We always thought of ourselves as Beatles, whether we recorded singly or in twos or threes." Mr. McCartney denied this.

He said: "One has only to look at recent recordings by John or George to see that neither thinks of himself as a Beatle." On his recent album John Lennon has listed things he did not believe in. One was "I don't believe in the Beatles."

Mr. McCartney stated that when the four entered into their partnership agreement in 1967 they did not consider the exact wording or give any thought to the agreement's legal implications. They had thought that if one of them had wanted to leave the group he would only have to say so. On the way in which the four had sorted out their differences in the past, he denied that it had been on a three-to-one basis. If one disagreed, they had discussed the problem until they reached agreement or let the matter drop. "I know of no decision taken on a three-to-one basis," he added.

Mr. McCartney denied that he and the Eastmans, the father of Mr. McCartney's wife and her brother, had obstructed Mr. Allen Klein in the preparation of accounts. Nor, he said, had the Eastmans been contenders for the job of manager of the group. He said he wanted them as managers, but when the rest of the group disagreed he had not pressed the matter.

Mr. Lennon challenged his statement that Mr. Klein had sowed discord within the group. Mr. McCartney recalled a telephone conversation in which he said Mr. Klein had told him: "You know why John is angry with you? It is because you came off better than he did in *Let It Be.*"

He added that Mr. Klein also said to him: "The real trouble is Yoko. She is the one with ambition." Mr. McCartney added: "I often wonder what John would have said if he had heard that remark?"

When the four had talked about breaking up the group Mr. McCartney said Mr. Harrison said: "If I could have my bit in an envelope, I'd love it."

Mr. McCartney also recalled the negotiations to acquire one of the NEMS companies for Apple. Mr. Klein, he said, had told the Beatles at the outset: "I'll get it for nothing."

That, Mr. McCartney went on, was a typical example of the exaggerated way Mr. Klein expressed himself to them. He added: "I became more and more determined that Klein was not the right man to be appointed manager."

Mr. McCartney ended his evidence by stating that none of the other three Beatles seemed to understand why he had acted in the way he had.

The short answer was that the group had broken up, each now had his own musical career, there were still no audited accounts and they still did not know what their tax positions were. None of these points, he added, had been denied by the other Beatles.

The hearing was adjourned until Monday, when counsel will make their final submissions.

1970

• • •

BEATLE PAUL McCARTNEY SAYS HE HAS QUIT GROUP

LONDON—Paul McCartney broke up the Beatles, the most fabulously successful band in the history of popular music, yesterday by withdrawing to concentrate on a solo career as songwriter, recording artist and family man.

The twenty-seven-year-old creative dynamo of the group thus made official what had been increasingly apparent in recent months: close as brothers when they were struggling in small night clubs, the four-some had acquired too many other interests along with wealth and world acclaim.

McCartney confirmed he was striking out completely on his own in written answers to questions sent him in lieu of a personal interview. His solo album, *McCartney*, will be released next Friday.

Two flat negatives ended the seven and a half year reign of the group, an era that changed the social history of the time, made millionaires out of McCartney and his songwriting partner John Lennon and rich young men out of Ringo Starr and George Harrison.

One of the factors in McCartney's decision to go it alone was his drifting apart from twenty-nine-year-old John Lennon who, since his marriage to Yoko Ono, producer of a film starring bare backsides, has been concentrating on a campaign for world peace.

It was Lennon who brought the group together in a smokey Liverpool cellar to point a new direction for popular music, to usher in the era of long hair and to revolutionize ballroom dancing by turning it into a solo recreation.

1970

• • •

The Final Sign-off

LONDON—The last of the faithful have disbanded. It's all over. The Beatles fan clubs in Britain and the United States have dissolved. A Beatles spokesman passed the sorry word: "It is unlikely that John Lennon, Paul McCartney, George Harrison and Ringo Starr will ever get together again as a group."

Explains Ringo Starr: "We don't want to keep the myth going that we're still a group because we're not."

Says Paul McCartney: "Please don't refer to me as a Beatle. That's part of my past."

The folding of the Beatles fan clubs marks the dissolution of a multimillion dollar musical empire which saw the Beatles zoom to and remain at the pinnacle for nearly ten years after they were discovered in 1961 performing in the Cavern Club at Liverpool.

What broke them up? Time and women, two factors which frequently destroy many all-male groups.

1970

• • •

Apple Bottoms Out

LONDON—Earlier this week the Apple Press Office was closed down and the two remaining employees dismissed. Since the breakup of the Beatles their Apple empire has diminished to little more than a center for collecting their royalties and dealing with their private affairs.

August 4, 1970

• • •

Stay Away from Pot

TORONTO—Beatle John Lennon warned teenagers to stay away from drugs, in a television interview in Toronto yesterday.

Lennon said his time on drugs was when he had no hope, and when a person was on drugs it was harder to find hope.

The Beatle and his Japanese born wife Yoko Ono appeared on the Canadian Broadcasting Corporation program, *Weekend*, as part of the couple's campaign for peace.

They are arranging for a "pop peace festival" at the Mosport auto race track, near Toronto, next July.

Lennon described Canada as the first country to help with his peace movement. He was astonished when Canadian reporters treated him and his wife like human beings.

JANUARY 17, 1970

• • •

BEATLE LENNON AND YOKO NOW VISITING LOS ANGELES

WASHINGTON—Beatle John Lennon and his wife, Yoko, have received U.S. visas and are now in Los Angeles "for business discussions," State Department officials said yesterday.

The Lennons will be in New York between May 7 and 16 "for further business discussions," the officials said.

They also said George Harrison, another Beatle, has also received a U.S. visa and was expected to arrive yesterday.

MAY 1971

• • •

BEATLE GEORGE STARTS A NEW LIFE WITH MODEL KATHY

GRENADA—Ex-Beatle George Harrison has split up with his wife Pattie Boyd, and sparked a musical chairs routine among some of the world's top pop stars.

For Pattie has moved in with rock guitarist Eric Clapton. And George is now living with model Kathy Simmonds, former girl friend of pop idol Rod Stewart.

"There comes a time when splitting is for the best," said Harrison. "None of us has time to waste, time to spend in an uncomfortable situation."

Friends say Clapton's relationship with Pattie Boyd formed the subject matter for much of his best-selling album *Layla*.

Break-up

Clapton recently described the woman in the album in an interview with *Rolling Stone* magazine. He apparently was talking about the break-up of Pattie and George's marriage.

"She was trying to attract his attention," Clapton said, "trying to make him jealous and so she used me."

"But I fell madly in love with her."

Pattie flew from England to join Clapton during a break in his recent American tour. They stayed in Tulsa, Okla., in a mansion owned by another rock superstar, Leon Russell.

Meanwhile, in a rare interview, George Harrison confirmed that he and Pattie had broken up, and added there was no chance the Beatles would get together again.

Tanned and relaxed, Harrison agreed to be interviewed in the luxury hideaway he was using in Grenada, West Indies.

Satisfied

The thirty-one-year-old musician talked about his personal life, his plans and hopes.

"The split-up of the Beatles satisfied me more than anything else in my career," he said.

"As far as I am concerned we will never perform again.

"The only circumstance would be if, God forbid, there were some vast debts incurred in the past and a farewell performance was the only way of clearing them."

As Harrison talked, Kathy Simmonds quietly served tea on the sunny terrace of their house high in the hills above St. George's Harbor.

"I haven't seen Pattie for a couple of months," Harrison said. "We are still very good friends.

"Work is the only thing that matters in my life.

"As soon as I return to London I am going to do something that has never been attempted before.

"I am bringing sixteen classical Indian musicians together to present a festival of Indian music."

Harrison reemphasized his work plans did not include joining with his former companions, John, Paul and Ringo.

"Please, it's insulting to me and to the other three to keep thinking of us as the Beatles," he said.

Meaningless

"That was so long ago, it doesn't mean anything now."

Harrison, the youngest of the Beatles, was also the last to marry. He and Pattie have been together for eight years.

A member of the Clapton tour, and a confidant of Eric's said that Pattie and Eric had become interested in each other several years ago.

Clapton has burst back on the pop scene after three years of inactivity caused by his fight to overcome drug addiction. He says he owed his cure to a woman psychiatrist who pulled him through.

Meanwhile, in London, Rod Stewart, left out in the game of musical chairs, didn't seem too upset.

He wished all the best to George and Kathy and Eric and Pattie.

1973

• • •

DEPORTATION OF LENNON BARRED BY COURT OF APPEALS

NEW YORK—In the twenty-four-page decision Judge Irving R. Kaufman issued a strong warning that the courts will not condone selective deportation based upon secret political grounds. This alluded to government documents that were submitted to the court, indications that the Nixon administration started deportation proceedings against Lennon in 1972 for fear that the former Beatle would make appearances in the United States promoting opposition to the then President.

In his summing-up and ruling in John's favor, Judge Kaufman said the court did not take lightly Lennon's claim that he was the victim of a move to oust him on political grounds.

"If in our two hundred years of independence we have in some measure realized our ideals, it is in large part because we have always found a place for those committed to the spirit of liberty, and willing to help implement it. Lennon's four-year battle to remain in our country is testimony to his faith in the American dream."

OCTOBER 8, 1975

• • •

BEATLES TO REFORM?

UNITED NATIONS—Will they or won't they? The Beatles are being urged by some highly placed United Nations officials to get back together for a benefit performance for Southeast Asian refugees. A spokesman said UN Secretary General Kurt Waldheim had spoken with Beatle George Harrison and that all of the Beatles had shown interest in the project. But a spokeswoman for Dark Horse Records quotes Harrison's manager as saying George won't be taking part in any Beatle reunion. If there is a concert, the Fabulous Four would perform in Geneva, Switzerland.

Beatle reunion fever hit what may have been an all-time high in late September when it appeared that even the United Nations had a stake in getting the Fab Four back together. At first, Rudolf Stajduhar, a spokesman for the UN, said simply that the Beatles "had been approached" about performing in a benefit for the Cambodian refugees.

Most reports had Paul, George, and Ringo set to perform with only John unsure. Dirk Summers, the L.A.

TV producer who was organizing the event for the UN said, "The ball is in John Lennon's court now." The concert was to be held in Geneva, Switzerland because, according to George Harrison, "The refugees are a planetary problem so the concert should be held in a neutral country."

Stajduhar said later, "If you're asking whether there is such an idea, yes, there is such an idea. It has been discussed by the UN and has the backing of Secretary General Kurt Waldheim. But if you're asking whether the Beatles have already agreed to such a concert, the answer is no. Klaus Feldman, a representative of the High Commission on Refugees at the UN stated that three Beatles had already agreed to perform and was quoted as saying that he 'can't understand Lennon's position.'"

Under Secretary General of the UN Genichi Akatani was then sent to a hotel to personally deliver a letter to Yoko (John's whereabouts were not known at the time). But by then Dirk Summer's assistant, Sabine Von Rogalla, said that Lennon had already broken off talks with the UN because he was "angry and hurt he was not asked to do the show before the news media informed him of it."

A secretary in the UN press office said, "The phone hasn't stopped ringing all day. The calls come in from London, Tokyo, Australia, all over the U.S." Another UN spokesman said Waldheim was "pleased and amused by the uproar."

But then the bubble burst. David Braun, George's attorney, said, "The story got started in the *New York Post* which quoted Dirk Summer's as saying he was promoting a concert that would reunite the Beatles and benefit the Boat People. The story spread like wildfire, but, of course, there's no truth to it whatsoever. No one gives much thought as to how to structure these benefit shows and the IRS takes a very dim view of them. Everyone is always so busy setting up the concert itself that tax consequences are never considered."

One of Paul's spokespersons, Carol Ross, said, "It's just not true, it's erroneous. I have checked with Lee Eastman who is Paul's attorney in the US and also his father-in-law. And he said there's no truth whatsoever in the reports."

And finally Paul himself said, "None of us wanted to do the concert because the Beatles are over and finished with. It would have been impossible to organize even if we'd all wanted to."

1979

• • •

UN MAKES APPEAL
Beatles May Stage Boat People Benefit

UNITED NATIONS—The United Nations is urging the Beatles to get together again for a concert to benefit Vietnamese "boat people" and other refugees, a UN spokesman said today.

Asked about reports that the famed rock group of the 1960s might reunite for a UN benefit, Francois Giuliani confirmed such a project has the backing of UN Secretary-General Kurt Waldheim.

He said Waldheim has spoken personally with at least one of the four Beatles, George Harrison. The project, he added, is being pursued by Los Angeles producer Dirk Summers.

Giuliani said the success of a rock concert by the Bee Gees last January for the benefit of the International Year of the Child had encouraged Waldheim to endorse the idea of a Beatles boat people concert.

The Washington Post in today's editions quoted a UN official as saying Harrison, Paul McCartney and saying Ringo Starr have agreed to play the concert probably in New York and that the fourth Beatle, John Lennon was considering the proposal. The New York Post said Lennon had agreed only to working on the same bill as his three former partners, and not to performing with them.

Giuliani said today UN officials did not know the status of negotiations with individual Beatles. The English group broke up in 1970 after a phenomenally successful career in the 1960s. Since then they have continued to perform individually, with two occasionally appearing together.

Funds raised through a Beatles concert would be used to help finance activities of the UN High Commissioner for Refugees, the agency responsible for caring for hundreds of thousands of refugees in camps around the world.

The Bee Gees concert, at the UN General Assembly hall in New York, reportedly has raised some $4.6 million for the United Nations through royalties on a record album and the sale of a television special of the performance.

1979

• • •

FAN, SEEKING TO FREE McCARTNEY, SLAIN WIELDING TOY GUN AT AIRPORT

MIAMI—Kenneth Alan Lambert had thirty cents in his pocket and visions of rescuing Paul McCartney, the rock star, from jail when friends dropped him off at Miami International Airport, detectives said.

Hours before the police shot him dead Saturday evening, Mr. Lambert told his friends he was flying to Tokyo to help Mr. McCartney beat some marijuana charges, Dade County Detective Jim McHugh said yesterday.

But Mr. Lambert, twenty-nine-years-old, had no plane ticket. He did have a *Bible* and a toy pistol, Detective McHugh said.

"Apparently he was a big Beatles' fan," the detective said. "He'd told his friends that one of three things would happen: He'd get rich and famous, he'd go to jail or he'd die."

Dade County officers killed him as he waved the toy pistol and cursed the clerk of an airport gift shop.

JANUARY 21, 1979

• • •

GEORGE HARRISON'S SHIVA "Ganges" Flows from Statue at 38-Acre Estate

HENLEY—Lord Shiva is sitting in George Harrison's garden. His life-size form was made recently by ISKCON artists at the First American Transcendental Exhibition (FATE), with branches in Los Angeles and Detroit.

Lord Shiva was installed as the center-piece and fountain of Friar Park, George's thirty-eight-acre estate in Oxfordshire, England, which he hopes will one day contain England's most beautiful gardens.

The *murti* is made from weather-proof fiberglass resin that simulates black stone aggregate. The "Ganges" water that flows from the top of his head produces a mystical, shimmering effect in direct sunlight.

After touring FATE's Los Angeles museum in 1978, which he said was "better than Disneyland," George began to consider the possibility of installing similar sculpted figures on his estate.

When Mukunda Prabhu visited Friar Park two years ago, George asked him to arrange for a meditating Lord Shiva to replace a fifty foot Roman goddess sculpture, then the fountain's centerpiece.

1980

• • •

CIVIC-MINDED BEATLE

HENLEY—George Harrison, the least-publicized of the ex-Beatles, is a very civic-minded individual. The guitarist is said to have invested money in *Vole*, a monthly magazine dedicated to improvement of the environment.

Harrison recently struck it rich with another investment, the Monty Python comedy *Life of Brian*. The controversial motion picture did well at the box office, particularly in Great Britain.

MAY 18, 1980

• • •

JOHN LENNON'S GARDENER COMES OUT OF THE WOODS

SAN FRANCISCO—"The new Albert Goldman book about John Lennon is filled with lies and distortions. For acquaintances have used it to gain prominence by standing on John's tombstone," said an angry Michael Tree. "Goldman has quoted people and described situations completely out of context. What may have happened on any one day is made to appear like days and years."

Mr. Tree was John Lennon's apartment gardener at the famous Dakota in New York City. He worked for Lennon during his years of seclusion and encountered him on a daily basis. "I always respected John's privacy and simply went about doing my job. It's interesting," he observed, "but not bothering him only made John curious about me. Slowly he began to initiate little conversations and in time we spoke about everything from the Beatles to his relationship with Yoko."

"Yes, John did use drugs," he said. "He smoked pot, but did not live in a haze as Goldman reported. In fact John would get up at dawn to meditate on the rising sun and enjoy the morning cityscape. Then sometimes in the afternoon he and Yoko would take a nap together with baby Sean."

AUGUST 30, 1981

• • •

BEATLES AUTHORIZE MERCHANDISING

LONDON—The Beatles disbanded fifteen-years-ago and their early fans are in their forties, but only now have the famous faces of the four Liverpool lads been authorized for use on goods such as T-shirts, lunch pails or bed sheets.

Determined Productions Inc., a San Francisco-based company that put Snoopy and Charlie Brown cartoon characters on people's chests around the world, announced an agreement last week to be the international licensing agent for all Beatles' merchandising.

1985

• • •

MONEY HUNGRY YOKO BOOTS JOHN'S POOR OLD UNCLE OUT OF HIS HOUSE
She's Loaded, he's broke—home was a gift from Lennon

LIVERPOOL—Cold hearted Yoko Ono is kicking John Lennon's poverty stricken uncle out of a house the dead Beatle bought him.

"My God! John left Yoko with several hundred million dollars," says Norman Birch, seventy-eight. "What could the few thousand dollars extra this place would bring mean to her? But it means everything to me. It's all I have in the world."

Lennon bought the three-bedroom house for Birch more than thirty years ago at the height of the Beatles' bonanza. "John was always generous," Birch says. "This house was meant to be a home for me and my family. Originally, the house was given to my wife, Harriet, who's since died. John saw it as an investment, but in the legal documents, I have always been the trustee. When my wife died, it was John's intention to give the house to me. We were very close. I got John into art college and even made all the arrangements for his mother's funeral. Of course, it all went bloody wrong when he got shot," he adds. "Now, out of the blue, I receive a letter from Yoko's attorney telling me to bugger off."

This letter informs Birch the estate wants to sell the property in Liverpool, England, "As swiftly as possible. We have been informed by Mrs. Lennon that, in view of the long years you have enjoyed the premises, we should offer you the opportunity to purchase it before it's put on the market," the letter from the lawyers explain. But Birch is too poor to buy the house.

"I wrote Yoko back several times, but my letters were always returned unopened," Birch says. "I've told her people I'm not going to last forever, probably another five or six years. I live on just a couple of tiny pensions, so there is no way I could buy another house if I had to. The purchase price of this house wouldn't even cover one of her fur coats. John told me the house was ours, but I've come to find the deed was never transferred to my name. When John was alive that was no problem. But he's dead now and Yoko sees this as an opportunity to make some extra money. Considering

her image of peace and love, you have to question her sincerity. If Yoko wants to make me an offer, I can probably get out of here if I had to. But if she tries to sell the house over my head, she'll have quite a job getting me out. I will be at the window making my stand. Where am I supposed to go? I have no savings anymore. I did have but when I sold my old house, but John encouraged me to spend it on the family. As long as John was alive, none of us had to worry. John always thought the world of me. If he was alive today he would say the same thing as when he and Yoko were here in my home and he didn't like something she'd said. He'd tell her off. He'd probably box her ears and hang her on the line to dry for being so nasty. This is my home. I have memories. But even if she succeeds in taking the place away from me, she won't be able to get those. I'll carry those happy memories to the grave."

1987

• • •

BEATLE GEORGE SNUBS DRUG-WAR COPS
Star refuses to join crusade to save kids

HENLEY—Former Beatle George Harrison has snubbed a police plea to join an anti-drugs campaign.

Officers are desperate to stamp out drug abuse in the posh area where he lives. His refusal to be involved coincides with publication of a book alleging he was once a cocaine user.

Police Sgt. John Shanahan said he approached Harrison after officers became alarmed that Henley-on-Thames in Oxfordshire, home of the Royal Regatta, had become "a floating sea of drugs."

Many showbiz stars have homes there.

He revealed: "I spoke to George Harrison personally, and asked him whether he'd do a warning message on our phone drug help-line.

"Harrison didn't want to put his name to it. He didn't want to know.

"He agreed it was a tremendous idea."

Hooked

"But he said that though he was concerned about the problem of young people getting hooked on drugs, he didn't want to get involved.

"That was it. I didn't push it. I knew that Harrison had been a drug user in the past.

"Minder star George Cole, who lives nearby, had no hesitation in recording an anti-drugs message for us."

Harrison was among showbusiness stars who in 1967 put their names to an advertisement in *The Times* stating, "The law against marijuana is immoral in principle and unworkable in practice."

He was once arrested in a raid by drug squad detectives when he lived in Esher, Surrey, and convicted of possession.

Dreaded

Sgt. Shanahan has read the latest allegations about forty-seven-year-old Harrison's past drug-taking in the book by American Beatles historian Geoffrey Giuliano.

Giuliano says he visited Harrison's 120-year-old Henley mansion, Friar Park in the mid-eighties. Called *The Secret Life of George Harrison*, the book has just been published in Britain by Bloomsbury and is already a big seller in the United States.

Giuliano says in the book: "George got too fond of staying up all night snorting cocaine."

He stood by his claims last night, but added: "George has straightened himself out now."

Giuliano told us: "I used to live near Henley myself, and the dreaded white powder (cocaine) was everywhere.

"Henley is like Katmandu. There are more dope dealers in the town than you can shake a Thai stick at.

"I lived for two years with George's best mate, 'Legs' Larry Smith, in nearby Hambleden."

The author claims: "Legs" often took calls from George in the middle of the night.

"The phone would ring and it would be George asking Larry to bring the Frenchman to Friar Park right away.

"That was their code for cocaine.

"Larry rushed around his small flat grabbing the stuff and putting it in a little green, handpainted case.

"Larry ran when George called. He never cared if he had a girlfriend staying with him or what was going on. George came first."

"He just didn't want to know"

Trendy

Smith was drummer with the hit sixties group Bonzo Dog Doo Dah Band.

Giuliano tells in the book how apparently a famous pianist arrived at Friar Park one night and Harrison was embarrassed to find he had run out of cocaine.

He writes: "With a flourish the pianist produced a small plastic bag containing five grams of best coke.

"He poured it on to a small mirror and politely invited George to go first. George inhaled the powder through a glass straw."

He says Harrison hid his coke-taking from wife Olvia.

Police are deeply concerned about the quantity of drugs pushed in some of the town's trendy pubs used by the sons and daughters of the wealthy.

Some users are very young, and Harrison's own son Dhani, twelve, will soon approach the danger age.

MAY 27, 1990

• • •

Yoko Suing U.S. Government

WASHINGTON—Yoko Ono and the estate of her late husband, John Lennon, are suing the U.S. government to contest a claim for back taxes in the amount of $592,288 US.

Most of the claim arises from an investment in a cattle-breeding operation.

As a side issue, Ono and the Lennon estate are quarrelling with the Internal Revenue Service over the value of a vintage, customized Rolls-Royce.

The bulk of the tax dispute is over the cattle investment in 1977, three years before Lennon was killed by a gunman.

Lennon and Ono bought 122 cows, ten bulls, real estate and equipment valued at $2.7 million US, for a cash outlay of $375,000. The IRS contends the operation was never intended to be profitable and existed only as a tax shelter.

1992

• • •

Harrison Plans Album

NEW YORK—George Harrison, who has just completed his first album in five years, attributes his avoidance of public attention largely to the Beatles' experience.

"We were loved for one period of time, then hated," after John Lennon's comment that the Beatles were more popular than Jesus, the guitarist told *Rolling Stone* in an interview for its October 6 issue.

Harrison's new album, *Cloud Nine*, ends an extended period away from the record industry. But Harrison said the stars of the 1960s still have plenty to offer musically.

"All these people, Eric Clapton, Ringo, Bob Dylan, whoever I come across of these old guys, we're not old, we're getting better," he said.

OCTOBER 1992

• • •

My Drugs Hell, by Lennon's Sister
John's Help Ignored

LONDON—John Lennon's sister Jacqui Dykins has told how the mega-rich star tried in vain to free her from a night-mare world of heroin addiction. Jacqui said she was so far gone as a junkie that she wouldn't listen to Beatle John's "lectures" and advice.

He visited her* with other worried members of the family in a bid to help Jacqui after she first started using heroin years ago. It was at the height of John's fame that Jacqui, now forty-one, dropped out of control, spending twenty pounds a day on her habit.

She said, "The family came round to my flat and tried to encourage me to stop but I thought I knew better."

Her sordid junkie lifestyle was a shocking contrast to the carefree days of the sixties when John was rolling in money and wanted his teenage half-sisters, Jacqui and Julia, to share in his wealth. He treated them to clothes, got them in the front row at Beatles' concerts and his first wife, Cynthia, took them on shopping trips to Harrods where they could have whatever they wanted.

Jacqui was still fighting her addiction when John was murdered. In desperation she contacted Yoko Ono for help.

"I'm not close to Yoko but she did give me some help. I have not asked for anything else."

Jacqui began winning her fight against heroin after going to see a psychiatrist. Later she was able to leave her home city of Liverpool and move into a flat in a London Suburb. She now works as a shop assistant.

Her friends, neighbors and work colleagues have no idea about her addiction or her famous brother. "I don't want people to know. I can see a change physically come over their faces as if they knew John was my brother. They expect me to be very rich, or something special, and I'm not."

1993

• • •

MANIAC THREATENS TO TORCH STAR GEORGE'S HOME

HENLEY—Terrified star George Harrison has been warned that an evil psycho is out to firebomb his £3 million mansion.

Detectives have told George a deranged American has been stalking him for six months, waiting for a chance to strike.

George, who has feared for his life since a crazed fan shot his Beatle pal John Lennon twelve years ago, said the madman even discovered his private phone number and talked to his fourteen-year-old son Dhani.

"This fellow said something and my son realized it was somebody who he shouldn't be talking to and hung up," said forty-nine-year-old George.

The weirdo has also contacted hotels where the star is booked to stay and phoned offices where he is scheduled to attend business meetings.

Now George is thinking of hiring a private investigator to track down the maniac before he has time to act. George has also ordered security at

---

* This is untrue, Lennon never stepped foot in Britain after he first left in 1971 and Ms. Dykins never visited America.

his thirty-four-acre Oxfordshire estate to be stepped up.

EX-BEATLE IS BEING STALKED

Video cameras scan the grounds and searchlights light up the approaches to the Gothic-style mansion. Guards check all visitors before allowing them through the huge electronic gates.

The chilling threat was revealed when George issued court documents during a US libel case against controversial Beatles' biographer Geoffrey Giuliano.

"I heard the local police had been told by the FBI that somebody threatened to burn my house down," he said. "He hasn't shown himself at all. Just purely by phone calls."

George said his forty-four-year-old wife Olvia tried to keep news of the psycho from him. "She didn't want me to know be cause she knew it would just get me crazy," he said.

The quietly-spoken star also revealed how a gunman vowed to kill him soon after mad fan Mark Chapman murdered Lennon in New York.

George told the court how seventeen police marksman surrounded his house to protect him.

"The death of John brought out a lot of crazies," he said. "But you have to take care in case there is the odd one—like Chapman—who will act upon his madness."

Past threats have led him to spend hundreds of thousands of pounds improving security at his homes in Hawaii, France and Australia.

But George says he hates being forced to take extreme measures to protect himself.

I'm peace and love, he said. *I'm not into violence.*

FEBRUARY 21, 1993

• • •

STORY BEHIND NEW ROUND OF BEATLEMANIA
George's $$ Blues Sparked Reunion

NEW YORK—Beatles fans can thank George Harrison's financial misfortunes for the Fab Four's much-heralded reunion.

Harrison, who became the owner of a movie company and a record label after his Beatles days, is down on his luck and his financial difficulties are the main reason for the Beatles "reunion," sources told *The Post.*

"Harrison told me once that being a Beatle was a nightmare," said biographer Geoffrey Giuliano, who's written twenty books about the group. "He's gone into this reunion kicking and screaming all the way, but he's going for the money."

It is estimated the upcoming TV documentary and six, CDs of unreleased Beatles songs will earn Harrison a much-needed $80 million next year.

The reclusive Harrison and John Lennon regularly objected to reviving the Beatles after the group broke up in 1970.

In 1989 Harrison said, "As far as I'm concerned, there won't be a Beatles reunion as long as John Lennon remains dead."

Frederic Seaman, who was Lennon's personal assistant from 1979 until his death, said yesterday that Harrison was the final element needed to put the reunion together.

"Paul [McCartney] wanted to do it and hustled Yoko [Ono] into giving him John's demo tapes so they could have a new Beatles single," Seaman said.

"Ringo [Starr] is easy going, so he was always going to go along with it, but George didn't want to participate until his accountant ripped him off for millions of dollars."

The seriousness of Harrison's financial situation was revealed on January 20 when he filed a $25 million suit in Los Angeles Superior Court against Denis O'Brien, his former business partner and financial manager.

Harrison, who hired O'Brien in 1973 to manage his finances, charged that the accountant had mishandled his investments and defrauded him for twenty years, cheating him out of at least $16 million.

Harrison and O'Brien, operating at Handmade Films, made a string of successful movies in Monty Python's *Life of Brian*, *Time Bandits* and *Mona Lisa*. But their later films, which included *Shanghai Surprise* with Madonna and Sean Penn, were costly bombs.

By normal standards Harrison is far from poor. He is believed to be worth less than $20 million.

WHERE IT ALL WENT

Here's how George Harrison's millions get eaten up:

Handmade Films: He had to sell the company for $5 million after some flops and is reportedly liable for debts of $10 million.

Denis O'Brien: Harrison claims the American money man defrauded him for over twenty years.

Friar Park: Harrison's 120-room Victorian mansion outside London is worth almost $10 million but is costly to maintain.

Harrisongs: Publishing company that collects royalties on Harrison's songs hasn't had a hit since 1987 and reportedly has 1993 liabilities of $5.12 million.

Dark Horse Records: The label's contract with distributor Warner Bros. has expired. Harrison admits his last record, "Live In Japan", didn't do "very well at all."

Grand Prix racing: He travels to the sixteen Formula One events every year and bought a $1 million McLarne last year.

Vacation property: He has a beachfront home in Maui, Hawaii; upkeep and travel runs up tens of thousands in bills.

NOVEMBER 16, 1995

• • •

NOW IT'S "SIR PAUL"

LONDON—Former Beatle Paul McCartney has been given a knighthood in the Queen's New Year's honors list. Last year Beatles producer George Martin also received a knighthood. In a brief statement Paul McCartney dedicated the award to fellow Beatles John Lennon, George Harrison and Ringo Starr.

1997

• • •

McCartney Cancer Terror

LONDON—It was announced today that Linda McCartney is suffering from breast cancer. After several treatments in England she traveled to Los Angeles for chemotherapy.

Paul's brother, Mike was quoted as saying, "Everything is going fine. She has more stamina than all of us, and Paul is there for her." Paul McCartney lost his mother to breast cancer when he was a teenager. We're all praying for Linda's full recovery.

1997

• • •

New Beatles' Film from Mr. and Mrs. Macca

LONDON—Despite Linda McCartney's ongoing battle with cancer she is apparently still hard at work. She and husband Paul are producing a film on the Beatles' utilizing Mrs. McCartney's never-before-seen shots of the group.

Beatle spokesman, Geoff Baker said, "Paul and Linda are currently editing through some 4,000 of Linda's pictures of the Beatles, all of which have never been seen, in order to make the new style of movie, which they call a photofilm."

The soundtrack of the film is rumored to include an unreleased recording session the Beatles laid down at the round house in Camden Town in 1968.

1997

• • •

Lennon Drawings Discovered

LONDON—John Dunbar, former husband of singer Marriane Faithfull, has discovered several drawings of John Lennon's. The former art gallery dealer apparently found the valuable sketches in a notebook he took with him on a trip with Lennon to Ireland in 1968. "I cannot believe," commented Dunbar, "most of John's drawings are frightful."

1997

• • •

Beatles on Killer's Hit List

NEW YORK—John Lennon's killer Mark David Chapman is reportedly intent upon murdering the three surviving Beatles according to a cell mate. Chapman has tattooed the words "John Lennon" and "Lonely" on his arm as well as a black gun, two red hearts and the initials F.F.Y.R.N. which apparently stand for: "Fab Four You're Next."

The former inmate commented, "He sounds so calm and peaceful, but he's nothing like the person who seemed so sane with Barbara Walters. When he talks about killing the Beatles, it's eerie. You'd think he was ordering a chocolate milkshake. And that's all he ever talks about—killing them all."

January 7, 1997

• • •

CHAPTER EIGHT

Late of Pablo Fanques
Fair/Family

Julian Lennon
SELECTED QUOTATIONS
London, 1984

My earliest recollections are when we all lived in Weybridge in Surrey. We'd drive to the gates to find hordes of screaming girls. I couldn't understand what was happening, but because it went on all the time, I thought it was normal. I took it all for granted, the other Beatles, lots of people, parties, and dad being away a lot.

• • •

Apart from rare visits, I lived from birthday to Christmas just to hear from dad.

• • •

Most of the time my life was ordinary but happy. I went to a private school and there were times when being John Lennon's son was very difficult. Older boys wanted to beat my head in because I was a Beatles' son, and others would force me to play the guitar and then poke fun at me because it sounded awful.

• • •

You'd go to a new school and the headmaster would say, "Here we have . . ." and everybody'd go *Boom!* And from that day on everybody knew. They point their finger and go, "Oooohhhh." It's hard trying to make friends with someone who already knows you from being the son of someone else.

• • •

I came downstairs the morning after dad died and noticed the curtains were still drawn. There must have been hundreds of photographers outside. My stepfather told me what happened. I refused to believe him. It was too much. But I had to comfort my mother. She had known him better then I had.

That same day I flew to New York to see whether everybody was okay, I worried about Sean. At the airports, I was hounded by photographers and journalists, but the worst part was the flight itself. All those people reading the papers that had the news about the assassination in huge capital letters on the front page. It took me quite a while to get over it. I was getting to know him a little better. That hurt more than anything.

• • •

187

Actually he was much more an uncle than a father.

* * *

Dad and I jammed together a couple of times, but it was never anything serious. I was too young. We hardly even talked about it; we were much too busy having fun.

* * *

Dad made me laugh a lot. He was a real comedian. He had a real sarcastic sense of humor, he could really make a fool out of people. I have to watch it a little bit, because I caught that habit from him. I was really fond of him. He was my idol.

* * *

Every now and then I'll go visit Yoko, but that's primarily because I'm concerned with Sean. He's getting caught up in all sorts of weird things. They still live in the Dakota building. It's very beautiful inside. Usually I don't stay very long. I see how Sean is doing and play with him a while. As soon as I get the chance I leave. Maybe when Sean is a bit older, we'll sit down and have a good chat. Sort him out a little.

* * *

Every penny I own, I made myself. Dad's money is in New York with Yoko. She determines what's to be done with it. All I can do is wait, patiently. I prefer to make my own living anyway.

* * *

There was so much music around my family, so many pianos and guitars, I couldn't avoid it. I was pleased to do it, because I like music so much.

Cynthia Lennon*
SELECTED QUOTATIONS
· ·

Cologne, 1992

For the most part, Julian was raised down south in London. We moved around a lot, then we moved back north again and he ended his school days in North Wales. So he still has his roots in North England. He has many of his father's mannerisms, his sarcastic and sardonic wit and he doesn't suffer fools gladly. He is very much like his dad in that way. His humor is obviously not as sharp as John's, because John came up a harder road than Julian. Julian had it a lot easier as far as financing and schooling is concerned. But, yes, he has a northern attitude.

• • •

The excitement of the Beatles was wonderful; the experience we all were able to share is something that a lot of people were very envious of. But I think the best times were before, the simplicity of life. The most devastating time was the death of Brian. That really threw everybody into total chaos. The pattern of life changed, the whole dream changed.

---

* Cynthia Lennon was John's first wife from 1962 to 1968

Pauline Stone

QUOTATION
· · · · · · · · · ·

Bristol 1990

John's Violent Tirade Against His Father at Tittenhurst Park, 1969

PAULINE STONE: The John we had known a couple of years ago was now unrecognizable. He sported a fiery red beard which gave him the appearance of a fierce, primitive warrior and made our birthday gift of aftershave laughably inappropriate. . . . Behind his granny glasses the pupils of his eyes were heavily stoned, maybe even on heroin which he admitted to sniffing occasionally when he was in *"real pain."* "I'm cutting off your money and kicking you out of the house," he snapped, stiffly taking a seat at the table and fixing on Freddie with his penetrating gaze. . . .

"Get out of my life, get off my back," he spat out in conclusion. . . . My initial reaction was that this must be some kind of sick joke, although it was clear from the look of sheer hatred in John's eyes he was deadly serious.

My glance turned to Yoko seated silently beside John, in the hope she might be able to calm him down. . . . Her detached air and deliberately averted eyes though left no doubt she did not intend to intervene. . . .

"It was your choice to give me an allowance," Freddie countered. These words seemed to act as a red flag stirring John into a further furious outburst.

"Have you any idea what I've been through because of you?" he yelled. . . . "Day after day in therapy, screaming for my Daddy, sobbing for you to come home. What did you care, away at sea all those years. . . ."

I felt genuine compassion for John and the trauma I knew he suffered as a child, but this was quickly replaced by a sense of indignation at the apparent unfairness of the attack on his father. "You can't put all the blame on your dad," I protested. "Your mother was just as much to blame for your problems."

Astonishingly, the mention of Julia triggered a vicious verbal attack on his mother, who he reviled in the most obscene language I had ever heard, referring to her repeatedly as a "whore". . . . Neither of us could believe it possible John could talk about his beloved mother in this way.

"Look at me!" he screamed at his father. "I'm bloody mad, insane! I'm due for an early death like Hendrix or Joplin and it's all your fault." At this point Yoko launched into a lecture on the seriousness of parental responsibility and the consequences to children in the event of separation from their parents. . . .

"Do you know what it does to a child to be asked to choose between his parents?" John roared. "Do you know how it tears him apart, blows his bloody mind?" I glanced at little David,* still playing happily on the floor apparently oblivious to the fearful atmosphere in the room and the blasphemies which flowed unchecked from his elder brother. As I considered the purpose of our visit, to introduce John to our son, it seemed a cruel twist of fate things had turned out like this. . . . "Father? You call yourself a father?" he sneered. "You think screwing some woman gives you the right to call yourself a father? You don't know the meaning of the word. You've treated me like shit, just like all the others. You've all ripped me off, the whole fucking lot of you!"

Noting I was about to tackle John again, Freddie wisely whispered to me to say nothing. I could see from his worried glances he was beginning to feel fearful for our safety. "Okay, John, I admit I was partly to blame and I understand your feelings," acknowledged Freddie in uncharacteristically subdued tones, hoping to calm John sufficiently to allow us to make our exit. . . .

"How the hell can you possibly understand how I feel?" he demanded. "How would you feel if you'd had nothing from your father all your life? How the hell do you think *he'd* feel?" he asked, pointing his finger furiously at little David who now began to cling to my legs, frightened by the growing violence in John's voice. "Lock him away from his parents and ordinary human beings and see how he'll end up, he'll end up a raving lunatic just like me!"

We were struck by the look of jealous rage which burned in his eyes as he glanced towards our son, a look which turned to pure hatred as Freddie anxiously picked up David and hugged him closely, gripped by the sudden anxiety that John might even vent his anger on the child. . . . I had taken as much as I possibly could, and despite Freddie's protests I was compelled to voice my indignation to John, although I knew I was playing with fire. "You've no right to treat your father this way," I shouted, feeling genuinely incensed. . . .

"Mind your own business!" he screamed with deafening force. . . . My distress left Freddie no doubt that neither of could handle any more of John's rage. . . .

John then lurched forwards across the table and grabbed hold of Freddie's lapel, confronting his father face-to-face. "As for your life story, you're never to write *anything* without my approval," he hissed. "And if you tell anyone about what happened here today . . . I'll have you killed!" A look of sheer evil appeared on his face as he went on to explain in extraordinary detail the procedure by which

---

* Freddie and Pauline's first of two sons.

he would arrange for his father to be shot. "And do you know what I'll do then?" he taunted. "I'll have you cased up in a box and dumped at sea right in the middle of the ocean, twenty, fifty or perhaps you would prefer a hundred fathoms deep?" He spoke these words slowly and deliberately, as if he had been rehearsing them for a long time. . . . It was as if he was actually taking part in the murder as he spoke. . . .

As I turned in horror towards Freddie I was struck by his sudden pallor and the expression of terror in his eyes. "Come on, pet," he whispered in an unfamiliar, empty voice. John hardly seemed to notice our departure and remained sitting at the table staring fixedly in front of him. . . . Only Yoko arose as we moved silently towards the door. "I'm sorry you have to leave this way," she said, an incongruous attempt at civility uttered in her soft, bland, Oriental voice. Throughout John's tirade I had been aware of her remarkably powerful presence as she sat close beside him and in this respect couldn't help but compare her with Mimi, herself a woman of powerful intensity. Although there the similarity ended, as Mimi was as narrow-minded in her attitudes as Yoko was outrageously avant garde.

Note: The above was excerpted and condensed with permission from *Daddy, Come Home/The True Story of John Lennon and His Father* with the kind permission of author Pauline Stone, who was married to John's father from 196_ until his death from cancer in Bristol in 1976. In addition to her writing, Ms. Stone is also a noted astrologer.

Fred Lennon

PRESS RELEASE
•••••••••••••••

London, 1967

Lennon's Dad Cuts Groovy New Record

For Immediate Release: Fifty-three-year-old Freddie Lennon, father of John, has made his first record. It is entitled "That's My Life (My Love and My Home")".

Mr. Lennon has been an entertainer in an amateur capacity for most of his life. He comes from a musical family, for his father was one of the original Kentucky Minstrels, and taught him to sing when he was young.

Most of Freddie's childhood was spent in an orphanage, for he was born into a large family and in those difficult times parents could not afford to feed so many children. At the orphanage, Freddie always took a major part in concerts, played his harmonica to the other children and generally showed an inclination towards the stage. He once sang at a theatre, but the orphanage authorities were dismayed at the thought of one of their boys going on to the stage, so Freddie's early dreams were quickly dampened.

After leaving the orphanage at the age of fifteen, Freddie worked in an office, but the call of the sea was strong, and he joined his first ship as bell boy at the age of sixteen. He stayed at sea for twenty-five years and travelled the world.

Freddie was always connected with entertainment on board ship, and has acted as compere, produced numerous concerts, sang in New York clubs and even conducted an orchestra in Lisbon. He has many interesting stories to relate about his adventures at sea.

At the age of twenty-five Freddie married, and his son John was born three years later. He was the only child.

When he left sea twelve years ago, Freddie took a job as a waiter, and later worked in holiday camps at Northern resorts. He came to live in London seven years ago. Over the years, Freddie was always interested in song writing, but never took it seriously. Six months ago he met Tony Cartwright who is now his manager. Together they wrote "That's My Life (My Love and My Home)", a story about Freddie's life. The song was taken to a music publisher, accepted and recorded.

Final Letter from Fred Lennon to John

1971

Dear John,

By the time you read this I will already be dead, but I hope it will not be too late to fill the gaps in your knowledge of your old man which have caused you distress throughout your life.

Despite your undoubted talents, your memories of your childhood appear to be non-existent and so I hope the reading of this story will help you establish what really happened in those early years. Of course, your only source of information has been your Aunt Mimi who for reasons best known to herself refrained from telling you anything about me. Consequently, as in Hunter Davies' biography of the Beatles, it wasn't so much what was said about me, but rather, what was left unsaid that caused you so much embarrassment and pain.

Since last we met on the occasion of your thirtieth birthday I have been haunted by the image of you screaming for your Daddy and it is my sincere hope that when you have read this you will no longer bear me any malice. Perhaps the revelations in my life story may bring you a clearer picture of how fate and circumstance control so much of our lives and therefore must be considered in our judgement of one another.

Until we meet again, some time, some place.

Your Father,
Freddie Lennon

Julia Baird*
REMEMBERING JOHN
· · · · · · · · · · · · · · · · · · ·
As Told to Geoffrey Giuliano, 1956–1980

1956

For my brother's wayward group of young ragtag musicians, "practice," as they say, "makes perfect," and that is exactly the path John and his comrades had diligently chosen to pursue.

"Where are we going, lads," John was known to suddenly cry out during their impromptu rehearsals.

"To the top, Johnny," was their enthusiastic response.

"What top is that, then?"

"To the toppermost of the poppermost!" was the final exchange in this, the baby Beatles' rhythmic war cry. Often times, with no other family willing to let the boys rehearse, John and his tea-drinking buddies would traipse along to our place for a little aid and comfort from Mummy.

"Julia was fantastic," admits John's long-time crony, Pete Shotton. "She was a kindred spirit who told us all the things we desperately wanted to hear. She made us feel welcome and always encouraged John to try and go as far as he could with his music. We loved her because she did everything for laughs. To her, nothing was really serious, except maybe having a good time.

"I can remember her walking up the road with us one day wearing an old pair of spectacles with no lenses in them. Whenever she happened to run into someone from the neighborhood she would casually slip her finger through the glasses and rub her eyes. Meanwhile, we would all be falling about in the bushes, pissing ourselves with laughter. Julia was definitely one of a kind."

As he grew older, John began to spend more and more time at our lively Springwood home. These were certainly not in any way considered "special" occasions, but more regular visits. If Jacqui and I happened to be outside when he arrived we would simply shout out, "Hi," and carry on playing. We never rushed in after him, or anything like that—he wouldn't have expected us to. Seeing John at home was a very natural and familiar thing for the entire family. As far as we knew, he was our big brother who just happened to have two homes.

---

* Julia Baird is John's maternal half-sister. She works as a French teacher in Chester, England.

It's difficult for me to try and judge just how Mimi might have been feeling about John's increasingly extended visits, but I can only hope she was happy to see him finally rediscovering his original family. In all honesty, however, she may have actually been a little uneasy with the obvious philosophical differences in child rearing between herself and Julia.

Mimi, a confirmed disciplinarian with a very strict view towards excessive permissiveness, certainly did not approve either of John's increasing involvement with music or of his newly adopted "teddy boy" fashion sense. Mummy, on the other hand, thought it was all smashing! Imagine the fun of defiantly thumbing your nose at authority simply by changing into a pair of winklepicker shoes and skin-tight trousers. If a little bit of hair cream could create such a delightful furor among grownups, what kind of fuss might be had by a little impassioned rock'n'roll?

"You're only young once," Mummy would often tell us. "Make sure you make the most of it!"

Without a doubt, one of the most memorable episodes in the Beatles' early Liverpool period, were their hilarious bathroom jam sessions with my mother at home in Blomfield Road. Our toilet was probably one of the tiniest in all of Great Britain, and to see John, Paul, George, Pete Shotton, Ivan Vaughn, and Mummy, all scrambling around inside trying to find a place to sit, was a wondrous sight indeed!

Perched precariously atop the commode, tucked like sardines into the bathtub, or tentatively sidling up to the sink, they somehow managed not only to fit, but to actually play. The door shut securely behind them, they enthusiastically tucked into a bevy of now classic tunes like "Maggie May," "Besame Mucho," "Alleycat," or the sneaky theme from *The Third Man*.

Paul McCartney remembers, "It was the best room in the house, hands down! Quite crowded, too, as I recall—don't forget it wasn't only us in there, but also our instruments, as well as a tiny pig-nose amp we used to carry around. Many a fine tune has been written in that little room, let me tell you. In fact, at home, I used to not only stand around with one leg on the toilet, but if perchance I had to actually go, I would lug my guitar in with me instead of a book. I remember me dad used to say, "Paul, what are you doing playing the guitar in the toilet?" And I'd say, "Well, what's wrong with that, then?"

In our humble john, however, there were absolutely no objections and the raucous musical free-for-alls sometimes meandered late into the evening. Their reason, of course, for choosing to tighten their chops in the bathroom was, like Mimi's front porch, that the room gave off a kind of natural echo which somehow seemed to enhance their offbeat sound. Occasionally, Jacqui and I were actually unlucky enough to be taking a bath when John's Beatle buddies suddenly felt the overpowering urge to let lose with a little homemade rhythm and blues. In that case, we were both unceremoniously hauled out of the tub to make way for these bathroom Beethovens.

Of course, we certainly didn't mind, as it generally meant we were allowed to go outside and play for an extra hour or so. (Bedtime being quite reasonably postponed, as it would have been virtually impossible for anyone within a one-mile radius to get any sleep!) The lineup for these unusual sessions was generally John, Paul, and George on acoustic guitar, Pete Shotton on string bass, and our uninhibited mother either on washboard, or playing percussionist with the aid of her favorite kitchen utensils.

Looking back, I suppose we had become a kind of refuge for John in his ever-increasing struggle to live amicably with Mimi. I don't wish to give the impression, however, that she was in any way callous or uncaring towards any of her family. In many ways, Mimi *was* the family. The unopposed, unspoken leader and advisor to us all. An extremely well-read, cultured, insightful woman, she was nevertheless very much the "elder" sister, and therefore took a loving interest in everyone's welfare. I know, for a fact, my brother was generally quite happy living with her and it was really only the normal sort of everyday, teenage uneasiness, about things that cropped up later in John's life, that ever caused them any difficulty.

If anything, our family will always be deeply indebted to Mimi for looking after John so well when circumstance so cruelly robbed our mum of the privilege. As Jacqui and I grew older, Mimi's home ironically became a kind of refuge for us, as well, during our own troubled teen years.

A little tale our cousin Leila liked to tell sums up the unusual nature of John's early years best. One day, John happened to be outside Mendips with both Julia and Mimi, when suddenly he turned to Mother and said, "I love you, Mummy." Then, pausing pensively, he softly spun around and whispered, "But I do love you, too, Mimi."

● ● ●

1958

Despite the apparent eccentricities of mother's family, all five of her sisters genuinely seemed to have found a level of peace and contentment in their lives which I greatly admired even as a youngster. All that was to change dramatically, however, when, in the sultry summer of 1958, a very grim reality came thundering down upon us all. It was sometime in the early evening, around six or seven o'clock, when Mummy quietly stepped outside with our Grandma Dykins to tell me she was off for a visit to Mendips.

"I'm just going to see Mimi," she said, bending down to give me a peck.

"Bye, bye," I replied. Jacqui, as I recall, was in the back garden playing with some friends when she left, while Daddy was inside with John, helping tidy up the kitchen after tea. I had been riding my bicycle with some neighborhood girls and for some reason just sat there watching them both ambling casually up the road. They were chatting, I remember and laughing as well. It was just another day, nothing special.

I'd seen both my parents hiking up that same road dozens of times. My father, on his way to work, would often turn round and lovingly wave or blow us each a kiss just before turning the corner. But tonight it was different. Something was terribly wrong, I just felt it.

Without thinking, I suddenly threw down my bike and ran like hell to the top of the road to try and catch her before she boarded the bus. By the time I got there, however, she had gone. I can still see them slowly disappearing into the twilight. Why I didn't ride my bike instead of legging it, I'll never understand, but I do know I desperately needed to see her again. And what would I have done if I'd have caught up with her? Pull her off the bus? Plead with her to turn around and come home? The truth is, I wasn't sure myself what I was so afraid of. It was dread, that's all, nameless, faceless dread.

Arriving at Mimi's, the two sisters from opposite ends of the earth sat down in Mendips' cozy living room for the traditional chat session they had so much come to enjoy. Julia adored Mimi for her bookish intelligence and insightful worldliness, while Mimi was in envy of her younger sister's uncluttered wit and easy charm.

Most nights, after an hour or two of conversation Mimi would accompany Mummy across Menlove Avenue to the bus stop, but this particular night she said, "I won't walk you, Judy, I'll see you tomorrow."

Mummy gave her a hug and replied simply, "Don't worry."

Nigel Whalley, one of John's long-time neighborhood friends, just happened to be walking down the street as Julia was crossing the road and paused for a moment to say hello. Stepping through the hedge in the middle of the dual carriageway, Julia was suddenly hurled high into the air by a passing automobile. She died instantly.

"An hour or so after it happened a copper came to the door to let us know about the accident," John later remembered. "It was awful, like some dreadful film where they ask you if you're the victim's son and all that. Well, I was, and I can tell you it was absolutely the worst night of my entire life. I lost me mother twice, once as a child of five, and then again at sixteen. It made me very, very bitter. I was just really trying to re-establish a relationship with her when she was killed. We'd caught up on so much, Julia and I, in just a few short years. We could communicate. We got on.

"Deep down inside I thought, 'Sod it, I've no responsibilities to anyone now.' Anyway, Twitchy* and I got a cab over to Sefton General where she was lying dead. Of course, there was no way I could ever bear to look at her. I remember rabbiting on hysterically to the driver all the way there. Twitchy went in to see her for a few minutes, but it turned out to be too much for the poor sod, and he finally broke down in my arms out in the lobby. I couldn't seem to cry, however, not then, anyway—I suppose I was just frozen inside."

Later that evening, after Jacqui and I had been put to bed by our father, I awoke to find Grandma silently climbing into my big, double bed. She cuddled up beside me and Jacqui was brought in, so I knew John must be staying over in her room. A few minutes afterwards the three of us were suddenly shaken by the horrific sound of Daddy sobbing and moaning uncontrollably in the next room.

Ironically, my sister and I hadn't been told anything, so we had no idea whatsoever why he was so upset. But we were terribly frightened and as such, didn't dare go anywhere near him. The next morning when we awoke, he was gone.

"Where is Mummy?" I asked Grandma on the way to school that day.

"We stayed with Mimi last night, that's all. Nothing to worry about, luv."

Stayed with Mimi? Never in my life had I known her to do that. She was absolutely always there in the mornings. Something very peculiar was going on. Jacqui and I both felt it, but we had no idea what. When we arrived at school, I was called straight to the headmaster's office and spent almost the entire morning sitting on his knee with him gently stroking my hair and kissing my forehead over and over. Later, another teacher took me into the loo and helped me wash my face and hands.

Apparently, Jacqui's teacher was showering her with lots of extra attention as well, so between the two of us we were now both completely bewildered. Finally, in absolute frustration, I screamed out at the headmaster, "What is going on? What's the matter with everyone?"

"I'm afraid your mother has been in an accident, dear," he said. "She's in hospital."

---

* John's naughty name for his mother's long time lover, Dykins.

The next thing I knew, I was running down the corridor to Jacqui's room, as someone from the school had offered to take us home. When we got there, however, we were completely and utterly shocked to find our Aunt Mater and Uncle Bert in our bedroom packing our clothes into two large suitcases.

"You girls will be coming up to Scotland with us for a holiday. Isn't that lovely," Mater offhandedly told us as she bent down to tie Jacqui's shoelaces. "Your mother is very ill, children, so of course you won't be allowed to visit with her just yet. In the meantime, you're coming home with us to Edinburgh."

I remember standing there being so bloody polite to them all when deep inside I knew exactly what was going on! A little later Daddy suddenly reappeared to tell us goodbye. It was obvious he was an absolute wreck and only stayed just long enough to have a little something to eat, talk with Mater a few minutes, and then immediately go back out again, as we were told, "to visit Mummy in hospital."

We stayed at Mater's in Edinburgh for a couple of weeks and then traveled on to their remote farm up north for another month or so. Still, nothing further was said to us about the accident, or even very much about Mummy, for that matter. Certainly not a word about the fact that she was dead. Still, as my brother John once said, "A conspiracy of silence speaks louder than words." In this case anyway, he was quite right.

I remember lying in bed at night, wide awake, knowing she was dead. Jacqui, however, was probably a little more innocent than I, and relied on me to reassure and protect her emotionally. Eventually, we did come back home to Liverpool, but the unforgivable charade continued.

● ● ●

1967

A few months after John moved out to his Weybridge sprawling estate, Kenwood, Cyn rang Jacqui and me at Harrie's to invite us down for a few days. Terrifically excited and very happy to finally spend some time with our big brother's family, we flew to London courtesy of NEMS and were picked up at the airport in John's spanking-new Phantom Five Rolls Royce. Whisked away from the curious stares of our fellow passengers, we went mad speculating just what they might be thinking. I'm sure the sight of two teenage girls being paraded through Heathrow by a uniformed chauffeur was a little strange, to say the least, but we thoroughly enjoyed every minute of it!

Eventually gliding through Kenwood's impressive electric gates and up the long, landscaped, semi-circular drive, we finally got our first peek at the fruits of

Beatlemania. "You've certainly come a long way from Gambier Terrace, John," I said to myself as the limo silently pulled to a stop at the main entrance. "Not too bad for a scruffy skiffle group from Woolton."

Once inside, we were both greatly impressed with the exceptionally well-appointed interior, but surprised to find there was, as yet, no kitchen. "I guess the workmen haven't gotten around to it yet," Cyn apologized. "Still, it's great seeing you and I know we're going to have great fun. John's out visiting Ringo at the moment, but he made me promise to ring him as soon as you arrived. He's really been looking forward to having you down for quite a while now, but never seems able to keep from working long enough to actually do it."

With that Cyn led us into a cozy rectangular room just at the back of the house. It had one huge glass wall and overlooked the spacious, well-manicured grounds and gently rolling park lands beyond. Crammed high with various eclectic mementoes of John's illustrious career, I particularly remember one well-placed bumper sticker pinned to the door of a bookcase which boldly declared, MILK IS HARMLESS.

Within minutes, it seemed, John returned and bolted through the kitchen into the back room. "Glad you finally made it, ladies," he sang out as he gave us hugs and kisses all around. "My, what smart young women they've become, Cyn. They'll probably form their own fucking group and knock us right off the charts!"

It was truly great to be home, once again, with our big brother. I know he was excited to show off his newfound success. "Mimi's often implied I was just struck lucky with the Beatles, like winning the pools, or something. But I think she may actually be beginning to see how hard we've worked. Especially after joining us on tour."

I will never forget the happy, wholesome, close family I experienced during that brief holiday with John. It was almost as if Mummy might come waltzing in the room any minute, carrying a tea tray full of freshly baked cakes, biscuits, and naturally, the all-important tea. Of course, now that lot fell to Cynthia, who did a fine job of making us all feel very much at home.

At the time of our first visit, John was not only busy with his many Beatle-related duties, but also very much involved in finally learning how to drive. Of course, not being able to really drive himself wasn't any great impediment to John in buying several fine automobiles! Among his collection was a mat black Ferrari, the Rolls, and a lovely all-white Mini with electric windows. Although he hadn't gotten round to actually taking his road test yet, that certainly didn't stop him from insisting on taking us for a ride.

"Might be a little risky actually driving on the road just yet," John slyly muttered, as Jacqui and I piled into the diminutive two-door. "Perhaps we would be better off simply going for a little spin on the local golf course."

"Oh, John, you can't," squealed my sister, laughing with delight. "You'll be nicked, for sure!"

"Are you kidding?" John said with mock indignation. "I'm a Beatle! One of Britain's national treasures. No one would ever dare say a word."

Although he was obviously only kidding, something in the way he said it struck me that perhaps he was finally beginning to understand the truly unique position he was in. At any rate, off we sped. Tearing into the moist, dew-laden turf with a vengeance. Up and over the hilly fairlanes and careening through the sand traps we all felt happy, wild, and free. Fortunately for us, it was still very early in the day and no one was really out golfing. Otherwise we might have had the opportunity to truly test John's theory of "Beatle infallibility."

More often than not John was away in London recording, so we ended up spending a lot of time with Cyn. She really was a lovely person. Not at all pushy or ambitious the way other people who came along later were. I always felt that if circumstances had been just a little different she and I would probably have become great friends. As it is, the last time I saw her was an unexpected, but certainly very welcome appearance at Harrie's funeral. In those days, however, we used to spend our time walking along the Thames together with Julian, feeding the ducks or simply waving to strangers as they passed in their canal boats.

For us, probably the biggest event of the entire visit was the opportunity to see the Beatles perform at the Finsbury Park Astoria. I remember riding into London with John that evening and commenting on how nervous he seemed.

"Just because I've been doing this rubbish since I was fifteen is no reason not to be edgy. You've no idea what these shows are like, Ju." Twenty minutes of out-of-tune madness underscored by an audience full of blithering idiots. None of us like it, you know."

Upon our arrival at the theater we were ushered backstage surrounded by what seemed like an army of Bobbys all walking arm-in-arm to ensure our physical safety. John was right, these concerts could get pretty bloody rough, but more on that later.

Once inside the dressing room I was surprised to find the other Beatles sitting down enjoying a quiet drink with, of all people, Mick Jagger. "I thought you lot were rivals," I whispered in John's ear.

"Only as far as the media is concerned," he confided. "In real life most of the groups are all the best of friends."

A few minutes later, after places were called, Mal and Neil (the Beatles roadies) showed Jacqui and I to a cordoned-off area in the front row of the theater. Very carefully they lowered us down from the stage, much to the surprise of the screaming girls in the audience, who for a moment actually thought we were part of the performance.

Once the show really got going, all hell broke lose. The by now hysterical crowd was totally out of control and soon started pushing its way forward towards the stage. "Get the girls," shouted John between numbers, "now!"

Instantly two of the Beatles security people leaped from the stage and hauled us both back up. After that little adventure we were quite content to watch the Beatles' manic performances from the wings. Later, we were all treated to chicken and chips in the dressing room with the rest of the group and then rode back to Kenwood with John.

Like all good things, however, our trek into the make-believe world of big-time show business came to an end, and within a few days I was back home in Liverpool preparing to sit for my A levels.

One of the most unfortunate incidents (as far as John and the family were concerned) was the sudden, totally unexpected reappearance of Alf Lennon back into John's life in 1965. Paul McCartney takes up the thread.

"It was certainly a great pity, when he showed up again after all those many years. We got to know about it from an article in *Sunday's People* which said something like, "BEATLES DAD WASHES DISHES AT THE BEAR HOTEL IN ESHER." I was with John at the time and he just kind of went, "Oooohhh. . . ." Luckily, we both had a good robust nature so we could say, "Oh, bloody hell, isn't it typical!" We managed to laugh it off like that. Eventually, of course, John did agree to see him."

The thing that disturbed John most about the whole affair was the fact Alf had never once tried to contact him from 1945 (when John was just five years old) until nineteen years later, after he had become successful. Apparently Alf had no idea about John's amazing career until 1964 when a workmate happened to point out an article on the Beatles to him and said, "If that's not your son, Freddy Lennon, then I don't know what!"

Almost immediately stories about Alf started turning up in the papers. Lennon, however, steadfastly denied he ever consciously sought the publicity. In his words, "It just happened."

John remembers the shock of first learning about his father's untimely reappearance. "I never saw him until I made a lot of money and he came back. I opened the *Daily Express* and there he was, working in a small hotel very near where I was living in the stockbroker belt outside London. He had been writing me for some time trying to get in contact. I didn't really want to see him, though. I was too upset about what he'd done to me and my mother and that he would turn up only after I was rich and famous and not bother before. So, originally I wasn't going to see him at all, but he sort of blackmailed me in the press by saying he was a poor old man washing dishes while I was living in luxury. I fell for it, saw him and I suppose we had some kind of relationship."

Contrary to most reports, however, John's mate, Pete Shotton, saw him almost immediately following his first meeting with Alf and says that at first, John was very encouraged by the outcome. "He's good news, Pete," John apparently reported. "A real funny guy, a loony just like us!"

That initial glow, however, quickly wore off after Cyn invited Alf to spend the night with them at Kenwood and it turned into three days of highly emotional scenes between John and his newfound dad. Mimi, of course, was not at all pleased to see Alf suddenly back in her nephew's life, but stoically resisted the urge to intervene.

Some three years later Alf again presented himself to John with the disturbing news he had plans to marry a nineteen-year-old Beatle fan by the name of Pauline Jones.

"I was terribly shocked when he first rang me up to tell me the news," remembers John's uncle, Charlie. "I said, 'Isn't one bad marriage enough for you? Do you have to go out and do the same thing again, and with a younger girl, at that?'"

Alf however, was adamant. He would marry the former Exeter University student, and he hoped, if John and Cyn were willing, that perhaps they might even employ the new Mrs. Lennon as their personal assistant.

John wanted to try and oblige his father as far as his admittedly troubled conscious would allow, so that is exactly what happened. John explains. "At fifty-six, he married a secretary who later did some work for the Beatles and ultimately they had a child. Which, I must admit, was rather hopeful for a man who had lived most of his life as almost a Bowery bum." The May/December union, however, was rife with troubles from the beginning, and after only five short months John decided it was time to cut loose from his troubled past and summarily dismissed Pauline. He wanted his aging father to be happy, though, and generously bought him a fifteen-thousand-pound house near Kew Gardens in London.

In addition, he also arranged for Alf to furnish his new home courtesy of Apple, as well as establishing a weekly payment of thirty pounds to help offset expenses. Eventually, though, the couple moved to Brighton, where John also agreed to cover their living expenses in a lovely flat near the sea.

The senior Lennon eventually had two children with Pauline: David Henry Lennon, born in Brighton in 1969, and Robert Francis Lennon, some four years later.

• • •

1975

By 1975 I was living in Wallasey and Mater, my aunt in Scotland, telephoned to tell me she had a surprise. John had been trying to get in touch with Jacqui and myself. She asked if I wanted him to contact me. "It would be lovely," I replied.

Apparently, John had been asking how "the girls" were and wanted to know what we were doing. Anyway, Mater gave me his hot-line number in New York and it was like trying to get in touch with God! That night, I telephoned, but couldn't get through. There was only a lot of strange noises and an American girl's voice saying, "Hello," but that was all I got.

I tried again the following evening at midnight and it was the same voice answering. "Can I speak to John," I asked. She wanted to know who I was, so I explained I was his sister. Could I give my name, please? Yes, Julia. She was still not satisfied. "Give me your father's name." By this time I was beginning to get annoyed. I had thought the hot-line number would get me straight through to John.

"Oh, forget it," I told her.

"Look," she said with more determination, "just give me your father's name."

I told her, "John Albert Dykins." Then she wanted to know where we used to live. It was too much for me. "Really, let's forget it, I don't . . ." Suddenly, there was John on the phone.

"Don't put the phone down, it's me," he yelled. "Don't hang up! If only you knew how many 'sisters' I had. . . ."

Together John and I shared a tearful, almost delirious reunion, even though I was in Wallasey and he was light-years away in New York. John wanted to talk about Mummy, and although I find it virtually impossible to mention her name, except to my sister Jacqui, it was easy to exchange memories with John.

We both revelled in the sunny days, the laughter, the idiotic humor, the tragedy of her death and its absurdity. And John discovered the ready-made family for which he had so long been searching. "All my life I've wanted a real family, and now I realize I've had one all along," he said.

"We all love you, John," I told him. "You know that. It's only our separate lives that have kept us apart. You'll always be close to me like we all still are to Mummy."

When I first heard John was trying to get in touch with me I must admit I was a little taken back. Since he moved to New York nobody in the family had really heard very much from him. What with the demands of a successful solo singing career, his well-known troubles at home with Yoko, and his well-publicized immigration hassles, he was no doubt thoroughly preoccupied. I, too, of course, was busy with my own career, but when Auntie Mater said he'd been writing recently inquiring about "the girls," I was thrilled.

"He says he wants to make everything up to you, Ju," said Mater.

"What on earth does that mean?" I replied. "He's got nothing to make up *for*. He's living his life and I'm living mine. What else is there?"

"I know, dear," she continued, "but he says he's been thinking a lot about your mum lately and he wants to try and do something for you and Jacqui."

"I don't understand what you're on about, Mater, but I will certainly speak to him."

"Listen, Julia," my aunt explained, "Your Allen is in business. John could set him up if he needed it. For goodness sakes, you know John would be glad to help. If you want anything, you mustn't be afraid to ask. Look at your cousin Stan—John gave him the money to start up his garage years ago and now he's doing very well. I'm not suggesting you dive right in and ask him for anything, but just think about it. If only for *his* sake."

Quite honestly, if it wasn't for John's great wealth we probably would have been in touch long before. We would have had a better chance of remaining close if he had been a sheep rancher in Australia or something. As it was, the seemingly gargantuan aura surrounding "John Lennon" made it difficult to maintain any sort of relationship at all. As far as I was concerned anyway, his financial situation only served to keep him more out of reach of his family. Moneywise, my brother was out there in the Milky Way compared to us.

That first phone call we probably spent at least fifty quid just crying and crying. John said, "I've thought a lot about you and Jacqui over the years, you know. I don't really know why we didn't stay more in contact."

"Remember what Mummy always used to say," I replied. "Don't think about it, Luvey, do it!"

"Yeah, you're right. There isn't really any excuse. I'm just sorry we lost so much time. You know, I realize now I completely screwed things up with Julian. He's really an amazing kid, though, in spite of everything I did to him."

"It's like Leila says, 'I hope John's new son inherits a lot more than his money and his genes!'"

"Too true," he said sadly. "I'm trying more with Sean now anyway. I tell you, Ju, I'm determined it's not going to happen again. Now that Sean's finally arrived he's going to get *all* my attention right from the word go. What about your little ones, then? What are they like?"

"Well, believe it or not, John, Nicky's* got Mummy's hair exactly. The same color, the wave, everything."

"Christ, that's fantastic! You've all got to come over soon. God, Sean and Yoko would love it."

"What about you then?"

"Are you kidding?" he giggled. "Allen and I would definitely be outnumbered with all those mothers and babies about. We'd have to get right down to the pub! Seriously, though, really think about it. Come anytime. Just let me know when and my office will make all the arrangements."

Sadly, that wonderful holiday to New York never materialized, but nobody was too awfully concerned about it as we always figured now that the family was back together again John would definitely be making the trip home.

"What about Jacqui's little boy, Ju? Oh shit . . . I've completely forgotten his name!"

"Then you've forgotten your own, silly. It's *John!*" We both laughed at this non-sensical little *faux pas.* So typical of John's often absent-minded nature.

"Do your kids look Irish, then?"

"I suppose. . . . Yes, I never really thought about it, but I guess they do."

"You know, Julia," he continued, "it's such a fucking, goddamn shame Mummy isn't around to see her grandchildren growing up. It still haunts me. There isn't a bloody day she doesn't cross my mind at least once."

"It's the same with me. It's horrible, her being dead. I hate it. Sometimes it's almost unbearable, but still, I know she'd want us all to carry on."

"I don't know. Sometimes it just kills me that Sean will never know his grand-mother. I mean, I'm always talking to him about her and everything, but. . . ."

"*I know,*" I replied. There was nothing more I could say. The frankness of our conversation was all at once both cleansing and extremely upsetting. Talk of Mummy predominated, with John digging deep to try and share with me his innermost feelings about the tragedy and irony of our lives. And, of course, the happiness.

---

* Julia's eldest son.

"Do you remember Mummy's pink party dress," he asked me softly, obviously trying to hold back the tears.

"Yes, of course. She looked beautiful. Daddy always said she was the most beautiful woman he'd ever seen."

"By the way, Julia, I'm very sorry to hear about Bobby's death. I only learned about it recently and it saddened me. They've written a load of crap about him and me over the years, but I was really always very fond of him. You know that. Things have been hard for you and I'm sorry."

"Thanks," I whispered. "It's been a crazy life, hasn't it?"

"You're not kiddin'. Look at the way the damned government is trying to boot me out of America. And for what? A couple of lousy grams of hash. From now on, every time I have a smoke I practically lock myself inside a fuckin' vault! Do you realize those bastards are actually tapping my phones? Some geezer here in New York recently gave me a special number that if you called it and it rang busy, then your line was tapped. So anyway, one day I did it and it was!"

"Well, I hope they're getting an earful now, John. With all this 'old home' stuff we've been talking."

"You do realize it's only all this immigration hassle that keeps me from coming home, don't you? Once I leave the country, chances are the bastards wouldn't let me back in again. My lawyers feel there is a very good chance that in the end we will win. But for now, anyway, it seems I'm trapped like a rat!"

"If they're hassling you so much, then why do you want to stay so badly?" I reasoned. "Why not just come home for good? You've still got your estate in Ascot, don't you?"

"Yeah. I don't know, Ringo says he's interested in the place, and anyway, who the hell wants to retire to sunny Berkshire after living in thundering Manhattan for so long? Five hundred years ago, or whatever, the center of everything was Rome, but now it's all happening here in America. When you come over you'll see what I mean. This is my home now, Ju. For better or worse."

All in all, we probably talked for well over two hours that night. Of course the phone bill was enormous, but Allen graciously paid it without saying a word. He was just happy, I think, that John and I had finally gotten together again. Ironically, it was John who finally ended that first call by gently chiding me for not calling "collect."

"What do you mean by '*collect*,' John?" I asked in all innocence of American ways and means.

He laughed. "It means that next time I'll be the one paying for the bloody call!"

"You mean, reverse the charges? Speak English, will you! You've certainly become very American in the last few years, haven't you?" I complained, taking the micky out of his mystifying New York jabber.

"You bet your sweet ass, baby! I'm in a New York state of mind," he retorted in his best Brooklyn cabby speak.

"You're obviously in some state, but I couldn't say what! Okay, then, John, I'll ring off now."

"All right, kid. When will you call again, anyway?"

"In a few days. . . ."

"Hey, and what about Jacqui?" he chimed in excitedly. "I want to talk to her as well."

"Yes, of course you do. All right, look, next time before I call I'll go round and fetch her over here to my place so we can all have a real family reunion."

"Great! See you do. And don't forget to give Allen and the kiddies a great big 'Howdy' from their loopy uncle in New York!"

"I won't," I said, missing him before we'd even hung up.

"See you, then."

"Bye, bye, kid."

Over the next few days all I could think about was John. I thought about him, Yoko, Sean, and their apparently happy life safe inside the fortress-like Dakota. About a week or so after I first spoke to John I finally managed to get hold of Jacqui, who was absolutely delighted to hear that our reclusive big brother had finally decided to pop his head back into our lives. As promised, the next call was a real family free-for-all with Jacqui, myself, John, and Yoko all jabbering together for a good couple of hours via transatlantic telephone.

Although our conversations often went on for hours, we probably only really talked together about a dozen times. He did write quite a bit, however. Long, dreamy letters, they were. The kind Mummy might have written and certainly would have loved to receive. "Dear Julia/Allen et al in walla walla sea side," began one of the first. "You'll find over the years I'm a bit erratic with answering letters even when I'm not pregnant . . . so don't get mad! o.k?" Unfortunately, I didn't keep any of them, but rather read them once and then tossed them in the bin. Much to the chagrin of collectors around the world, who probably would have had me preserve them in the British Museum! What Lennon fans fail to realize, however, is that to me, these were simply personal little notes from my brother to me. Not the inspired writings of the cultural leader of a generation!

● ● ●

1980

Our life in Chester was exceedingly normal and satisfying. Allen had his work which he thoroughly enjoyed. I had mine at home with the kids and together we made a very happy family. On the morning of December 9, 1980, Allen went off to work as usual, Sarah* and Nicky were dropped at school and little Michael* sat playing with an old jigsaw puzzle in his kitchen high chair. Around eight o'clock I thought I heard a very slight tapping on the front door and ambled over to investigate.

To my surprise it was one of the neighbors, a lovely girl called Sylvia, who came to tell me my cousin Leila was on the phone. At that point we had only just bought the house and decided not to rush right out and have a telephone installed. Instead, we had arranged it with Sylvia to give out her number to our closest friends and family to be used only in the event of an absolute emergency.

"Leila," I thought to myself. "What on earth does she want at this hour of the morning?" Dashing across the street to Sylvie's, I ran to the phone, but strangely stopped just short of actually picking it up. Why, I don't know. It was just a feeling of dread. That selfsame feeling of total helplessness I first experienced that balmy summer's eve when Mummy knelt down and kissed me goodbye for the very last time.

"Hello . . ." I finally stammered. "Leila, what is it?"

"Then you haven't heard?" she asked.

"No . . . What is it? What's happening? Are your kids all right?"

"Julia," she cautiously continued, "it's John. I'm afraid he's been shot."

I was stunned. Although I hadn't seen John in years, the words cut through me like a knife and I felt as though my right arm had been suddenly sliced off. I stared down into the phone in disbelief. She had to repeat it several more times before I finally, very slowly, began to take up the thread. "Is he all right?" I asked.

"No, Julia, he's dead."

"Are you coming over, then," I said trying to hold back the tears.

---

*   Sarah is Julia's daughter and Michael her youngest child.

"Yes, I am. I'm coming straight away. Just sit tight until I get there."

"All right," I promised, trailing off into nothingness as I carefully placed the receiver back on the cradle. "All right."

As the news spread that chilly December day, Leila and I sat together in my kitchen talking of old times. "Do you remember that secret whistle John always had to call for his mate, Ivy, through the garden?"

"And how he loved fishing for salmon with Uncle Bert when he visited Mater in Scotland?"

So many memories. So many tears and laughter. The world had lost a superstar that day and it was grieving. But I had lost my only brother and I was simply numb.

Rushing home from work, Allen did his best to comfort me, but I was inconsolable. There would be no visit home. The only family reunion we would have now would be to share our mutual grief. John was lost. Lost to the demented dreams of one nameless nowhere man. Taken out of this world violently and without mercy. By now it was kind of an old story after Mummy, Uncle George, Daddy, and Harrie all passing away with very little warning. But it never got any easier to deal with, nor did it hurt any the less.

Allen and I, still shocked and saddened by the terrible irony of it all, told the children the following morning. Afraid they would hear it casually at school, we sat the two oldest down and broke the news.

I remember thinking, "Michael is our third baby and John still hasn't seen any of them." None of children ever knew their uncle, and that to me was a very great shame. There was Nicky, the spitting image of my mother, same bright eyes, same curly red hair, and John had never even met him. To the children Uncle John was simply one of four smiling faces staring up at them from the cover of a Beatles LP. And now, of course, it was forever too late. A reality I struggle to accept even to this day.

Angela and Ruth McCartney*
INTERVIEW
• • • • • • • • • • •
Buffalo, 1994

ANGELA MCCARTNEY: I remember when Ruth and I went to London once when the Beatles were recording "All You Need Is Love." We stayed at Paul's house, and when he and John got home they were in the weirdest state, the very strangest mood. I assumed they must be the coming down from an acid trip.

GEOFFREY: How did they act?

ANGIE: Just very woozy, flighty and *weird*!

GEOFFREY: What do you remember about the breakup of Jane Asher and Paul?

ANGIE: At the end of Mike and Angie's[†] honeymoon, we were flying back from Austria into Luton, in England. The *Sunday Express* was on the plane and we were sitting with the drummer for the Bee Gees and he opened the paper and handed it to Mike. In it there was a piece on Jane Asher having been on the "Simon D Show" saying her engagement to Paul was over, which was a complete surprise to all of us. When we landed we called home and asked Jim if it was true and he said, "Yes, Paul's here, actually, and he's got somebody with him." Which turned out to be Francie Schwartz, the girl that used to work at Apple.[‡] We got home in the wee hours and my mum was there and she filled me in on the details. She said Paul had come home with this little girl and it was evidently all over between he and Jane. Francie hung around for a day or two with Paul and he basically ignored her. She was like a spare part. She'd just stand there or he'd go out in the car and not speak to her. He brought her home and then she was an embarrassment to him. I felt sorry for the poor kid. He actually took her out once to Auntie Jinny's because Jim had said, "Look, you brought her here son, you just can't ignore her." I remember Paul said to her, "I'm going to Auntie Jin's, do you want to come?" That was the only interaction between them. After that we never saw Francie again.

• • •

---

* Angela McCartney is Paul McCartney's stepmother. Ruth McCartney is the former Beatle's adopted sister.
† Angela Fishwick was brother Michael's first wife.
‡ Francie Schwartz is a respected freelance writer and businesswoman who had a short-lived relationship with McCartney in 1968. She later wrote a biting memoir of that time entitled *Body Count*.

ANGIE: There was another time when Paul came down to Rembrandt* on the train. He called and asked for us to pick him up. He spent a few days with us and then decided to go back to London. He asked me to book a whole compartment because he didn't want to be bothered. I asked him what name he would like to use and he said, "Arnold Kack"—now "Kack" means shit, like "ka-ka." I said "Oh, I'm not going to say that." He said, "Go on, I insist." He was joking but he wasn't. When I booked it and they asked for a name and I said, "I'll have to spell it for you, it's a South African name, it's K-a-c-q-u-e." I wasn't going to say Kack! He had funny little ways of being slightly amusing.

RUTH MCCARTNEY: And slightly obnoxious.

ANGIE: And always embarrassing someone! There was a time Paul and Linda were up in Scotland. Jim phoned to speak to Paul and Heather answered. Jim said, "Where are your mum and dad?" And she said, "They're out in the fields, I think they've had a fight." Jim asked if she was all right and she said, "Oh, yes, I'm fine, Mary and Stella are in bed." Jim was worried and called the next day and got Linda. He didn't ask any direct questions, just small talk and then said, "Can I speak to Paul, is he around?" and she said, "No, he's not. As a matter of fact, he's been gone a couple of days. I don't know where he is." Of course the bottom nearly fell out of old Jim's world. She asked Jim to call if she heard from Paul and he said "Of course." That went on for two or three more days, when finally Paul showed up unshaven and tatty. He didn't have a key, so he rang the bell and I answered it. He said, "Hi, Ang'," and walked right past me as if he felt quite guilty.

The phone rang and it was Linda. I didn't say anything, I just asked Paul if he wanted to speak to her. He said "Okay," and went upstairs in the bedroom and talked to her for a long time. He came down, had a long conversation with his father and then said, "Good night Ang', Linda's coming down tomorrow with the kids."

Well into the evening of the next day, Linda turned up with two taxis because to drive all the way out to the farm and then come down to Liverpool and back again took two drivers. Besides, she had so much stuff in the car she barely had room for the drivers.

RUTH: Linda, Heather, Mary, Stella, the dogs, Lucky, the dalmatian, Martha, and tons of luggage. It's about a twelve-hour drive.

ANGIE: When she came in the door she looked just awful, shocking. I put my arms around her and said, "You poor little thing" and we both cried. She said she was all right and let's just forget it. Obviously, I wouldn't dream of asking any

---

*   The name of McCartney's comfortable Liverpool home on Baskerville Road, the Wirral. Paul still owns it to this day

questions. What the hell it was all about I still don't know. But when people malign Linda I always say, "Look, her life can't be easy. It can't!" She was up there bewildered and alone with the kids in such a remote place. It's unbelievable.

• • •

GEOFFREY: Did Paul often smoke pot at Rembrandt?

ANGIE: Out in the garden and in his bedroom.

RUTH: I still associate the smell of pot with a sort of clandestine, *Don't let Ruth know* thing and bad moods. Dad would say to Paul, "Don't do that shit here." Then it would break into "Whose house is this, anyway?" Paul would say, "It's my bloody house, I'll do what I want as I paid for it!" Now I always associate the smell of marijuana with a fight.

GEOFFREY: When Paul smokes, does he get mean?

ANGIE: He becomes oracle-like. He'd get to where he knows everything and everyone else is just an idiot and if you dare argue with him there's a fight. It's exactly the opposite of everything I ever understood about marijuana, the happy, hippy, love and peace drug.

• • •

GEOFFREY: Describe a day in the life of Paul and Linda at Cavendish Avenue back then.

ANGIE: They'd get up around lunchtime. Linda would let the dogs out into the back garden, make tea, and leave a trail of tea leaves all over the place. She didn't use a strainer.

RUTH: She'd make a fucking mess.

ANGIE: They'd be in the bathroom a very long time. They'd hit the phones, usually, come down about one or two with wet hair and Linda would cook breakfast, you know, bacon and eggs, fried tomatoes, mushrooms. Then they tended to go upstairs and look at television.

GEOFFREY: Did they look after the children?

ANGIE: No, not really, Rose* was there.

GEOFFREY: How were Paul and Linda with the fans outside Cavendish Avenue?

ANGIE: Pretty cold, really.

---

* Rose was the McCartney's long-time housekeeper from the early Jane Asher days. She stayed with the family until her retirement.

RUTH: It depended on their mood, really. Sometimes they'd stop and talk to them.

ANGIE: But not often.

RUTH: Generally they treated them like trees.

• • •

GEOFFREY: What was Paul's bedroom like at Rembrandt?

RUTH: Just a bed and a stolen blinking light. He ripped off one of those hazard lights from the motorway. They dumped it in the back of the Rolls and put a coat over it as wouldn't stop blinking. You could see the bloody thing flashing through the curtains and my dad used to have a fit.

• • •

ANGIE: I remember Paul waking us up in the middle of the night and saying, "Dad, Ang', wake up, I've got some demos." One of them was "She's Leaving Home." I wept when I heard it. It was such a beautiful song. I thought of it in terms of how I'm going to feel when Ruth leaves home, but she hasn't. We're still together.

RUTH: I remember when he played us "Hey Jude." We were all looking at each other like this was the emperor's new clothes. It was a good song and then it started into this "na-na-na-na-nananana" and went on and on for about seventy-two bars.

ANGIE: He asked, "Ang,' what do you think?" and I said, "Well, all that repetition at the end doesn't really cut it, take it out." And that was the biggest-selling song they ever had! So after that he'd always say, "Ask Ang' anything you want about our songs—if she hates it, it will be a hit." I remember something else he was very proud of was "Norwegian Wood," which was John's, mainly. That was another time when he got us up in the middle of the night. It was a great song, but it didn't really mean a lot to us. He told us it was based on a real experience of John's.

GEOFFREY: "When I'm Sixty-four" was composed in honor of Jim's sixty-fourth birthday, correct?

ANGIE: No, it was written when Paul was sixteen. He first played it to us on Cavendish Avenue on the eve he announced his engagement to Jane. He'd bought her an engagement ring. It was that year Jim was going to be sixty-four and Paul said, "I've got a song to play you."

RUTH: How true do you think it is that Paul wrote "Hey Jude" in his Astin-Martin on the way to Weybridge?

ANGIE: We always understood Paul wrote "Hey Jude" about Julian [Lennon] when he was planning to go and ask Cynthia [Lennon] to marry him. When Cynthia came home from holiday and found Yoko sitting at her kitchen table wearing her bathrobe, Paul evidently felt some responsibility. John wasn't taking care of her, so it was his job. He apparently brought her a single red rose and then drove out to where Cynthia was staying and asked her jokingly to marry him.

● ● ●

GEOFFREY: Jim was quite ill a lot of the time, wasn't he?

ANGIE: At that time, the plan was for Jim to go to a hospital which was close to the house to have some more tests done. The final day Paul and Linda were there, they were flying out of Manchester to New York. Paul helped me to lift his father into the car and drive him to the hospital. When we got there, Paul lifted his dad out of the car and into a wheelchair and wheeled him into the hospital. Meanwhile, while I did all the admission paperwork, he took his dad up to the ward and helped him into bed. They were both very tender, emotional and teary-eyed with each other. We all had to leave so they could begin the tests and Paul and Linda had to get ready for their flight. So, we drove home—both of us were very quiet all the way. I remember just outside the house Paul squeezed my hand and said, "I'll never forget you for what you've done for my dad."

We went in the house and made breakfast. I'd kept Ruth home because of Jim and Paul and Linda's flight. Anyway, I was in the kitchen and Paul went out into the dinning room to the piano. He started playing "The Long and Winding Road." Jim used to say how much he loved that song and how it reminded him of the drive up to Scotland to the farm. To this day, when I hear that song it still upsets me because it reminds me so much of Jim.

● ● ●

GEOFFREY: Tell me about the creation of "Blackbird" and your mother.

ANGIE: My mum Edie used to live with my sister Mae in Liverpool, but my sister took ill and had to go to hospital. Paul kindly suggested we order a private ambulance to pick up my mum, drive her through the Mersey Tunnel to stay with us at Rembrandt where I could look after her. While she was there Paul came home for a few days and used to go into the back bedroom and sit on the end of Mum's bed and talk to her, as did Mike—they were both very sweet and tender with Edie. She happened to say, "I can't sleep. This bloody blackbird, in the dead of night, 'cheep cheep,' it sings all sodding night." We all laughed about it. One night Paul said, "Let's record this." So he took a small hand-held tape recorder into Mum's bedroom, held the mike outside the window, and recorded the sound of the blackbird. Ultimately the song "Blackbird" was written which incorporated that recorded bird song. It makes me very happy. Paul was very good to my mum. So to me, the two songs that are very special are "The Long and Winding Road" and "Blackbird."

GEOFFREY: What was the "Golden Slumbers" story?

RUTH: I was such a lousy, bloody piano player. I was seven and going to piano lessons—I hated theory. I had "Golden Slumbers," the original lullaby, in a book and I was practicing it there in the dining room, which is right off the kitchen. That's where the old scrambled eggs story came from, breakfast and scrambling eggs while Paul was playing around with the piano when he was writing "Yesterday." It became "Da-da-da dadadadadada scrambled eggs." Anyway, I was in there one day practicing theory with the old medieval song "Golden Slumbers." I remember Paul saying, "You're butchering that bloody song—what are you trying to do in there?" I told him I was practicing my lessons. He said, "Well, let's have a look." He sat beside me on the bench and we were both staring at the music, and it might as well have been Chinese. We're both looking at these dots and neither of us could read music. Anyway, we ended up learning to play it together and he said, "That's nice, what's that called?" I said, "Golden Slumbers."

GEOFFREY: This is around the *Paul Is Dead* time—tell me about that. Was it amusing to you?

RUTH: Not at all.

ANGIE: Paul was horrified. They went up to Scotland to get away from it. It was pretty sick.

GEOFFREY: What did he say about it?

ANGIE: He thought it was absolutely sick, weird. I mean why would somebody start a rumor like this? It shows you how people latch onto anything and everything even remotely connected with the Beatles, including a lot of sickos. They're like the Star Trek Trekkies. They literally live, breathe, eat, and sleep the Beatles. *Paul Is Dead*—it's nuts. I know he was very distressed by it. It grew to such ridiculous proportions. It petered out in about five days. I believe the repercussions for Paul emotionally were pretty great.

• • •

GEOFFREY: What can you say about the Beatles' breaking up.

ANGIE: It was pretty grim. When they had that court case and Paul went to sue the other Beatles, it distressed Jim to such an extent he broke out in shingles. We only knew what we read in the press. Jim would speak to Paul occasionally and he was pretty uptight and didn't want to talk about it. It was like a particularly messy divorce, a lot of recriminations and a lot of mudslinging.

CHAPTER NINE

Don't Allow the Day/ The Early Years

John "Duff" Lowe*
SELECTED QUOTATIONS
....
West Derby, February 21, 1993

Paul and I didn't know each other until our forms coincided and we started to do some common subjects together, like music. When we were about ten, we both applied to join the Cathedral choir. They hold auditions every six months and my parents put me back in again and I got in. Paul said he didn't want to go in anyway, so he made his voice crack during the audition. I don't think he ever tried again. So when we were about fifteen, Paul asked me if I wanted to play in the band. I'd been playing the piano since about six. I didn't know what the format of the band was. I didn't know who John Lennon was. This was during a break, I think, walking across the schoolyard. He just said he had a band called the Quarrymen and would I like to play in it. I think, in fact, they were re-grouping because it had been a skiffle group and it didn't just change in one week from skiffle to rock. The skiffle stopped and they rebuilt it, as it were. We started practicing on Sunday afternoons at Paul's house in Allerton. It was on the opposite side of town to me, so I used to get the bus over there. Whereas George, John and Paul all lived in the same area. We would practice with Paul's father sitting at the side of the piano and he would wave his hand at me if we were getting too loud. Because the house was in a terrace, he was worried about the noise and kept us well down. Of course; there was no amplification, so the piano could drown everything out if it was played too loud. I'm not sure if John was too fussy about having a piano. We used to go out gigging, which was generally the following Saturday. I can't remember gigging on a weekday.

I can remember a gig at the Woolton Hall, we played in the interval. All these places had jazz bands on because that was the thing then. Rock'n'roll was just coming in so we just used to get the interval spot. We'd get about a half an hour. On this particular occasion John had some sort of throat infection. But the teds must have known he could sing, especially the more raucous Little Richard things. John was saying, "I can't," but they wouldn't take no for an answer, so we had to do it. Somehow we got through it. I remember one of them came up to me and said, "That was great vamping on the piano." I think that was the only time the piano was picked out for special mention. Of course, Jerry Lee Lewis was very popular and the piano was becoming more credible as part of a band. It's well-documented that Paul says he asked me to join because I could play the

---

* John"Duff" Lowe was an original member of John Lennon's group, the Quarrymen, an early incarnation of the Beatles. (The Quarrymen were John Lennon's first school boy group.)

arpeggio at the start of "Mean Woman Blues." I mean, anyone could play an arpeggio, but that's what he said.

● ● ●

I remember we used to get good acoustics in [Julia Lennon's] bathroom. I remember it vaguely now you've reminded me. I can remember now at the Institute George and Paul and I used to play in the music room. We did little gigs at the end of term. I read in Ross Benson's biography of Paul that we did it to cheer up the guys who hadn't done well in the O Level exams. I don't remember doing it for that particular reason though. I also remember we used to go to the working men's clubs . . . I think on Sunday afternoon. We wouldn't practice; we'd arrange to meet. Certainly we went to a couple in Walton near to Everton Football Ground. It would be a showcase. You'd have ten to fifteen minutes to do some numbers. Paul said to me in 1981, "Do you remember at this club there was a guy eatin' glass?" I'd forgotten that, but yes, there were some strange acts and yes, guys eating glass were popular on the clubs. I suppose we were a bit of a strange act as we were a rock'n'roll band and at the time there weren't many around."

● ● ●

The Quarrymen didn't do a lot of gigs. I remember doing a school hall somewhere; there was a stage and the piano was stuck down the side of the hall. So I was stuck down the side of the hall because there was no way we could get the piano on the stage. My parents never knew I was in the Quarrymen. It's only the last ten years they've known anything about it. I wasn't allowed to have a pair of jeans, so John Lennon used to lend me a pair. I'd put them on at home under my other clothes and nip off out, as they thought, to the cinema. If it got very late, I had problems because I'd miss the last bus back. I remember on one occasion leaving and only John and Paul were left. They carried on with the Everly Brothers' "Devoted to You." It wasn't so much that you had to be in early, but public transport dictated you couldn't be out late. That was probably one of the reasons why I eventually started to think I couldn't be bothered. You'll probably find that most people working in bands lived close to each other. They weren't dotted all over the place.

Bob Wooler*
INTERVIEW
· · · · · · · · · ·
Liverpool, 1983

GEOFFREY: When did you first meet the Beatles?

BOB WOOLER: At the bus stop in Penny Lane, I met George and Paul. Harrison was going from Gaston to Speke. He lived in Speke. That was at 8:59. And they said, "We're in a group." Gerry and the Pacemakers were off, and I met the Beatles. I didn't know them, really. But I knew their drummer Tommy Moore. He used to work at Gosendox on the railway with me, and he was very keen on drumming.

GEOFFREY: Is he still around?

BOB: He is dead now. I went to his funeral in 1980. He was older than the Beatles. He suffered through various Beatlizations in Scotland at the hands of Lennon and McCartney. My fourth meeting with them was in the Jackaranda Club in December 1960. They explained to me that they had been to Hamburg and this is where they first began to happen. At the time I was working with a local promoter by the name of Brian Kelly and I said, "Why not give the Beatles a half-hour spot at the Litherland Town Hall as an extra?" I asked Kelly for eight pounds and, of course, he collapsed. He said, "Four pounds." So I said, "There are five Beatles, actually." Neil Aspinall was a kind of Beatle. He drove them around, but he didn't go on stage and play. So there were actually six Beatles. So, of course, four pounds was a ridiculous sum—it's not even a pound per man. Anyway, after a lot of hoggy-boggy, it became six pounds. Now because I as handling that particular show I controlled the order of the groups at the venue. I was able to give them a very good spot, not too early and not too late. The reason why a late spot is bad, is because people are starting to go home. Anyway, I placed them right in the middle. Of course, they transfixed the audience, and that was the beginning of what was later to become known as Beatlemania.

GEOFFREY: You were actually their first manager, weren't you?

BOB: I have never passed myself off as their manager, but I was very close to the Beatles throughout 1961 and was certainly their advisor.

GEOFFREY: What kind of advice would they come looking for?

---

* Bob Wooler was the Beatles' first unofficial manager, mentor, friend, and compere at the Cavern Club in Liverpool. Since that time he has been a great friend to all Beatle People everywhere.

Bob: For instance, if you had met them, they would come to me and say, "Well, what do you think of him?" They would consult with me about the order in which they appeared on stage.

Geoffrey: What made you get involved with them?

Bob: Actually, I wrote an article about them in August of 1961, a couple of years before thy exploded in your country. I assessed what they meant to the local scene, because after all, nobody else wanted to know. London didn't want to know. Your country didn't want to know. You were still digging your Fabians and Frankie Avalons. But *we* had the scene and this group more than any other, was playing havoc with the emotions of the audiences. The Beatles were clearly calling the tune. Of course, it wasn't exactly their tune, as McCartney and Lennon weren't yet composing at this stage. They were still doing cover versions, but unlike other groups, they were choosing the more obscure B sides of their R&B favorites.

Geoffrey: Who do you think came across the strongest to the audience?

Bob: That would be a bit unfair, I'm not able to speak for the audience. I did say in an article I wrote, however, that they appealed to both sexes, which they did.

Geoffrey: Tell me about their first appearances at the Cavern.

Bob: Well, originally I joined the Cavern for their lunchtime sessions and I'd been onto the owner Ray McFall about this group, the Beatles. I was really rooting for them. I said to him, "Furthermore, they are able to play lunchtimes because they don't work, you see." Unfortunately, he wasn't a very easy person to get through to. Now if you think I am sort of prim and proper, you should meet Ray! He really is the typical English gentleman. You wouldn't expect to find a person like Ray getting involved in the pop scene. Eventually, though, he agreed, and they played their first lunchtime session for the whopping sum of six pounds so they could give Neil something. They always regarded him as part of group. That's why they took him to Apple with them.

Geoffrey: What was Stuart like?

Bob: I did talk with him, though I only knew him a short time because they all went back to Hamburg in April 1961. Of all of the Beatles, Stuart Sutcliffe and I used to relate. We used to talk, not just rock'n'roll, but about films, books, and paintings. He was quite a painter. Art was really much closer to his heart than the guitar.

Geoffrey: What was his relationship with John Lennon?

Bob: Stuart wasn't a meek and mild person by any stretch. He could be quite verbally aggressive. He used to stick up for himself because John used to have a go at him when he was in the mood, as did Paul. They used to shut him down quite often. Of course, it wasn't really a falling out. It was simply an establishment of position, of pecking order.

GEOFFREY: What was their persona when you encountered them after Stuart died?

BOB: A lot of things happened to them because Epstein was with them and lots of glowing things were going to happen to them, so in a way, they were rather full of that. In other words, they had rather got out of their emotional feelings for Stuart by then when I next saw them.

GEOFFREY: They had the ability to rather easily leave people behind, didn't they? They were a bit cold, weren't they?

BOB: Oh, yes.

GEOFFREY: That was probably necessary for them in making it.

BOB: Being ruthless, you mean?

GEOFFREY: Did you feel they were ruthless?

BOB: No more than other people in show business. I have thought about this. The Beatles don't ever entirely forget a person. But they assess the *value* of that person and they think, "Well, what can that person contribute now?"

GEOFFREY: Mike McCartney has said their attitude was, "What's in it for me?"

BOB: When they are surrounded by all this wealth?

GEOFFREY: Perhaps that becomes an end unto itself.

BOB: Well, money attracts more money, doesn't it?

GEOFFREY: How did the Beatles leave Liverpool?

BOB: They would be coming and going between Liverpool and London throughout 1963. They had been away on tours around the country. Therefore, they disappeared from our vision outside the Cavern. They didn't suddenly announce, "We're leaving tomorrow, folks," there is a tearful farewell at Lamb Street Station. Hollywood would do it that way, but not the Beatles. They actually departed lock, stock, and barrel from Liverpool at the end of 1963, when Epstein set up shop in London where all the publishers and television people are. He was, of course, preparing for the Fab sixties invasion.

GEOFFREY: When they first hit in America, was it a surprise to you?

BOB: Well, your country was the ultimate, the Shangri-la for any pop musicians. They had been extremely big in this country, nationally. Therefore, if you take it in a logical progression, fantastically big, locally, even bigger nationally, headline news and all that. They would rather sweat the significance of Kennedy's death in this country, which to you is tremendously important and there is no question about it, but the same year, this country was becoming *Beatlized*, generally. Even the older people talked guitars and strings, most of which was rubbish because they got it wrong. Nevertheless, you wouldn't find these people talking this way a year before, so they were fantastically big in 1963. It seemed a logical step, but I had no idea that you would be swept off your feet. After all, they played venues in this country which had only a couple thousand capacity, and in the States it was sixty-five thousand, or something. When the press was taken away, for a moment, they were shit scared, but they were driven because they knew the show must go on. Of course, Lennon complained and Harrison was always concerned about his guitar breaking and McCartney used to say, "Just go through the motions," and that is all they did. They were very much an *image* both on record and in concert.

GEOFFREY: An image which has prevailed for over twenty years.

BOB: A fantastic image.

GEOFFREY: How long do you think it will go on?

BOB: They had a Beatles day here awhile ago and I was asked the exact question. I said, "I never cease to be amazed at the number of books, films, videos, and all the rest of it. How long is this going on for? It's twenty-five years since the Beatles first exploded on the universe. So you tell me, Beatle fans." And one of them said, "Why, forever," and that was good enough for me. Of course, we know that nothing is forever.

GEOFFREY: How did you first hear the news that John Lennon was murdered?

BOB: I was, perhaps, that last person in Liverpool to hear of his death. I had a bad cold and I didn't get up that day. I switched on the twelve o'clock news on the radio, and, of course, it was the first thing they mentioned. He died about eleven o'clock.

GEOFFREY: 10:49 actually.

BOB: They tried to contact me.

GEOFFREY: Who?

BOB: Various radio stations to get me on the air, but I was unavailable. You know how debilitating a cold can be.

GEOFFREY: How did you feel when you first heard about it?

BOB: Devastated. So much so, that despite the way I felt, I prepared myself. I came into town. It was Bob Cook at the Grapes Pub who said, "Where on earth have you been? I've been inundated. All the television have been at the pub asking for you."

GEOFFREY: What have we as a people lost by John's passing?

BOB: When the Beatles broke up in 1970, they went their separate ways. McCartney and Lennon stayed up there doing their own thing. They were basically fine with each other. I've always felt that Lennon's songs were far better than McCartney's. There was much more to his songs than what Paul achieved. They just appealed to me more. Some of the songs Paul did were just ordinary sounds, whereas John Lennon, like for instance, the melody of "Jealous Guy," were marvelous. I said to a press guy in the *Daily Post,* "At the end of this century they will choose a hundred people who were part of the twentieth century like Einstein, Roosevelt, Churchill, or Hitler," and so I said, "You can rest assured John Lennon will be one of them." And he said, "Do you really think so? You'd be saying the same thing about George Harrison and Paul McCartney." I said, "Well, naturally if you're going to include Lennon, you must mention McCartney and the other Beatles." But it's Lennon, really, because he was a very considerable figure, especially when he met Yoko Ono. I don't know how great a power behind the throne she was. I did a tribute to John after his death. I called him a "shooting star" when he was shot. There are millions of stars in the sky, and there are even millions more you will never see, and this is like the human race. You do, however, see a shooting star. It does make its presence known. It's very brief, but then life is, too. I set it to the tune of the New World Symphony. It's very brief, it goes: "Shooting star, shooting star is a teardrop in the sky. You struck sparks, your name will not die."

CHAPTER TEN

I Only Want What I Can Get/ Applegate

George Martin*
INTERVIEW
• • • • • • • • • • •
London, October 31, 1995

QUESTION: The June 1, 1966, session for *Yellow Submarine* was most unusual, wasn't it? The production needed sound effects. It was the trap room in Studio Two that gave *Yellow Submarine* its unique seagoing flavor. Could you give us a little history on the contents of the trap room and what was used to enliven Ringo's vocals?

GEORGE MARTIN: It all sounds very technical, but actually it was a very bootlace affair. In those days Abbey Road was a pretty primitive studio by today's standards. Long before the Beatles came along I had worked on spoken-word and comedy records, in particular Peter Sellers and Spike Mulligan, *Beyond the Fringe*, as well as people like Peter Cook and Dudley Moore and so on. So I was quite used to using sound effects. In those days there were no such thing as samplers, digital effects, or even tape cassettes. If you used recorded effects they generally came off discs, so we tried to make our own. We used all sorts of things like roller skates to make train noises over rails. I remember once trying to effect the sound of someone having their head chopped off—I used a cabbage, which was very effective. Studio Two was underneath the stairs and generally filled with percussion instruments, like you find in the kitchen of a symphony. There were tambourines, gongs and that kind of thing. Even a cupboard that opened and shut, so you could get the noise of a door opening and shutting. It was really like a junkyard, or an antique shop. We used to make up our effects as we went along. For *Yellow Submarine* we used chains and, of course, bowls of water with straws to simulate the effect of a sub surfacing. It was nice because we were all being inventive—it was fun, like a party really, good fun.

QUESTION: I understand that the June 1, 1966, session for *Yellow Submarine* had numerous friends and musicians that contributed. I believe it ran about twelve hours that day. Could you mention a few names of the people who joined in that production?

GEORGE: I honestly can't remember. I do remember a lot of people did come in—you'd probably know better than I.

QUESTION: Probably some of the Rolling Stones and I think Brian Jones.

GEORGE: Yeah, I remember the Stones came down.

---

* George Martin was the Beatles' charismatic record producer. Today he runs Air Studios, a successful recording facility in Central London.

QUESTION: Your contribution to the *Yellow Submarine* LP was an entire side of music you composed using a forty-one-piece orchestra. It is this music I'm most interested in; but first let's talk about the movie. What kind of outline were you provided and how did you sync your pieces to what was transpiring in the film?

GEORGE: When the project was first mentioned the Beatles didn't like the idea and didn't want any part of it at all. When Brian [Epstein]* committed them to the picture, it was a part of a deal he did with United Artists. He'd done it so they'd provide new songs. But they said, "We're not going to write any decent songs, we'll give them the rejects." I was asked to do the score by the director, a charming Canadian, a really nice guy, George Dunning was his name—he's dead now, unfortunately. The people on the ground, who actually did the production in England, were headed up by John Kurtz, and curiously, I'm talking to you from Air Studios in London and downstairs John Kurtz is working. Dunning got me in saying, "Look, we're going to need all the help we can from you because we haven't much time"—we had a year, which isn't much time for a full-length animation. He said, "We're going to give you all of our sketches, our storyboards, and as soon as we're anywhere near finishing a reel I'll give you what we have and let you decide what you want to write for a score." I said, "Don't you want to give me any direction?" He said, "No, be as imaginative as you can, do what you want—it's going to be complete pop art." We did it that way because we had such little time. We didn't have the luxury of finishing the film and then me adding the score over it. I'd have reel four one week and reel seven the next and then reel six, and so on. I knew which reel was which—I had my script. I wrote what came out of my head, that's what it amounted to. We collected all the scores together, recorded and hoped for the best. It seemed to turn out okay.

QUESTION: About the music you composed—the first selection is called "Pepperland." It conveys a kind of uplifting and a longing—how was this achieved?

GEORGE: It was working strictly with the film where you had this lovely land of brightness and color and butterflies flittering around. It was that kind of image, a dream world, really. It was slightly old-fashioned—everyone was wearing dresses that didn't seem very contemporary—but that fitted the dream, too. So, I felt it needed a classical approach. I felt I must convey a theme that was lilting, light, but something classically orchestrated with a happy feeling at the end of it.

QUESTION: Then there is the "Sea of Holes" and the "Sea of Time," which is the longest and starts with East-Indian music.

GEORGE: Well, yes, that was really George Harrison putting his little aura on it. George and I get on very well, and certainly he is the reason Indian music was ever

---

* Brian Epstein managed the Beatles from their climb to stardom in Liverpool until his death in 1967.

featured in the Beatles. Whenever you'd see George in *Yellow Submarine,* you'd hear Indian music. So, I used a tambura drone and composed my strings with bending notes that sound like the delruba. I tried to convey the effect of Indian music.

QUESTION: You'd already done some previous work with Indian musicians—is that right?

GEORGE: Yes, that's right. Even before I'd met George I'd been doing some Indian work. Again, going back to Peter Sellers, one of the tracks I did with him was a spoof with him singing "Wouldn't It Be Loverly" from *My Fair Lady* as an Indian doctor. He did the accent and it was really quite funny. To do that I used a group of Indian musicians, tambura, tabla, sitar, and added classical Western instruments to them. So, I'd got used to using Indian musicians long before George came along.

QUESTION: Do I detect some use of backwards music in that piece?

GEORGE: Well, I certainly used backwards music in "Sea of Monsters," but I don't remember about "Sea of Time"—I might have. I tended to do all sorts of weird things just to get effects. In "Sea of Monsters," the backward noises were very useful because it fit the vacuum monster that sucked up things from the sea floor. It ends with the monster sucking himself up from the corner of the screen. I thought it needed a "sucking up" sound. I always thought that backwards sounds were funny "sucking up" kind of noises. When you have a drum cymbal, for example, backwards it becomes kind of "schooomp." It almost sounds like someone inhaling. So I thought I could do that with a whole orchestra. I wrote a whole section that lasts about three minutes. Of course, to record it you've got to turn your film round back to front and record the music back to front and play it back the other way. What actually happened when we recorded it with a large orchestra in the studio as I saw the film was that in order to turn it back to front it also turned out being upsidedown. That never occurred to me, so I was watching an upside-down film at the same time. The engineer I used had a great sense of humor. At the end of the tape he didn't switch the red light off immediately and I noticed him saying something into the microphone. It turned out that he had taken the time to figure out a backwards bit which, when played forward, was something like "Yellow Submarine," take three."

QUESTION: There is a classical section ending with drums and a laughing sound—can you identify that?

GEORGE: Oh, yes—in England we used to have a popular television advert for Hamlet Cigars which used a very famous Bach section which I religiously copied because the monster, in particular, was smoking a cigar which explodes. So I used this Bach piece when the cigar exploded, the drums and the laughing sound, as a gag, really.

QUESTION: "March of the Meanies" achieves a great military sound. How did you achieve that?

GEORGE: I was using all the brass instruments in the orchestra, tubas and trombones. I gave a very staccato feel to the strings; a sort of choppy beat to it, not unlike what Hitchcock's Bernard Herrmann used to do when he used to score for strings, or what I did in "Eleanor Rigby" to a certain extent. The brass gives a certain sinister feel to it all. There are also notes written on the score of the piano for the piano player to hold his sustaining pedal and crop the strings of his piano with a metal bar, which makes some pretty nasty noises, too. I was trying to convey the wasteland that had been left after the war—stark scenery, no birds, no trees, no leaves, nothing living and thus emptiness. In scoring it I was trying to give that empty, devastating effect—the feeling of hopelessness. Music for me is like painting a picture. When putting sound to tape, you're effectively using the palette of color your orchestra gives you to paint that picture.

QUESTION: In your book, *With a Little Help from My Friends*, you relate a story in which one day Paul McCartney came to you and said, "I've been listening to Beethoven and I've just sussed it out. You know the beginning of the fifth symphony—there is only unison, there are no chords. Everybody's playing the same notes—what a great sound!" "Of course, it is!" you rejoined, "the whole orchestra speaks with one voice, that's the genius." Were you actually making your whole orchestra speak with one voice in the end of *Yellow Submarine*?

GEORGE: It was a triumphant end and everyone was happy again. And "Yellow Submarine" was a good tune to blare out. In fact, they weren't all playing the same notes, because there are chords in it. It was interesting Paul didn't realize you didn't have to have a whole lot of different notes with an orchestra. If you get them all playing the same notes, it's pretty effective.

QUESTION: In your mind, is *Yellow Submarine* no more than an adventure of four lads restoring hope, love, and beauty to a defiled, overrun utopia, or does it still have meaning for the young today?

GEORGE: I think it does! One of the nice things about the *Yellow Submarine* movie is that people seem to enjoy watching it from each generation. In a way, it's like the Beatles themselves. The Beatles always find an audience in each generation. I think it fits into that category—it's kind of timeless. It is good and evil, and I'm a believer in good and a great believer in hope for people that goodness will prevail.

QUESTION: An interesting point is that nobody dies in the movie. . . .

GEORGE: I know, not even a Blue Meanie.

QUESTION: I'd like you to expound on a point in your book, *With a Little Help from My Friends*, in which you say that the *Sgt. Pepper* album spoke for the sixties.

GEORGE: I think that was one of the successes of *Sgt. Pepper*, it was enormously timely. The young people in the sixties identified with it immediately, because the youth had years of repression and felt that after the war everything was stale with so many rules and regulations. So for the first time in the sixties, young people were saying, "Hey, hold on! We want to live a bit. We want color in our lives. We don't want to dress the way our fathers did." I think *Sgt. Pepper* gave them an opening, along with other things like the Mary Quant spirit and the Carnaby Street era. People were realizing they had their lives in their hands. *Sgt. Pepper* led the way by showing you didn't have to conform all the time—you could be adventurous and successful. It didn't convey the message that many people misinterpreted it as—the way to do this was drugs. A lot of people said that *Pepper* was a drug album. It wasn't for me, I can tell you that. If it was, I can assure you it wouldn't have been made like it was.

QUESTION: The entire planet is standing by for the *Beatles Anthology*. We are especially eager to hear the first new Beatles recordings in twenty-five years, "Free as a Bird" and "Real Love." Can you tell us how this came about?

GEORGE: Paul had gone to New York for the Rock'n'Roll Hall of Fame induction of John Lennon, met up with Yoko, and they got on fine. Paul and Yoko have had their differences in the past and it seemed this particular visit cemented their relationship. During the course of that weekend Yoko said that John had been working on a few songs before he died and she played him some of them on tape. "Free as a Bird" was the first thing he thought was really pretty good. It wasn't finished. The main part was there, but a lot of the words weren't. Yoko said, "If you could do anything with it, I'd be grateful." So Paul came back to England and talked to George and Ringo. I spoke to him about it, too. He said we might be able to use this tape. The tape Yoko had given him was just a straight demo John had done by literally putting a cassette recorder on top of a piano and playing. So the technical quality wasn't very good. We have the best engineers here and Paul was able to filter out a bit of the piano, but not much and also get it in time because John's demo was all over the place. Then they set out to overdub their playing. They did it at Paul's studio—I wasn't asked to join them because it wasn't really necessary. To be honest, I wasn't all that keen on doing it. I was a little uneasy. I wasn't too keen on Natalie Cole singing with her father, and I wasn't sure how this would work out. George and Ringo joined Paul for a whole week and stayed in a nearby hotel. I heard the result and was knocked out. I thought it was absolutely super. Of course, Ringo, Paul, and George laid down a beautiful track, needless to say. George does a great guitar solo, and the voices George and Paul added to it and the lyrics make it a complete whole. When I heard it I said to Paul, "This is what you would have made if John had been alive." Paul justified it by saying, "You know, George, this is the only way the Beatles can ever make any more records."

Derek Taylor*
INTERVIEW
• • • • • • • • • •
London, November 6, 1995

QUESTION: During the late 1960s consciousness was focused on putting an end to all wars, particularly those in Southeast Asia. Fortunately, the musicians of that era worked unanimously toward world peace. How would you evaluate the consciousness of the nineties?

DEREK TAYLOR: The consciousness of the nineties is directed largely to people doing the very best they can for themselves, lining their own pockets, paying hardly any tax and generally being selfish. Of course there are vast exceptions to the rule, but this is certainly not the sixties or seventies. Students now are not like students then. There has been quite a move towards selfishness. I think it began with the drift toward the "Me Generation." This is not unusual—people have been like this for most of history—but in the sixties we did have a window where we believed the world could be a much, much nicer place.

QUESTION: I thought it would last much longer than it did.

DEREK: Well, it just shows you how starry-eyed and foolish we were—however, I'm not a cynic.

QUESTION: Why do you believe the film, *Yellow Submarine* was so successful, even with such minimal input from the Beatles?

DEREK: I always saw *Yellow Submarine* as a symbol for a vessel that would take us all to safety. The overall message of the movie is that good can prevail over evil, which is quite an old one. There is enormous hope, reassurance, color, and vitality in the movie. Also, there is a very clear delineation between the naughty and nice people, the Blue Meanies and our heroes. It ends on a very high note and makes people feel extremely good and full of energy.

QUESTION: Do you remember seeing the film for the first time?

DEREK: Yes, I do. I remember thinking it was terrific. It was quite coolly received by the English public and very warmly received in the United States.

QUESTION: How was it received by the Beatles?

DEREK: Well, they liked it. There was a hippie, psychedelic ethic in *Yellow Submarine* that may have seemed, by mid-'68, a little passé. However, it's

---

* Derek Taylor was the Beatles' capable press officer, who rose to prominence during the group's heady Apple days. Mr. Taylor passed away recently following a long battle with cancer.

acknowledged now by the band, as far as I know, to have been a worthy effort—Ringo certainly liked it very much. At the time it came out, there was so much going on. Apple was getting very busy, taking on too much in an endeavor to help people get recording contracts or see their paintings hung. We were trying to get books and poems published, music recorded—all the promises that were made, we were trying to fulfill. By the summer of 1968 when *Yellow Submarine* came out, there were great stresses and strains around the Beatles and Apple that made it very difficult to concentrate on *Yellow Submarine*. It was a time of great office stress. Stress in the Apple offices was quite extreme because of the working hours and calls coming in and the number of callers to the building. In our eternal world "Yellow Submarine" suffered from a lack of attention—our response suffered from inattention. But it's a wonderful piece of work and still looks great today. It will live forever—there's no doubt about that. *Yellow Submarine* is a real good piece.

QUESTION: What can you tell us about the *Beatles Anthology*?

DEREK: I didn't go to the sessions. I tend not to go to recording sessions because there isn't much to do for people who are not recording. What happened was that there was a feeling around 1993 that they should record linking music for sections of the *Anthology*. The three of them considered this at some length, and there is no doubt when they get together they can pick up the instruments and get to it. All of that remains, all of that relationship and many other aspects of their relationships, have been renewed as well. But the obvious missing element was John—obviously there could never be Beatle music in his absence. Somewhere around the end of 1993, Yoko offered two tracks with John on piano—there is even talk of a third. They went to Paul's studio with Jeff Lynne and considered how best to do it. John was at the piano and the others were at the studio with their instruments and their old Beatles feeling and now they were four, albeit with John only on tape. They did what he would have wanted them to if he had gone on holiday and left them with this cassette and said, "Well, I'm off now. Finish this up—it's a nice tune with nice words. I trust you to do what you think best for it"—and that's what they did. It's truly a great Beatles record of today and, of course, it will be number one.

Alistair Taylor*
INTERVIEW
• • • • • • • • • •
New York, September 1984

GEOFFREY: How did you first come in contact with Brian Epstein and the Beatles?

ALISTAIR TAYLOR: I had a very boring job in an office when I saw an advertisement for a shop assistant at NEMS which I applied for—had an interview with Brian, and he offered me a job as his personal assistant. That was long before the Beatles—we'd never heard of them. This guy Raymond Jones came in and asked us to get this record called "My Bonnie," which we did from Germany.

GEOFFREY: Were you there when he came in?

ALISTAIR: Oh, yes, I was there every day. We got a box of twenty-five, then another twenty-five and they just kept selling as fast as we could import them. Then a few weeks later we went down to meet this group at the Cavern, or rather to hear them. So we just took it from there.

GEOFFREY: What was your initial reaction to the personalities of the Beatles? Did they seem very ordinary?

ALISTAIR: No, they were sensational. I hated pop music at the time—I was into jazz and the classics. I still am, really, but they were just so fantastic. Not necessarily musically—as a matter of fact, they were bloody awful as musicians, then anyway.

GEOFFREY: So we couldn't have gone to Woolton back then and found four other guys who had the same buzz?

ALISTAIR: Liverpool was full of guys like that at the time, but the Beatles had something else. Charisma—I call it "Ingredient" I don't know what it is, but they certainly had it!

GEOFFREY: Was Brian very enthusiastic about his discovery of the Beatles? Playing at managing a pop group was a total departure for Brian. It must have changed his whole life.

ALISTAIR: Yes—a lot has been said about how he went around saying they were going to be bigger than Elvis. But I don't remember it being as blatant as that.

---

* Alistair Taylor was with the Beatles from almost the very beginning in Liverpool and stayed with them through their Apple days in London. He has since published both a book and audio tape of his adventures.

As a matter of fact, when we went for lunch that same day, we sat and talked about what we should do. I think it was something just new and fun.

GEOFFREY: Was it a toy for him?

ALISTAIR: A little, perhaps.

GEOFFREY: Queenie said recently that if Brian were alive now he wouldn't have been as tortured a soul as he was, because now everyone's gay so it's no big deal.

ALISTAIR: Right. He was a very complex man, and I think there's far more to it than his just being gay. He wasn't happy at that. He tried very hard *not* to be.

GEOFFREY: He had a girlfriend for awhile.

ALISTAIR: Yeah, he did, more than one. You know, twice I had a phone call from him saying goodbye, he was committing suicide. I've often said in many ways I would have been happier if he had.

GEOFFREY: You don't think he did?

ALISTAIR: No. I know he didn't. Accidental death. End of quote. I mean I was *there* behind the doctor, by thirty seconds. The times I've been asked the question, "Why did he commit suicide?" Well, I want someone to tell me where it says he committed suicide. The verdict by the coroner was accidental death. The whole investigation indicated accidental death. Remember, there were only two people in that room—the doctor and myself, right? I've never said it was suicide. I've heard stories there was a note found, but I didn't find it.

GEOFFREY: What about when the Beatles changed their public persona from lovable moptops to the psychedelic lords of London? We know they turned on long before the public ever knew about it. I just met a guy who said Lennon used to chop up every goddamn thing he could find in a little mortar and pestle and snort it up.

ALISTAIR: Oh yeah. He probably did. Look, if you weren't there, you can't begin to understand the pressure and their way of life. I don't give a damn how many books you've read or how many people you interview, I can't convey what it is like. I mean, I was close to them and even *I* was under pressure, and I was not remotely in their league. It was unbearable and they just had to do *something*. Imagine—you can't walk down the street, you can't go out in a car, you can't do *anything* without being torn to shreds, day in, day out, night in, night out. In the early days, possibly even before I knew them, I know they were on pills, but that was just youngsters experimenting. We've all done it, but the real development, I think, came as an escape. It was fun. They could afford it and they mixed with people that said, "Hey, try this." I mean, Lennon spent three weeks trying to persuade me to go on a trip, but I never did. But John and Derek would spend hours trying to persuade me. "We'll be with you—it's great." It was all done in fun, really.

Certain people have come out with that statement that John Lennon was high every single day of the sixties! Well, when in the hell did he find time to write songs, make movies, go on tour, do interviews, television shows, write books?

GEOFFREY: There was a poster issued by Apple playing all these instruments, like a one-man band. What was it all about?

ALISTAIR: That was Paul's idea. McCartney was very much the man with the ideas. We had just set Apple Corp up and we wanted to get tapes and projects in from unknown people. You know, I'm the guy who actually said to them one day, "Look, this is stupid. We cannot manage this business!" Let me tell you something. One Sunday we were sitting in Hilly House, Brian's private office, having an Apple meeting. It was just the Boys, myself, and Neil, and suddenly they just picked up the phone and said, "Hey, let's get ahold of Derek!" And they rang Derek Taylor—it was when he was with the Beach Boys. They said, "Pack your bags and come on over." Well, I said, "What's he going to do?" "Oh, ah, we don't know. We'll find him something." Later, when Derek arrived, he said, "Okay, let's set some kind of business up." There was talk about doing one of those dispatch express rider delivery things. They've accused everybody of ripping them off, but they just gave carte blanche to everyone. People were buying genuine antique desks for their offices—I mean, really! Ron Kass had this incredible all-white office which cost the earth—I mean, it was unbelievable! Peter Asher had real old masters hanging on the wall of his office. It was, "The Beatles have plenty of money, so let's spend," you know? We had this crazy idea of the cordon bleu chefs in residence. I went along with it very much. I think it was probably my idea, because here we were entertaining people spending a lot of money in restaurants and I said, "Look, this is much more sensible. Here we've got this beautiful house on Savile Row—let's have our own cooks!" They were two girls out of the cordon bleu school, but it was never used for that. We *still* took people out to lunch, and the only people that dined at Apple were Peter Brown and Neil Aspinall, who were having eight-course lunches with expensive wine. There was this huge metal cabinet full of vintage wine and champagne. You'd go in and there were just them, no visitors. Great stuff!

GEOFFREY: So what about this wonderful idea the Beatles had about saving the world with Apple and giving all the young artists a break? What happened when you started getting billions of audition tapes by post?

ALISTAIR: They collected dust in the corner. We just couldn't cope. Yes, we tried. Obviously we got hold of a few people—Billy Preston, James Taylor, Mary Hopkin, my darling Mary. The kids were sending tapes and sheet music in. You'd come in the morning and switch on the answering machine and get some guy auditioning on the tape. We used to send a lot of them around to the Grade Organization.

GEOFFREY: Was there a time when you said, "Hey, I guess we're not going to save the world with Apple?"

ALISTAIR: It was never meant to save the world! Let's put things into perspective, right? Apple was set up purely as a tax-saving project. Instead of paying nineteen and six on the pound, we paid only sixteen shillings. In the beginning when there was an executive board at Apple, the Boys and Brian didn't want to know. It was Clive Epstein, myself, Geoffrey Ellis, a solicitor, and an accountant, and the idea was we would just quietly announce to the tax authorities that we would be opening a string of shops. The original idea was greeting cards. Gradually they started drifting in on meetings and Apple Corp evolved from there. Later it was turned into this silly philosophy, admittedly. Even then it was not designed to save the world—the idea was to get rid of the hassle of big business. I mean, why couldn't business be fun and pleasurable?

GEOFFREY: Why do you think the Beatles broke up?

ALISTAIR: They were breaking up from day one. More than once in the early days I had to go off and find George. He'd say, "I'm not doing this," and he'd piss off. I think the pressures got so bad toward the end, I'm astonished they stayed together as long as they did!

GEOFFREY: So how did you feel about the Beatles and the way it all turned out? John was assassinated and they all married ladies from the States.

ALISTAIR: I find it sad. Why should it be considered bad? Aren't we only concerned because they're the Beatles? Isn't it simply life? There's thousands of people walking the streets of New York who would have noticed otherwise? We're only aware of it because it's John, Paul, George, and Ringo.

GEOFFREY: How did you feel when you heard John was killed?

ALISTAIR: Appalling. I heard it on the news at five o'clock in the morning. My wife just yelled—she was next to the radio and she just said, "John's dead," and I knew who she meant straight away. It was just awful.

GEOFFREY: Even if you hadn't seen him in all those years, did you still feel close to him?

ALISTAIR: Oh, yeah. You don't wipe out those years—you don't wipe out a living with a legend. And you don't wipe out being part of it and helping create it. I've tried turning my back on it. You find yourself name-dropping when you've lived with someone like that. I worked twenty-four hours a day, seven days a week with them. When you work for them, you really *work* for them. I went on holidays with them. We were friends—I just wasn't an employee. It was such an important part of our history.

Mukunda Dasa Goswami*
INTERVIEW
•••••••••
Toronto, February 1983

GEOFFREY: How did the Hare Krishna devotees first come to England?

MUKUNDA DAS GOSWAMI: Well, it was a mutual idea between Syamasundar, myself, and Gurudas. We went there back in September of 1968 along with our wives. We didn't know anyone in London, but we had our guru's blessing so it was all right. It wasn't easy though—we spent an entire year just looking for a place to start a temple.

GEOFFREY: Who was your first link to the Beatles?

MUKUNDA: Syamasundar happened to meet George Harrison while we were living in the warehouse on Betterton Street. I think it was in December, or perhaps January—anyway, he was our link. He came down to the temple a month later, and sometime after that we were all invited to his home in Esher†. George had a very nice meal prepared and afterwards we all chanted with him and Billy Preston.‡

GEOFFREY: Can you remember anymore about that first night at George's?

MUKUNDA: Well, it was a very long session. I would say we chanted for somewhere between two and four hours. Billy was playing a very early type of Moog synthesizer, George was playing his guitar, and we were, of course, playing drums and kartals. I remember doing a bit of cooking together that night, and I think George played us a Lenny Bruce record.

GEOFFREY: How did your experiences of the Beatles compare to the popular images of them projected by the media?

MUKUNDA: Well, George was the one we really knew and he actually seemed to fit what we had thought about him prior to our meeting.

GEOFFREY: I'm going to shoot a few names at you and you just give me a line or two on each, okay? Derek Taylor.

MUKUNDA: Very friendly and helpful. Imaginative, creative and kind.

GEOFFREY: Pattie Boyd Harrison.

---

* A sanyassi in the renounced order of life, His Grace Mukunda Dasa Goswami is a long-time friend of the Beatles, in particular, George Harrison. In April of 1996, they traveled to India together on a spiritual pilgrimage.
† Kinfauns, on Claremont Drive in Esher.
‡ Keyboardist Billy Preston played extensively with the Beatles during their final days together.

MUKUNDA: Also a very friendly person. She really seemed to like the devotees a lot. Always very gracious whenever we talked to her.

GEOFFREY: Mal Evans.

MUKUNDA: He played piano on one of our songs, "Prayer to the Spiritual Master." He was playing a drone kind of thing. A nice guy. Happy-go-lucky. Big and tall. Died tragically.

GEOFFREY: Yoko Ono.

MUKUNDA: She seemed to be into a kind of Buddhist-inspired impersonalism but relatively interested in all spiritual matters.

GEOFFREY: Linda McCartney.

MUKUNDA: She once came into the recording studio with Paul while we were working with George, and they both sat down and fiddled with the controls for a few minutes. I think they made some comments on how they thought it should be mixed, as well. She often visits our restaurant "Healthy, Wealthy and Wise" in London. Both Linda and Paul have been strict vegetarians for years now.

GEOFFREY: Neil Aspinall.

MUKUNDA: Neil always seemed like a very competent person who was very helpful to Apple in general and George in particular. When we were recording for Apple, he used to haul us around town to the sessions.

GEOFFREY: Billy Preston.

MUKUNDA: He was a very enthusiastic musician. He liked to sing songs about God. It seemed to me that was his very favorite music. He loved playing on the sessions with us, too. I think he actually played another session with us at Trident Studios in Soho.

GEOFFREY: Overall, did George strike you as sincere in his spiritual yearning?

MUKUNDA: Obviously he was very sincere. He was naturally that way even before he met us. He'd been to India and he used to talk about how he had always thought about God. As far as Pattie went, she was friendly, but didn't particularly exhibit any kind of overt spiritual characteristics.

GEOFFREY: What about drug usage in the Beatles' inner circle at that time?

MUKUNDA: It wasn't something I was intimate with them about. I know George once told me he had visited the hippies in Haight Ashbury and was a bit appalled at the depths of self-destructiveness they seemed to have reached via their drug use. George really seemed to have his head screwed on when it came to drugs and that sort of thing.

GEOFFREY: The Beatles seemed very accessible to almost anyone who wanted to see them back then, right?

MUKUNDA: They put a notice in the paper that they wanted to help other people and not just keep all their money for themselves. They wanted to support the various charities and causes they believed in. Naturally, millions of people came on to them asking everything under the sun, so it was pretty crazy. When we first went up there, I believe we saw Peter Asher* in A&R and told him what we wanted to do. We needed to get a building and needed a cosigner for the lease. In London it's not that easy to go out and rent something. They want to know who's behind you and of course we didn't have very much money. So we asked if Apple would do it, since they were publicizing the fact that they wanted to help charities. Asher immediately said, "Well, as far as I'm concerned, I can't do anything about it, but I'll talk to George." So that was our first encounter with him—a very nice meeting. When we did finally meet George, he offered to help. I would say Apple was a very happening place at that time.

GEOFFREY: What is Harrison's home Frair Park like?

MUKUNDA: Thirty-eight acres, mostly lawns. There's topiary gardens, sculptured bushes, lots of shrubbery, rhododendrons, lots of big trees, but as I say, mostly rolling green lawn. There's a series of lakes and a waterfall. In the back there's a replica of the Swiss Matterhorn with water coming down. It's very well kept. There's an underground system under the waterfalls, lakes and some caverns from before. A guy by the name of Frank Crisp built the place and he ran it as something like an eighteenth-century amusement park. He brought boulders down from the north country and made it a little wonderland. Then it was taken over by nuns and they covered a lot of the original stuff over. George actually excavated the whole thing after he found the plans to it. He discovered there was a whole waterfall, underground cavern system and a lot of things the nuns didn't want, so they had them covered over. There are also some beautiful rose gardens. In another section, the house is three stories with a fourth story added on. I don't know how you could describe the style, but it's mainly Gothic brick on the outside. It has a look of a Friary with lots of stained glass.

GEOFFREY: Getting back to George and his chanting. Did he chant regularly?

MUKUNDA: He did at one time, but I wasn't really keeping tabs on him. Syamasundar was the one who spent the most time with him and taught him how to chant.

GEOFFREY: How about John Lennon's interactions with the devotees at Tittenhurst?

---

* Late of Peter and Gordon fame.

MUKUNDA: He was pretty much alone with Yoko, keeping to themselves in their house. We were over in the cottages, which were probably servants' quarters at one time for the Cadburys. We weren't seeing much of him. Usually when he was there he was with Yoko somewhere and we didn't see him. We actually had very little contact with him because he had it organized that way.

GEOFFREY: Were you ever in the main house?

MUKUNDA: We were working there for a little while when we first came, stripping the walls down.

GEOFFREY: Tell me about the devotees' participation in John and Yoko's Montreal Bed-in.

MUKUNDA: The devotees were on the record "Give Peace a Chance." They were very well received and John and Yoko seemed to really like their presence. The media noticed them and liked them as well. They gave a real nice flavor to the whole thing.

GEOFFREY: Did Lennon ever chant that you know of?

MUKUNDA: He never chanted the Hare Krishna mantra except when singing with George.

GEOFFREY: How did that property which is now Bhaktivedanta Manor fall into the hands of the devotees?

MUKUNDA: We were looking for a bigger place ever since we got to our first real temple at Bury Place, because Prabhupada said it wasn't big enough. Dhanajaya went to one property after another through estate agents and various contacts, driving around all over the countryside. By that time George had committed himself to helping. They showed him a few other places—at least one place very near Tittenhurst Park which he didn't think was worth the money. It required a lot to fix it up. Then we got the Manor. They approached George and thought it was very good. I think he negotiated the price down quite a bit and proceeded to pay for it. We moved in on March 7, 1973.

GEOFFREY: How about his new wife Olvia and son, Dhani—have they changed him much?

MUKUNDA: He seems much happier than he was before, when he was with Pattie. George and Olvia seem to be very domestic. They really seem to vibrate on the same wavelength.

GEOFFREY: Has George ever told you of his travels in India?

MUKUNDA: He once met Guru Dasa and Srila Prabhupada in Vrndavana. He came with Ravi Shankar by bullock cart, and Guru Das took them around to see our new temple which had just been built. George talked with Yamuna Dasi and seemed very happy to be there. He loved the temple and spent a lot of time talking with Srila Prabhupada.

GEOFFREY: What has Prabhupada said about the Beatles' past lives?

MUKUNDA: There was a letter from Prabhupada which said something about John Lennon being a wealthy businessman in Calcutta in his last life.

GEOFFREY: How involved in the music scene is Harrison today?

MUKUNDA: Not very. I think he has to produce another record from Warner Brothers—I don't know what his plans are after that, however.

GEOFFREY: Anything to say about George's apparent disillusionment with some of the Hare Krishna devotees over the years?

MUKUNDA: George knows the philosophy is greater than anybody's particular frailties, so I wouldn't really call it disillusionment.

GEOFFREY: When and where did the sessions begin for the Radha Krishna Temple album?

MUKUNDA: The "Hare Krishna Mantra" began in EMI's Abbey Road Studios in April of 1969. There was also a practice session at Trident Studios a month or so before that.

GEOFFREY: What studio musicians were on the album, and who played what instruments?

MUKUNDA: Well, John Barnum did some of the string arrangements on "Govinda," and there was also an Indian violinist. Klaus Voorman played bass, I think, and of course, George was on guitar and Billy Preston on keyboards.

GEOFFREY: How was the lead singer chosen?

MUKUNDA: We had an internal audition and it just turned out Yamuna seemed to have the best voice.

GEOFFREY: What promotion was done for the project?

MUKUNDA: They had a big media party, mainly. The press were all bussed from Apple out to Signum Hill to a big tent behind a huge house. We had fabulous prasadam and, of course, all chanted together. George was there—he spoke and we gave out promo copies of the record. I think George went on the radio once for us, and there were these huge posters up in the subways—the usual stuff, you know. We were on "Top of the Pops" twice, which was the best promotion you could ever get. It was the most popular show in the country!

CHAPTER ELEVEN

It's Been A Long Time/
Friends

Brian Jones*
INTERVIEW
●●●●●●●●●●
London, 1968

QUESTION: What do you think of the Beatles' *Sgt. Pepper*?

BRIAN JONES: I think it goes to show what great writers John Lennon and Paul McCartney are. The fact that somebody like Joe Cocker can pick up a song like "With a Little Help from My Friends," which let's face it, nobody thought was very good and do something marvelous with it is great.

QUESTION: Experimental pop music didn't bring much success for your group. Will you return now to the commercial beat, to your old style?

BRIAN: Well, I understand by that question that you're talking about *Their Satanic Majesties Request*. I think everybody should experiment. And we don't consider that we have failed. We haven't gone back on our new album to a very, very funky "crash bang." It doesn't mean that we failed, it just means we don't want to continue along a tangential line. Every now and then we want to go out and experiment.

QUESTION: What do you think your generation has offered to the world?

BRIAN: Our generation is growing up with us and they believe in the same things we do. Our real followers have moved with us, some of those we like most are hippies in New York, but nearly all of them think like us and are questioning some of the basic immoralities which are tolerated in present day society, the war in Vietnam, persecution of homosexuals, illegality of abortion and drug taking. All of these things are immoral. We are making our own statement; others are making more intellectual ones. Our friends are questioning the wisdom of an almost blind acceptance or religion compared with total disregard for reports related to things like unidentified flying objects, which seem more real to me. Conversely, I don't underestimate the power or influence of those unlike me, who do believe in God. We believe there can be no evolution without revolution. I realize there are other inequities; the ratio between affluence and reward for work done is all wrong. I know I earn too much, but I'm still young and there's something spiteful inside of me which makes me want to hold on to what I've got. I believe we are moving on to a new age in ideas and events.

---

* Brian Jones was the founding member of the Rolling Stones. In July of 1969 he was found
  dead in his swimming pool.

"Legs" Larry Smith*
INTERVIEW
• • • • • • • • • •
Hambliden, Oxfordshire, 1983

"Legs" Larry Smith is a wonderfully eccentric person. He dresses crazily, says very amusing things and is completely "over the top." When I met him I thought, "Hello, this guy's funny!"'

GEORGE HARRISON

• • •

GEOFFREY: Tell me about Vivian Stanshall. Where did you meet him?

"LEGS" LARRY SMITH: Mr. "Standstill" was standing still on a traffic island in Oxford when we first met. He was in town to buy some paint. Actually we got on quite well from the very start.

GEOFFREY: How did you come to join the Bonzos?

LARRY: Viv said, "If you want to join Bonzo Dog, you'd better get off your ass, man and get sucking a tuba." Anyway, thanks to British Rail he sent one down, so I sat on the carpet for a week trying to play the damn thing. Somehow I managed to get three notes out of it, so I was in. I wasn't really much on actually playing it, but I could damn sure work up a great shine on the mother! I was *very* good at cleaning it.

GEOFFREY: Wasn't there some pretense to great, conceptual art in the band at this point?

LARRY: No, indeed not. I was much more into horse racing, gambling, and women. I did have a book on Rembrandt and a few early Picassos lying around the flat, however. For culture, I used to listen to the *1812 Overture of Franklin McCormack* continuously.

GEOFFREY: What was your name back then, sir?

LARRY: Trevor Tearbreaker.

GEOFFREY: Tell me, Trevor, what were those early Bonzo gigs like?

---

* "Legs" Larry Smith was a founding member of The Bonzo Dog Do Dah Band.

LARRY: Well, we used to jump into a car after college and drive to various pubs in the East End of London. The cockneys never took no bullshit from no one, so we'd jump on stage and just play totally insane songs for an evening. People tended to get drunk, strangely seemed to enjoy themselves and us! We once played "Brazil" for twenty minutes, which we had never even attempted. We thought, "Well, it's a nice summer evening, so why not?" We mixed a few cocktails, sat down, and played.

GEOFFREY: When did you become their drummer?

LARRY: Well, we were constantly playing twenties and thirties novelty songs, wonderful though they are and I wanted to move on and "go electric, man," just start playing a bit of rock and roll. I remember our manager, Reg Tracey, saying to me after I put the idea forward to the guys to do a couple of Elvis numbers, "Larry, if you want to play rock and roll, then I suggest you join a rock and roll band." Thank God I nearly did!

GEOFFREY: Got any Keith Moon stories? He was a very big Bonzo fan, wasn't he?

LARRY: I will reserve my Keith Moon stories for later, when I've returned from the paddock.

GEOFFREY: What's a paddock?

LARRY: Where they keep the horses. Don't they teach you anything in America?

GEOFFREY: So tell me about the *Magical Mystery Tour* film you guys did.

LARRY: Well, we were sitting in Manchester (which is a nightclub in the north of England where it always rains when the roof is off) and we heard the Beatles had asked Bonzo Dog to be in their new TV movie. We were naturally quite delighted until we actually got to make the film and *really* found out what the Beatles were like!

GEOFFREY: So how was it, making the film?

LARRY: The film was fine.

GEOFFREY: Did anyone screw the. . .

LARRY: Projectionist?

GEOFFREY: Yes, and the stripper?

LARRY: The film was shot in one day in a strip club in Soho—it was a very heavy schedule and quite remarkable.

GEOFFREY: The Raymond Review Bar.

LARRY: Indeed. It still exists and Raymond has just done a wonderful thing for our lucky troops that went off to the Falkland Islands to fight the good fight. What *were* we fighting for? He's offered a pound off any scotch and Cokes the troops would care to purchase whenever they come to the Raymond Review Bar. Which I think is wonderful. Anything that increases alcoholism is fine by me!

GEOFFREY: What about the party for *Mystery Tour?*

LARRY: The party was in fact more fun than making the actual segment! We all ended up at a big hotel—it was a fancy dress evening and that is what we gave them! I turned up as a World War Two officer from the South Pacific in a white U.S. Marine outfit and white ducks. I also wore a lovely little porkpie cap and had an equally lovely dogshit tattooed on my chest. Vivian turned up as a transport cafe, which is a cheap place to eat over here. He had plastic fried eggs and plastic strips of bacon glued onto a bright yellow Day-Glo oilskin jacket. I think Paul and Linda were . . . no, it wasn't Paul and Linda then, was it?

GEOFFREY: I believe it was Paul and Jane at that point.

LARRY: Paul and Linda were yet to be. Paul and Jane Asher were in attendance, however.

GEOFFREY: As buskers.

LARRY: Buskers, yes, the pearly king and his pearly queen. John Lennon was a rocker—it was wonderful, a terrific night. There was a jam at the end—everybody jumped on stage and it was fab gear!

GEOFFREY: What about Lulu—did she make any phone calls?

LARRY: Lulu made several phone calls to me at my table. *(Looking out the window)* Oh dear, someone is riding a horse in my field.

GEOFFREY: John's father, Freddie Lennon, was at that party, wasn't he?

LARRY: Yes, John's father, quite right old boy.

GEOFFREY: They did a wild dance together.

LARRY: They certainly did. Somebody gave them the bill!

GEOFFREY: So let's talk a bit about "Urban Spaceman."*

LARRY: We asked Paul McCartney to produce a track for us. We had about five or six songs we thought he might like to record. He chose "I'm the Urban Spaceman," which was written by Neil Innes. The day of the recording at Abbey

---

* The Bonzo Dog Do Dah Band's one and only hit single, written by co-founder Neil Innes.

Road, Paul arrived and we were all hanging around somewhat nervous of this great event, wondering what was going to happen. Just wondering if we were really good enough to cut this disc and crazy things like that. Anyway, Paul arrived looking rather casual and then we roared into a three-hour marathon session with Paul showing just how wonderful he can be in charge of production twiddling those little control knobs.

GEOFFREY: So tell me, do you like our policemen in America?

LARRY: I have met many fine policemen in connection with the worldwide tours I was part of during the seventies. Actually, to step out of a plane and onto a bit of tarmac, into a bit of black limousine with two policemen escorting you is quite outrageous. We whizzed through Chicago that way once, just like the Democratic Convention!

GEOFFREY: You've done tours with many famous individuals. You've tapped with Eric, Elton, and you've probably even tapped a bit with George once or twice. . . .

LARRY: I certainly have.

GEOFFREY: You've tapped with the best of them.

LARRY: . . . and I've tapped with the worst of them. In fact, I was just tapping yesterday in one of George's new movies. I hadn't tapped in about five years— very distressing indeed.

GEOFFREY: And you still dare to go by the name of "Legs"?

LARRY: Isn't that wonderful? I tapped with a band of ruffians, rapscallions, and ragamuffins. It's crazy, but we didn't even have a name. We were making this movie, *Bullshot*, a kind of super-thriller for Handmade Films. There was Zoot Money, Ray Cooper, myself, and two other wonderful gentlemen who were in this band of lovable street urchins and buskers. We spent half the day wanking and the other half dancing.

GEOFFREY: What about your recent art work for our beloved son and comrade, Señor Harrison?

LARRY: Yes, well, I go through periods of being absolutely drunk and periods of great sobriety and this, happily, is my sober period coming up. I always do things in tens, so I spent ten years drinking and now I'm on my second year of being sober. Anyway, I'm beginning to work a bit more these days, and last year I was offered a chance to design an album cover for George. In fact, design the entire campaign, which included the songbook, two posters, and basically overseeing the whole *Gone Troppo* campaign.

GEOFFREY: So, did you work closely with George?

LEGS: We did, yes. I kept whizzing over every couple of weeks as the album tracks were forming—so were the designs and stuff in my head. George took a real interest in the process. He knew a lot about the process of album covers, obviously, because he's done so many. But he was very involved in this particular one.

GEOFFREY: I understand you've also been doing some design work on Derek Taylor's forthcoming book, *Fifty Years Adrift*?*

LARRY: Yes, I'm art director. I'm just beginning to sort out all the visual references, facsimiles, and millions of highly polished Beatle photographs they want to use. That's going to be the last of my art things for awhile, though, I think.

GEOFFREY: Let's talk about life after Bonzo. You did a tour with Eric Clapton—when was that?

LARRY: That was in 1974. We did a little tour of Scandinavia and all the low-lying, high-kicking countries of the Netherlands. Eventually we ended up in America doing a wonderful tour. We had our own jet, you know.

GEOFFREY: How about Elton's tour—when was that?

LARRY: 1972.

GEOFFREY: Anything memorable in that?

LARRY: The whole thing was memorable! It was a wonderful experience—very nice to go on what I term "a first-class tour" instead of the sort of chewing-gum, spit-and-shit tours with Bonzo Dog we used to wade through. They were all wonderful evenings once we finally got on stage doing the show, but the buildup, the backup, the let's-go-ahead pace of the Bonzo tours was quite appalling. It pissed everyone off and that's one of the reasons we stopped touring. But to do Elton's tour was wonderful because first of all there was an awful lot of money, a good road crew, facilities for this and that, and I could make pizzas right on stage. Why, I even had my own bedroom (which I used to carry around in my suitcase). I had four helicopters . . . just for my shoes! Plus we had three luxury liners permanently going from South America to North America just in case we wanted a bit of sea breeze, you know, a bit of toot. It was wonderful in that respect.

GEOFFREY: What numbers did you dance to?

LARRY: I danced to a number called "I Think I'm Going to Kill Myself," one of Elton's songs with lyrics by Bernie Taupen.

---

* A pricey, leather bound memoir published by Genesis Publications of Guildford Surrey.

GEOFFREY: Do you think all this madness you've been involved in over the years is healthy?

LARRY: It's made me a better person.

GEOFFREY: Do you ever think of doing something normal with your life?

LARRY: I now know how to tie bandages, I know how to treat people for electric shock . . . if somebody has a fit, I know exactly what to do.

GEOFFREY: In the many years we've know each other, what is the one thing about me that annoys you the most?

LARRY: Your ability to arrive before you've left.

GEOFFREY: Why do you detest interviews so much?

LARRY: Because I believe like religion that when photographed, part of the soul is sucked up to sky and the same goes for the radio microphone. I think that when one's interviewed on the radio, particularly, part of your shoe is somehow transported to Australia.

GEOFFREY: Aren't you glad the sixties are over?

LARRY: Well, no, actually—they're in the next room. Here, I'll just bring them in. "Hi, Mrs. Sixty, Mr. Sixty, sir! Come in, please. It's a real pleasure being black in your country. I love your wonderful policemen. Thank you, no, I mean that sincerely."

GEOFFREY: Well, thank you very much, Mr. Smith, for your great insights and superlative anecdotes.

LARRY: It's been a pleasure. Sorry I couldn't have given you more time, but I have some gardening and I've left a rice pudding in the oven—it's a problem.

Jo Jo Laine*
REMEMBERING PAUL & LINDA
As Told to Geoffrey Giuliano, 1972–1980

1972

Paul and Linda looked up as we approached. Instead of pausing for a brief introduction and then moving on as I expected, Denny was gesturing me to slide onto the bus seat opposite the McCartneys. Tongue-tied and sweating bullets was not how I'd imagined meeting my childhood idol. How was I possibly going to live through the next several hours!

There I was, sitting before rock's premier legend, stoned from a joint I'd had earlier that morning. If Paul noticed, he didn't let on, politely chatting as any two strangers who meet on a bus. He was so nice, in fact, I relaxed and began to converse as if he were any ordinary guy.

Linda, on the other hand, I couldn't figure. She smiled, joined in on the conversation and appeared genuinely friendly. But there was something I couldn't put my finger on. A coolness, an underlying mistrust, even. And then when Paul asked, "Where are you from, Jo?" and I responded, "Boston," I caught a lightning-quick shock on Linda's face. Something was way out of whack.

It didn't take me long to find out, at least part of it. On a pit stop, she joined me in the ladies room. As we stood before the mirror, I drew out my brush and began to untangle my windblown locks. I was aware of Linda quietly studying me. Casually she ventured, "Oh, do you know Jane Asher?"

A bit startled I replied, "Sure. At least I know of her."

"What do you think of her?" she asked.

"I think she's very beautiful."

Linda's face fell like a cement block. Suddenly it was so clear. All the while Paul and I had been chatting Linda's mind had whirled into a panic: "Who's this girl? How long's she gonna last? She's got long red hair just like Jane Asher's. She's after Paul, not Denny. What am I gonna fucking do!"

---

* Jo Jo Laine was Wing's collaborator Denny Laine's wife.

If only I'd known how that first meeting would set the stage for our turbulent history. I was on top of the world, basking in the glow of being on the Wings tour, totally mad for Denny, when the bubble burst. After the gig that night, Denny came back to the hotel and sat me down.

"I've just had a talk with Linda," he said. "She asked me to her room to tell me they're very uptight about you being around. Linda says you're after Paul and you're a groupie. . . . She says you're just using me to get to Paul."

I sat there absolutely stunned. "Of course I think Paul is wonderful, but I'm here because of you. If you want me to leave, I will, but I want you to know I care very much about you and I don't care what this woman is saying."

Denny trudged on with obvious discomfort. "Linda also said you're trying to flirt with Paul."

"That's a lie!" I fired back, now outraged. "If anything, I hate them both for what they're doing."

After a long silence, Denny sighed, "I don't know what to think."

Hurt and anger began to steamroll over me. Not ten minutes ago in the limo riding back to the hotel, the McCartneys had been so friendly. To think I'd looked up to Paul all those years!

The next onslaught came in an unlikely form. One night on the ferry crossing to Norway there was a knock on my door. Standing there was nine-year-old Heather McCartney. "Could I have a word with you?" she asked tightly. She came right to the point. "You're making my mother and father very uncomfortable. We all know you're only here for Paul and we all know where you come from."

I studied her carefully. "Do you really? Do you also know how much I've come to care for Denny?" No response. "If you want my honest opinion, I think Denny's far sexier than your father. And there was a time I considered your father the sexiest man in the world." She left the room without another word. If Linda didn't put her up to it, she planted one hell of a wicked seed. Sending off a child to do her dirty work. All because I looked a bit like Jane Asher?

• • •

The night of August 10th was a particularly festive one. I caught a glimpse of Jim McCartney, Paul's dad and his brother Mike passing in the hallway. Then around midnight I heard the band stomp back to the hotel all abuzz about something. Denny rushed in and dropped a bombshell. "You'll never believe this— Paul's been busted!"

I shot up. "What about you? Did they get you, too?"

Denny shook his head, obviously distressed. "For Christ's sake, Jo, Paul's in jail! He took the rap for all of us." Apparently, seven ounces of dope had been addressed to Wings guitarist Denny Seiwell at the hotel. The cops found out and busted Paul in the dressing room after the show. As it turned out, he only had to spend nine hours in jail, but paid a rather hefty fine of £1,000.

But that obviously didn't faze Paul and Linda. As I quickly discovered, pot was their thing. Actually, they were a fair bit nicer when they were high. But they did smoke their share on a daily basis and never stingy when rolling their joints. This was especially true on the tour bus, where borders lay only hours away and time was ever so fleeting.

"Smoke as much as you can," hailed Denny as we desperately plowed through a giant bag of the stuff. Then Paul would say, "Look, lads, we're coming to the border. We've got to get rid of the shit." Then we'd all scramble to the open top of the bus and toss the precious contraband to the wind. Anyone watching would have thought we were scattering someone's ashes! It killed me to watch hundreds of dollars fly off down the highway. I was always tempted to keep a few joints, but Denny was quickly at my side to growl, "Don't you fucking dare!"

As the Wings tour continued through twenty-six cities in ten countries, we lived like kings. One of our accommodations in Scandinavia was a medieval castle complete with a banquet hall and guards in armor. Passing down one of the dimly lit corridors one night, I heard guitar strains wafting from one of the chambers. It was the McCartneys' room. I paused in the doorway, enjoying the hearty "busking." In fact, Paul spotted me and nodded an invitation to join the impromptu jam. As they launched into the old Beatles chestnut "Eight Days a Week," I chimed. How often had I sung along on the radio, never dreaming I'd actually one day sing it with one of the Beatles!

My happiness, however, was short-lived. A few nights later in the dressing room following the performance, Linda decided to test her superiority over me. The room was strewn with flowers showered on the band by adoring fans. Linda promptly snatched the nearest bouquet and shoved it against my chest. "Here, Jo Jo, put these in a vase." This was no polite request, but rather, an order to a servant! I was steaming. With all eyes on me, I sarcastically cooed, "Why, Linda, do you really think I'm worthy of doing this for you?" I then dumped the flowers in the sink and stormed out of the room, leaving everyone in shocked silence.

The one really dicey incident on the tour happened in Sweden. The band was relaxing in a basement club adjacent to the hotel, sitting at the bar having drinks. Suddenly, a young man in a suitcoat walked up to Paul and declared, "I've got a gun in my pocket right now, and I'm going to shoot you!"

Though I didn't hear the remark, I watched Paul's face turn a ghastly white. He murmured something to the road manager and then whispered to Denny, "Some guy has just threatened my life." Before I knew it, Denny and Henry had sandwiched this crackpot, who turned out his pockets and cajoled, "It was all just a lark, mates. I was just trying it on. No harm done." When we left the club, I saw Henry placing a long thin knife back into his thin boot. I remember thinking how Paul should be the one carrying it and how prophetic that would later turn out to be.

The tour ended and we all headed back to England. It was just a natural progression for me to move in with Denny. He leased a quaint little mews at 19 Kenway Road, Earls Court, which was sorely in need of a woman's touch. I shopped for weeks at Portabello Road Market, furnishing the place with new curtains, quilts and other bits and bobs. Little did I know our first guests would be the Macs. When they pulled up in their green Rolls, I watched as Linda perused the place with a scrutinizing eye. This was no housewarming visit, but rather a chance for Linda to snoop, to try and show up "the little upstart."

When Paul remarked approvingly, "It's nice and cozy here, Jo. You've made it just like home," it took the wind clear out of Linda's sails!

● ● ●

We were off to Scotland for the band to rehearse up at High Park, the McCartney's 300-acre farm in the Mull of Kintyre. I was so excited as we drove through the rolling heather-strewn countryside at the prospect of spending the summer on Paul and Linda's remote estate. After the twelve-hour drive, we pulled up to a large cement-block structure I assumed quartered the McCartney's livestock. But when Denny began unloading the van and carting our gear inside, I couldn't figure out what the hell was going on.

I stepped down from the VW and trudged into the building. I couldn't have been prepared for what awaited me—bare concrete from ceiling to walls to a stone and dirt floor, portioned off in sections like a maze. When I caught sight of an old mattress on the floor and Henry and Sheila McCullough peering out from behind a wall, it finally hit me: Welcome to the Hotel McCartney, the finest in bunker accommodations! Incredibly, this is how the world's richest and most famous musician housed his band.

Camping out in our cozy van had been heaven compared to the daily drudge on "Junior's Farm." Mind you, there were no kitchen facilities, nor indoor plumbing. We were forced to use outhouses. And baths? Each night we'd all boil water so one person could take his weekly bath. Here I was, eight months pregnant, tromping up and down hills carting buckets of water like it was "Little House on the Prairie." We took this roughing it just so long until Denny bought a trailer where we could at least cook our own food.

The roadies, too, had their own cottage at the top of the hill. We would visit Trevor and Sarah Jones and Ian Horn and take turns sitting in the lone chair. The running gag centered around the evening's "entertainment." Trevor and Ian had drawn a picture of a television set on the concrete wall and pretended they were watching TV. Of course, that's when they weren't engaged in a rousing "air darts" competition on the dartboard sketched on another wall!

There were no such hardships, though, for feudal landowners Paul and Linda. Although their house was admittedly modest, at least they had all the modern conveniences. Still, I couldn't accuse them of extravagance. The kids used to bop around in unmatched socks; little Stella in the same worn red-and-white checked dress I'd seen Mary wear. They were happy children, though and by all accounts Paul and Linda seemed wonderful parents. I never saw Paul lift a hand to any of the girls. He adored those kids.

It was hardly the same story, however, with his musical cohorts. Paul was dictator on the good ship Wings and made sure his subjects were stifled creatively, financially, and every other way. One by one the entire band would all fall like dominoes.

● ● ●

1973

It was the day my sister Maureen had come to the farm to meet the band and help me with the baby, which was due in two weeks. We were standing outside the rehearsal barn when Henry McCullough came flying out, slammed down his guitar, and told Sheila, "Get the car packed up. We're getting the fuck out of here!"

The final straw came over a certain riff Henry wanted to play and Paul insisted, "No, play it this way!"

"The way Paul wanted it was too bubble-gum," Henry admitted to me as he flung his gear into the car. "I tried to tell him my bit was better. There was no reason for Paul not to let me play it. We always have to do what he says. We can't take it any more."

I watched them speed off down the road, never to be seen again.

That afternoon Maureen arrived on the farm. We were standing outside our trailer when the McCartneys came trotting over the hill on their horses. I tried to hide a smug little smile as Paul and Linda got their first glimpse of my sixteen-year-old sister standing in the woods. Long blonde curls and a Brigitte Bardot pout had earned her the nickname "Susie Creamcheese." As introductions were made, I studied Paul's reaction. Like everyone, he couldn't take his eyes off her.

The real show, though, was Linda. She'd suddenly become a fount of friendliness, gushing over this gorgeous creature, when we all knew she'd like to bury her in the nearest manure pile. She breezily proclaimed, "You're all invited over to our house tonight. Dinner's at six."

"So, Linda," I asked, "what are we having to eat?"

Without missing a beat Paul quipped, "How about Maureen?" I could barely contain myself. Linda promptly reined her horse around and galloped off in a huff, Paul reluctantly, but dutifully, following. A week later Denny and I reciprocated with a barbecue outside our caravan. It was our last night on the farm before returning to London to await the baby's arrival. It remains the fondest memory I have of the McCartneys—why I can still today feel so bittersweet about our relationship.

I couldn't have romanticized the scene any better. The mild starry August night, roasting marshmallows, a blazing bonfire, all of us smoking joints. The sounds of our harmonies echoing over the Scottish hills as Paul and Denny took up their guitars strumming old Beatles tunes.

"It won't be long now," Paul nudged Denny, referring to my swollen abdomen. He was crooning a takeoff on the Wings song "Mary Had a Little Lamb": "Linda had a little lamb, her name was Mary. . . ."

"You're in for an experience you'll never forget," exuded Linda, taking a long slow toke.

"I was there for both the girls," revealed Paul, smiling in remembrance. "I got a camp bed and kipped right there in the hospital. In fact, we had to search around to find a hospital that would let me sleep in her room. I never left her side. It's the greatest experience in the world when you see your child for the first time. That baby's gonna make all the difference in your lives—you wait and see."

Anyone peering in on that campfire would have pictured old dear friends basking in each other's company. I was so hopeful, so optimistic that night. Who knew? Maybe once Linda saw I was about to have Denny's child, the friction would be gone for good.

Around midnight the party broke up. There were hugs and kisses all around. "Good luck in London," hailed Paul. "Good luck with the baby," beamed Linda.

● ● ●

I'd scarcely gotten into motherhood when Denny was off to Lagos, Nigeria, to record *Band On the Run* which would become Wings' breakout album. The night before they were set to fly, Denny and I stopped by the Seiwells' basement flat just down the road. Out of the blue Denny dropped the bombshell, "It's time to move on. I don't like this setup anymore. I love the band, I want to be with you, Den', but all the games, the way everything's been handled . . . it's just too much."

What was he saying? Was Denny S. thinking of leaving, too? As we stood there, Denny was on the horn to Paul. "Listen, Mac, I don't know how to tell you this, but I don't think I can go through with the Lagos gig. I think I'm just going to pack this thing up. . . . What can I say?"

We sat there stunned. This, right on the heels of Henry's departure! Just like that, the next day Denny and Sheila were gone, back to America. We did meet up with them a couple of years later in Chicago, where Denny was happy and thriving as a top session drummer. "Who would be next?" I wondered disturbed.

Paul covered his disappointment with typical bravado, telling Denny, "Oh, they can go fuck off. Who needs 'em anyway?" For all the chaos of the situation, the trio of Paul, Linda, and Denny tackled EMI Studios in Africa scarcely missing a beat. Not that Linda did much more than adding a harmony here and there. But the two guys were able to overcome a recording facility out of the Dark Ages where "half the stuff was hanging off the walls." Later on, the woodwinds and strings were added, but what became the acclaimed *Band On the Run* was in essence very much a McCartney/Laine production.

The most disturbing incident Denny wrote about in his letters was the harrowing robbery. Paul had been warned about taking to the dangerous Nigerian streets after dark, but like a bloody fool went out anyway. Sure enough, a couple thugs jumped Paul, putting a knife to his throat. "They had expensive cameras, cassette players, tapes, Paul gave them everything," wrote Denny. "He talked them out of it like he does and they let him go. It could have been very nasty. For robbery, because it's a military set-up, the authorities take the guys down to the beach and publicly execute them tied to a pole. So it was to their advantage if they were going to rob you to kill you. Then you couldn't recognize them in a police lineup." Paul must have been shitting himself. This time it wasn't a drunken prankster in a bar. It was a miracle he wasn't stabbed to death.

●　●　●

1974

1974 began as a magical year. *Band On the Run* proved an international smash, producing several hit singles. At long last we were seeing some substantial money. I was on such a high, going on wild spending sprees for me and our baby, Laine, I scarcely paid attention to Denny's concerned face as he went over the royalties one evening.

"This isn't right, Jo," he told me. "Damn it, it's not what Paul promised." I vaguely recalled Denny recounting a night up on the farm in Scotland where he and Paul were sitting on a hillside sharing a joint. "Just think of all the money that's going to be coming in from this album," Paul said. "You'll get a quarter of a million easy, Den', when the ol' royalties start rolling in." It was the first time he'd offered Denny a defined percentage. I remember my common-law husband coming back and swinging me in the air, so excited at the prospect. "We're gonna be millionaires, Jo!" he'd hooted.

"This is one hell of a difference from what Paul promised me that night," he now soberly discovered. He was obviously upset, but at the time it didn't affect me. All I could see was a small fortune starting to pour in. The warning lights were flashing red, but I was blind to them. And that's exactly how Paul wanted it.

• • •

I'd been planning to accompany Denny to Montserrat in the Caribbean where Wings were recording *Tug of War*. I should have seen it coming when my husband approached me with that sheepish look and familiar opening line, "I've got something to tell you." On orders from the high command, I was forbidden to come on the trip.

"What!" I railed. "You're not letting those bastards get away with that! Denny, c'mon, you didn't go along with it, did you?"

"What could I say? Listen Jo, you need to see where Paul's coming from right now. Lennon's murder has got him very paranoid about security. After all, he's had several death threats. You coming would only compound things and draw unwanted attention. He just can't handle any bad publicity right now."

I whirled around. "Is that how you see me, Denny? As bad publicity? I'm the mother of your children, for fuck's sake!"

He fell silent, refusing to look at me. He couldn't even muster the old standby: "Don't you see, Jo, I'm doing this for us. I know sucking up to them doesn't seem fair, but just think of the money, of what we can have. . . ."

"I don't care anymore about the money," I'd always wail back. "I just want us to be together, back to the way we were."

We couldn't even argue like Jo Jo and Denny any more!

I'll never forget the day Denny finally left the band. The tension had been building for a year, but because of my own problems, I hadn't picked up on it. It started with Paul's infamous drug bust in Japan in January of 1980. I wasn't on tour with Denny, preparing instead to attend the Midem Festival in France to promote my "Dancing Man" record. He called me in London, blurting out, "You'll never guess what! Fuckin' McCartney's been nabbed for grass at Tokyo airport!" The news struck me as neither here nor there, my interest in the Macs having long since waned. The immediate fallout was bad enough. Paul in the slammer for nine days and the tour cancelled. The band members didn't get one lick of the $100,000 compensation they were due, either. That really pissed off drummer Steve Holly, who'd given up a chance to play with Elton John for the Wings gig. As for Denny, he felt he'd been betrayed. He later said, "I felt I was entitled to an explanation from Paul, but I never got one."

I had no idea of the bust's long-range ramifications. Paul made a stir about Denny leaving him in the lurch and joining me at the festival, but what was he supposed to do? Sit around some swanky Japanese hotel while Paul stewed over his own damned stupidity? With immediate plans up in the air following the bust, Denny and I went into Rock City Studios in Chertsey with Drew to record the album *Japanese Tears*. We worked long and hard on the project, with me contributing backup vocals and even a solo number ironically entitled "Same Mistakes." The title track was a pretty tune Denny dedicated to a distraught fan who'd waited outside for days to see Paul. "There is a tap on my shoulder from a tiny yellow hand . . . with tears in her eyes . . ." went the infectious lyric. Paul had the nerve to turn his nose up at the album, saying we'd cashed in on the bust. Tough shit! This from the fucking skinflint who didn't offer anyone a penny because of his own neurotic need for a constant supply of high-powered hemp.

It all came to a head when the trio of Paul, Linda, and Denny became a band of three, literally hobbling into the studio that February on broken wings. To me, *Tug of War* reflects the whole mess. I think it's a terrible piece of fluff; to this day I can't stand to listen to it. The whole Montserrat business meanwhile, bored a big hole in Denny.

Finally, one morning he couldn't even go into the studio. Wings roadies Trevor Jones and John Hammel kept ringing the house all day. At last Denny picked up the phone and said, "I'm not speaking to *anybody*! That's it. I'm finished with *Tug of War*. I'm finished with the band. I'm leaving Wings."

I sat there numb. As Denny put down the phone, our eyes met. So you finally blame Paul and Linda, my gaze silently told him. Unfortunately, it was eight years and one marriage too late.

Later in the day the phone rang again and it was Paul. "Is Denny there?" he inquired coolly.

"He can't come to the phone. He asked me to give you and everyone else the message because he finally realizes the damage all of this has done. He's lost me now and it's too late."

Paul tried to interrupt, but I snapped, "He can go to the studio with my blessings, but he doesn't want to."

"You fucking cow," he snorted, "like it's all my fault!"

"No. Sorry, luv, this time it *is* your fault." I hung up the phone and just like that, after ten years it was all over. The press feasted on the bust-up for months, fueled by various denials and rumors of Denny's imminent return. But the fact was that Wings, the biggest group of the seventies (outgrossing even the Beatles in record sales), was permanently dismantled. I think it's no coincidence the band survived every musician's departure except Denny Laine's. That in itself speaks volumes about Wings' great success, not to mention their seventeen gold and platinum discs. Still, even to this day I find it all very, very sad.

Bob Gallo*

INTERVIEW

•••••••••••

Toronto, 1983

BOB GALLO: The fact is that Pete might not have had the charisma Ringo had. The story goes that after Pete was tossed out of the band, Paul went around Liverpool trying to find the ugliest drummer he could that happened to have his own drum kit. In those days it was very tough to find someone with a full kit. Anyway, along came Ringo, so there they were with an ugly drummer and a great kit to boot! Now to be honest, between Ringo and Pete, technically Pete is a somewhat better drummer, but he probably lacked the overall appeal Ringo had.

GEOFFREY: Yet George Martin has always maintained Ringo's drumming was far superior to Pete's.

BOB: I think Pete is a very decent drummer. His timing and feel were very good and as a producer doing an entire album with Pete, I thought he was just a little bit better than Ringo. The point I'm trying to make is that according to Peter, it was jealousy that started the whole thing, *not* musicianship.

GEOFFREY: What did you think about the album you cut with Pete? Did you feel he was really good enough to make it big?

BOB: Well, I certainly hoped he was! After flying them in from England and putting them up in a hotel for over two months, you could say I had a vested interest in their success! As a producer, I think I could have done a lot better with them if we had more time. Both bands had a lot of original material, but the music frankly didn't come out as well as I would have liked. Then there was the fact most teenagers really hated Pete.

GEOFFREY: Were you aware of this at the time?

BOB: I don't think so. We all thought he would be riding the Beatles' tail, and he did, too, for a while. Then some people in the business started talking, and the first thing you know, poor Pete was poison.

GEOFFREY: How would Pete react to media coverage of the Beatles' various exploits? Did he follow their careers?

BOB: To be honest with you, he wouldn't do anything but kind of hang his head and look the other way. He would try to change the subject or ignore the situation, but deep inside I knew it was eating him up.

---

* Sixties producer Bob Gallo was reponsible for Pete Best's solo LP, *Best of the Beatles*, released on his own Savage Records in the mid-sixties.

Afterword
A GOOD DAY'S NIGHT
. . . .
Charles F. Rosenay!!! *

Whenever people ask, "Why the Beatles?" my response is inevitably, "The music, memories and magic." Millions of words continue to be written about the wonderful sounds the Beatles gave us, but the memories, too, are another important element of the phenomenon. Inevitably, though, it is the magic which is most difficult to define. That intangible, undeniable *something*, which made the Fab Four stand out from every other act of the era and, arguably, any period of recorded music.

Part of that X-factor was the magnetic personalities of the four, as well as the many charismatic people surrounding the group. A unique combination of wit, charisma, savoir-faire, and a delightful mix of subtle, sexual magnetism with boy-next-door charm helped define John, Paul, George, and Ringo as the bona fide heroes of now three generations.

Elements of great personality could likewise be detected in their looks and the way they carried themselves, but most importantly, in the interesting things they said. So much of the brilliance of the Beatles both as a group and individuals was in their everyday words and thankfully, now here in Geoffrey and Vrnda's *Things We Said Today*.

Interestingly, the one aspect of the Beatles that *hasn't* yet been adequately covered is the magic of their words—not their lyrics, but in interviews and daily life—as well as the many words that have been spoken about them by others close to the phenomenon. To date Messrs. McCartney and Starr have not devoted the exhaustive effort necessary to penning proper autobiographies. George Harrison, though, took a stab at it with his 1980 lyrical memoir, *I Me Mine*, and John Lennon frankly left a far better autobiography in his songs, poetry, artwork, campaigns and everyday chat than he ever could in a mere book.

Many of those who surrounded the Beatles, too, have similarly committed their lives to paper: Pete Best (the Beatles' original drummer), siblings such as Mike

---

* Mr. Rosenay has made the preservation of the Beatles' memory his life's work. He publishes the insightful magazine *Good Day Sunshine* and produces Beatles conventions worldwide. For the truly devout, Mr. Rosenay packages "Magical Mystery Tours" to London and Liverpool so fellow aficionados can visit various Beatle sights on a professionally guided tour. You may contact Charles c/o Liverpool Productions, 397 Edgewood Avenue, New Haven, Connecticut 06511, USA.

McCartney (who actually says more with his marvelous photographs than words could ever convey), Julia Baird (Lennon's sister), Allan Williams (*The Man Who Gave the Beatles Away*), Cynthia Lennon and many others.

For the serious fan, the music historian, or even the casual student of rock and roll, there can never be enough words about the Beatles. Just like the devoted fan who thrives on hearing every last version from the extended *Get Back* sessions, there are those, too, who hang on every word spoken about the Beatles. A book of conversations by and about the Beatles is as welcome and important today as it was in the late sixties . . . and as it will be years from now. If the music of the Beatles is truly timeless, then so is intelligent discussion of their turbulent, eventful lives.

Cheers,
Charles F. Rosenay!!!
September 1, 1997

Index

●●●●●●

About the Authors

GEOFFREY GIULIANO (JAGANNATHA DASA) is a top international celebrity biographer and popular culture authority whose over twenty previous books include *The Beatles: A Celebration*; *John Lennon: My Brother* (written with

Lennon's sister, Julia Baird); *Dark Horse: The Private Life of George Harrison*; *Blackbird: The Unauthorized Biography of Paul McCartney*; *The Beatles Album: Thirty Years of Music and Memorabilia*; *Rod Stewart*; *Vagabond Heart*; *The Rolling Stones Album: Thirty Years of Music and Memorabilia*; *The Illustrated Series*; *Paint It Black: The Murder of Brian Jones*; *The Lost Beatles Interviews*; *Behind Blue Eyes: A Life of Pete Townshend*; and *Two Of Us: The Passionate Partnership of Lennon and McCartney*.

In addition, Giuliano can be heard regularly on the Westwood One Radio Network, and he has created a line of audio rocumentaries for Durkin Hayes Publishing and a series of biographical CD boxed sets and video documentaries on various popular musicians for Laserlight Digital. He is also a twenty-five-year student of Vedic culture and philosophy and a dedicated animal-rights activist.

VRNDA GIULIANO is co-author of *Not Fade Away: The Rolling Stones Collection*; *The Illustrated Series*; *The Lost Beatles Interviews*; and *The Lost Lennon Interviews*.

Her forthcoming lacto-vegetarian cookbook, *Compassionate Cuisine*, is soon to be published. Vrnda is also a pilot and lectures on nonviolent lifestyles.

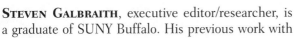

STEVEN GALBRAITH, executive editor/researcher, is a graduate of SUNY Buffalo. His previous work with the Giulianos includes *The Lost Lennon Interviews*. He makes his home in Buffalo where, in addition to his own writing, he composes and records music.

SESA GIULIANO (SRI DEVI DASI), associate editor/researcher, has assisted on virtually all of Geoffrey Giuliano's books. Returning from an extended sabbatical in rural India, Sesa is currently studying audio and video production. In addition, she is an experienced professional photographer.

Her first child, Kashi Nath Narayan Jones, was born on July 25, 1996.

If you would like to write the Giulianos, their address is Indigo Arts, Post Office Box 305, Lockport, New York 14095-0305, or you may visit them at their web sites at http://www.neonblue.com/sri or http://www.neonblue.com/indigo.

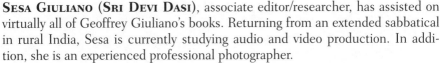